The Killer Within

THE KILLER WITHIN
In the Company of Monsters
Philip Carlo

THE OVERLOOK PRESS
NEW YORK

In Memory of Ben Byer and Jenifer Estess

This edition first published in hardcover in the United States in 2011 by

The Overlook Press, Peter Mayer Publishers, Inc.
141 Wooster Street
New York, NY 10012
www.overlookpress.com
For bulk and special sales, please contact sales@overlookny.com

Library of Congress Cataloging-in-Publication Data
Carlo, Philip.
The killer within : in the company of monsters / by Philip Carlo. — 1st ed.
p. cm.
1. Murderers—United States. 2. Murder—United States.
3. Monsters—United States. I. Title.

HV6529.C374 2011   364.152'3092273—dc22   2010041079

Book design and type formatting by Bernard Schleifer
Manufactured in the United States of America
FIRST EDITION
2 4 6 8 10 9 7 5 3 1
ISBN 978-1-59020-431-3

"He who fights with monsters should be careful lest he thereby become a monster. And if thou gaze long into an abyss, the abyss will also gaze into thee."

—FRIEDRICH NIETZSCHE, *Beyond Good and Evil*

Killer: 1 : one that kills
      2 a : one that has a forceful, violent, or striking impact
       b : one that is extremely difficult to deal with

—*Merriam-Webster Dictionary*

Amyotropic Lateral Sclerosis: Commonly known as ALS, it was first described by Charcot in the nineteenth century, and is a relentlessly progressive, presently incurable, neurodegenerative disorder that causes muscle weakness, disability, and eventually death. ALS is also known as "Lou Gehrig's Disease," after the famous New York Yankee baseball player who was affected with the disease.

—**Lauren B. Elman, M.D., and Leo McCluskey, M.D., MBE**
Clinical Features of Amyotrophic Lateral Sclerosis,
June 19, 2009, UpToDate.com

More than 300,000 Americans alive today will die of ALS.
—**The ALS Association**

This book is dedicated to my wife, Laura Garofalo Carlo.
Without her help, love, guidance, and support, not only would this
book never have been possible, but the frame of mind needed to
write the book would not have been possible.

The Killer Within is also dedicated to my assistant,
confidante, and friend, Kelsey Osgood,
who gave voice to me after I lost my hands
and my ability to hold a pen.

Contents

Introduction

In trying to understand and write comprehensively about what motivates professional killers, serial murderers, Mafia bosses, and mob hit men, I have gone into prisons across the country, sat down opposite some of the most notorious criminals of modern times, and picked their brains. I am not a cop, FBI agent, or from any branch of law enforcement. I did this to learn the intimate secrets and idiosyncrasies these people have and to tell their stories with unvarnished candor. Always careful not to point fingers or make judgments, I managed to gain their confidence—not an easy task.

I extensively interviewed California's notorious Richard Ramirez, aka the Night Stalker, at San Quentin's death row. I spent over two hundred hours at Trenton State Prison with Richard Kuklinski, the Ice Man, a six-foot-six, 320-pound contract killer who, during his forty-three-year "career," murdered over two hundred people. For many months, I worked with Anthony "Gaspipe" Casso, the head of the Lucchese crime family, and learned not only what makes a Mafia boss tick, but the culture of La Cosa Nostra, its mindset, rhyme, and rhythm—how it became the most successful criminal enterprise of all time. More recently, I wrote *The Butcher: Anatomy of a Mafia Psychopath*. This was the story of Tommy "Karate" Pitera, a drug-dealing capo in the Bonanno crime family who killed over fifty people, dismembered them, and strategically buried the pieces in federally protected bird sanctuaries throughout the tri-state area. I managed to slip in and out of these people's world without doing damage to myself because, I think, I was born and raised on the mean streets of Bensonhurst, Brooklyn—ground zero for the New York Mafia. It was in Bensonhurst where, as a boy, I came to know sudden, deadly violence up close and personal. It was in Bensonhurst that I graduated from the school of hard knocks with honors.

However, as I write this, everything has changed. A monkey wrench has been thrown into the mix, for now a stone-cold killer is stalking me, a remorseless murderer far worse than any I have yet met, written about.

Because of this killer, I was forced to flee New York and settle in South Beach, Miami, Florida. The warm weather here is better for my health, though I did not escape unscathed. In New York, this killer ravaged my limbs and robbed me of the use of my hands. I cannot even hold a pen now. I am only able to continue writing with the help of an assistant, someone who can readily deal with the in-depth violence I write about, and take flawless dictation. I posted an ad for such a person on a Columbia University bulletin board. After interviewing a dozen different candidates, I found Kelsey. She has a perfectly heart-shaped face, unusually large eyes the color of Tupelo honey. Kelsey is extremely well read, particularly attentive. An aspiring writer herself, she can get on paper my thoughts faster than I can say them. We work like a bow and fiddle.

As I now dictate this to Kelsey, we are on the beach, sitting on comfortable lounges in South Beach, Miami, under the subdued shade of a big, yellow umbrella. The sun shines brilliantly. To my left is the surprisingly clear Atlantic Ocean, a clean aquamarine color. Before me is a long stretch of white beach. Above is a pastel blue, cloudless sky. It is over eighty degrees, though a pleasant breeze off the ocean makes it comfortable. However, lurking somewhere behind me, where I cannot see because I am unable to turn my head due to atrophy of the muscles, is the killer I talk about. I shiver at the thought. I feel its icy breath on the back of my neck. Despite the killer's unsettling presence, the beach is an idyllic place to write. If it weren't for the breathing machine I'm using, a passerby would see nothing wrong. I am tan and surprisingly healthy looking, but where there were once large bicep muscles, there is now only a gathering of thin skin. I look down at my legs. They are little more than bones covered in loose flesh. They have become so weakened by the killer that I can no longer walk or support myself.

I turn to Kelsey. Our eyes meet. The clean, fresh smell of the ocean is all about us. This is somewhat awkward. I have already written two books with Kelsey's assistance, but now, for the first time, she is actually a character in the story. I plan to be brutally honest here, and I fear it could be embarrassing, even hurtful, to her. I do my best to take a long, deep breath. I turn my attention to Kelsey, sentences and thoughts, images and emotions swirling about inside my head. I will soon give them all life and breath.

"So I'm ready. Are you, K?" I ask.

"Yes," she says.

"Chapter One," I say, knowing this will be painful for me, not sure if I have the wherewithal and strength to put it all on paper, I take the first step . . .

PART ONE
The Roots of Evil

1. Napoli

I am now sitting in my motorized, all-black, fancy Permobile wheelchair on Via Nuova Marina, at the northern end of the glorious Bay of Naples.

Stretched out endlessly before me is the majestic Tyrrhenian Sea, a clean, deep blue-green color, calm and friendly today. The Tyrrhenian looks more like a pristine ocean you would find in the South Pacific rather than here in the Mediterranean. Its fertile waters have kept Neapolitans and southern Italians well-fed since time immemorial. From where I am sitting, I can see the island of Capri ahead of me and off to the left a bit. If the Tyrrhenian Sea has a precious stone, it is surely Capri. The island has such inherent beauty, is so well placed in the heart of the Mediterranean, that the Caesars of ancient Rome lived there, coveted and loved the island for its unusual beauty, temperate sea, and bounty of all things edible.

Tiberius Caesar, perhaps the maddest of all the Caesars, a bona fide, psychotic serial killer, an extreme sexual sadist and pedophile, lived on Capri. There Tiberius had legendary, ongoing orgies involving both male and female children. When Tiberius tired of any particular child, he had him or her tossed onto jagged, terracotta-colored cliffs on the northeast side of the island, tearing them apart, maiming them horribly, killing them. Cormorants, gulls, and vultures then gleefully, indifferently fed from them, eyes and tongues first. Beyond this exquisite island holding the darkest of secrets is the volcanic, amazingly fertile island of Ischia. Like Sicily, Ischia is part of the breadbasket that feeds the whole of Italy. Roman legions went there for the medicinal powers Ischia's sulfur hot springs afforded. People still come from all over the world for the miraculous healing powers of the sulfur springs.

Off to my left is the infamous Mount Vesuvius. A lazy, blue-gray plume of smoke issues from Vesuvius. Directly behind me are neatly cut terraced hills, *viale,* and *piazzae.* There, too, are palm trees and their giant leaves sway sensuously in the warm breeze languidly coming off the Tyrrhenian Sea.

Contrary to the inherent beauty of Naples are gunshots, loud and too close for comfort. This is the home of the most feared of all the Italian organized crime groups—the Camorra. The Camorra are more ruthless and cunning and dangerous than even the Sicilian Mafia. The Camorra kill the young, kill women, kill without logic, oblivious to the political and sociological ramifications of murder out in the open. The Camorra kill with the mad abandon of Tiberius. Perhaps, I think, they are the descendants of Tiberius. They surely kill as though they are. When I hear the gunshots, I flinch. I know only too well the destructive power of bullets. I have been studying all types of mortal wounds for some thirty years now. At autopsies at the office of the medical examiner in New York, I was allowed to see inside the skulls of people shot to death by bullets to the head. I know that a .22-caliber at close range is not powerful enough to enter and exit the cranium, thus the bullet bounces around inside the skull and causes massive damage. It is an assassin's caliber of choice.

Off to my right are the docks and piers from which, at the turn of the century, Italian immigrants left Italy in dire need of a better life. They were fleeing plague and drought, government tyranny, corruption, and poverty. Between 1890 and 1920, some 4.5 million Italians fled Italy from these very docks, most of whom landed on New York's Ellis Island. It was this mass migration, these people who took with them nothing but what they could carry, of which I am a descendant. Both my maternal and paternal grandparents were part of this huge exodus. When they left Italy, they were not only searching for a better life for themselves, but for their children and grandchildren as well. Back then, New York was so far away from Italy in terms of culture and food, language and social customs that it could readily be likened to the moon. As I close my eyes now, I can see them—as the steam ships slowly pull out—waving to those they are leaving behind. Calling over the widening gap, "Momma! Pappa!" as tears run copiously down faces. They knew they'd never see one another again. Over one hundred years later, hot tears hurry down my face as I think of that time, see it vividly in my mind's eye.

To these people, Italians, *famiglia* was more important than anything else. With family, you never stood alone; there was always somebody to watch your back. With family, the chances of success were proportionally increased.

My father, Dante Carlo, had seven brothers and three sisters; my mom, Antonina Mandato, had six sisters and three brothers. Between the two families, I have some thirty-five first cousins. In a sense, I became the by-product of the American dream. To describe here the blood and sweat, toil and tears my grandparents, aunts, and uncles went through to make a go of it in America would take a large volume unto itself . . . the poverty, World War II, drug abuse, my cousin Andy Carlo murdering my father's brother Willie would fill a thick book— a Brooklyn *Gone With the Wind*.

My parents settled in Bensonhurst, Brooklyn. For the most part, Bensonhurst was a nice neighborhood. The streets were clean and well kept. There was an abundance of shopping on nearby 86th Street. The B train quickly shuttled people from Bay Parkway to Manhattan. There were many churches and synagogues. It was a good place to grow up, but Bensonhurst also had a dangerous underbelly. The huge Italian-American community, drawn to its tree-lined streets and avenues, included many mafiosi and their associates. Bosses, underbosses, captains, lieutenants, soldiers, and Mafia assassins all lived there. La Cosa Nostra regularly celebrated birthdays, weddings, christenings, and holidays and mourned their dead in Bensonhurst. When I was growing up, the streets of Bensonhurst were safe. A woman could walk alone and not be accosted. Rape and burglaries were, for the most part, unheard of. However, mafiosi had no inhibition or compunction about killing their own in broad daylight—killing when and where and how they pleased. They, too, killed like Tiberius. It seemed like some strange intimacy with murder ran in their blood— perhaps was in their very genes.

It is late in the afternoon. I am tired of writing—dictating to Kelsey, who has been sitting on a wooden bench next to me. I look at my hands. They are painfully thin. Atrophy is beginning to twist the pinkie fingers on both hands. Damn, I think. The sound of the waves has lulled me into a pensive, introspective mood. I feel torn between laughter and tears. I again think of my grandparents. I know in my heart that if any one of them could see me in the condition I am in now, they'd be brokenhearted beyond words. I know better than to dwell on such thoughts. I look away from the pier and see my wife, Laura, walking toward me. She has been shopping and is carrying two bags. Laura is some twenty-six years my junior, vivacious and athletic, exceedingly attractive. Her father's family hails from Sicily. Her mother's family is Norwegian. This interesting combination made for an unusually beautiful woman with a high, broad forehead, wide, Slavic cheekbones, blue-green eyes the color of the Tyrrhenian. The strain of my sickness is taxing on Laura, though she is strong and stoic and, for the most part, deals well with this beast that has taken hold of me.

Kelsey, Laura, and I head off to find a trattoria. I will not eat where there are any tourists. With this basic guideline, we have come across some excellent restaurants in offbeat places with amazing wine and relatively inexpensive, glorious food. The cuisine of Naples is so good that it is worth a trip just to come here and eat. As we make our way along the Via Ernesto Capocci, the smell of strong espresso, fresh baked bread, and pizza permeates the air. Naples is a scenic city with well laid out piazzas and squares. Palm trees line most every street and avenue. Yet, still, I hear the sounds of gunshots off in the distance. None of us speak of them. I wonder if they are my imagination, or perhaps a car backfiring. I know better but I prefer to think that it is rather my imaginings than someone being suddenly dropped by a bullet to the head.

We are here, in Naples—the place my grandparents left over one hundred years ago—to do battle with the killer that is destroying me. I find myself thinking it is a cruel irony, the meaning of which eludes me.

We find an unassuming trattoria on Via Loggia di Genova, adorned with statues of famous Neapolitans, take comfortable seats at an outdoor table. I must remain in my wheelchair. It is no longer possible for me to stand. In Naples, as in most of Italy, the food offered by restaurants is customarily displayed on long, hip-high tables. You are expected to walk up to the table and point to whatever tickles your fancy. Everything looks mouthwateringly good. There are grilled vegetables—stuffed artichokes, zucchini, carrots, seared cauliflower, broccoli rabe. There is also a large variety of fish—shrimp, lobster, and branzino. Next to the fish there is an assortment of meats—hot and sweet sausages, thin slices of different cuts of steak all marvelously laid out, there for the taking. We are hungry and we happily make our choices and go back to our table with a bottle of wine from nearby Sorrento. While we wait for our food, we sit and watch the Neapolitan world go by.

Throughout all of Italy, eating is a slow, unhurried affair. We have an antipasto, a pasta dish, a meat dish, and, for the last course, a salad—comprised of arugula, radicchio, and finocchio—fennel.

Sadly, at this juncture, I cannot hold a knife and fork, and Laura patiently spoons the food into my mouth. People around us act like they don't notice but out of the corner of my eye I see them sorrowfully watching as she feeds me. The age difference between Laura and me is such that I could very well be her father. I am sure the Neapolitans think she is a good daughter feeding her papa, but I don't give that much thought. Instead, I think about the food and savor it. In a sense, eating here in a family-run, off-the-beaten-path trattoria is like eating at one of my grandmother's homes. We learn that the restaurant is owned by a Signor Vittozzi. He and his five daughters and his wife work the kitchen and what they produce simply and honestly and quickly, without argument or fanfare, is some of Italy's finest cuisine.

Suddenly, as we eat, the rat-tat-tat of automatic gunfire comes from off in the hills to our left. No one seems to notice, react, or care. Murder is part and parcel of daily life in Naples. I thought growing up in Brooklyn's Bensonhurst had left me jaded and street savvy, but in Naples, murder has taken on a far different sociological meaning. Here in Naples, those in organized crime don't live and die by the sword, they die by a long list of cruelties, the least of which is the gun. I push the thoughts of murder away, and I focus on the lemon-infused veal Milanese adorned with toasted pignoli nuts Laura is placing in my mouth.

We've made the difficult trip to Naples for a cutting-edge drug known as IPLEX—mecasermin rinfabate. In order to help secure the drug here in Italy, I was forced to hire an Italian attorney. He explained that southern Italian courts are much more apt to grant a request for IPLEX, the only drug available to help me combat the killer intent upon taking my life, little by little, a piece at a time. IPLEX is manufactured by an American company—Insmed out of Richmond, Virginia. Though it is an American-made drug, it is only available in Italy. To secure the drug as an American, you have to go through all kinds of protocols and leap through rings of fire. We had to first get an Italian doctor to write a prescription, a residence in Naples, and a lawyer to petition the Neapolitan courts. If I can prove that my stay in Italy is for work—the writing of a book—namely this book, *The Killer Within*—and that the killer is just behind me and intent upon stealing my life, there is a *possibility* the court will approve my petition. Essentially, IPLEX is an esoteric, jazzed-up steroid that is supposed to rebuild—generate—muscle ravaged by the disease. We have come to Naples knowing this is a long shot, but sadly it is the only shot we have at this juncture.

I push thoughts of the disease away and focus on the glory of the food before us. I no longer eat as much as I used to, but ALS does not affect taste buds, and I am still able to swallow. Inevitably, down the road, the muscles that enable me to chew, eat, and swallow will diminish and I will have to be fed through a tube surgically inserted into my stomach. There is a diabolical laundry list of horrors that the killer has in store for me. I have seen them up close on other people stricken with ALS. But like I said, I don't allow myself to dwell on these thoughts—those realities. I think of sunrises rather than sunsets. Though I have written prodigiously about murder most foul for many years, I now somewhat obsessively focus on life, tomorrow rather than yesterday.

After dinner, they bring us a small plate of sweets, which I take with the best espresso I have ever had; this followed by a large shot of ice-cold Limoncello and the meal is finito. All of us pleasantly satiated, we make our way back toward the private home in which we are staying. By now it is dark and a vivid, golden half-moon hangs over the Tyrrhenian Sea, laying a glistening lunar highway on the calm water. It is a beautiful sight to behold, a vision no doubt my grandparents saw over one hundred years ago. The beauty before me is much in contrast to the violence, the murder, and the subjugation the Camorra cause throughout Naples and its surrounding provinces.

Tomorrow we plan on going to Ischia to begin the wait. Over and over again, I have heard about the wonderful healing hot springs there. My Italian doctor has written the necessary prescriptions; the papers have been filed with the Neapolitan courts. All we can do now is be patient and hopeful. Meanwhile, we will wait on one of the most beautiful islands in all of the Mediterranean. As we slowly make our way to our quarters, each of us complimenting the dishes we ate, there is a tumultuous explosion. The Camorra are fond of bombs, and I am certain they just blew something up—the home of an enemy, the shop of an enemy, the car of an enemy.

"I don't want to be here," Laura says.

"I know," I say.

Kelsey remains mute and quiet, not wanting to make an already difficult situation more difficult—as is her way. It really is ironic that I came here, we came here, for a life-giving drug when all around us, people are killing one another. How, I wonder, can they be so fucking stupid? How, I wonder, can they throw their good health to the wind? When I see people smoking, I want to walk up to them, admonish them, yell in their faces, "Stop—you have your good health! Are you crazy?"

Sadly, the Neapolitans have taken destroying one another to new heights. I want to go find the heads of the families and say to them, "No amount of money is worth your health. Make peace. Make friends. Make money without tearing each other apart, killing one another." When you see the upper echelons of the Camorra strutting about Naples, they are amazingly healthy, virile men in the prime of life, broad-shouldered and muscular. They dress impeccably. Many of them have the inherent natural good looks of movie stars of old. Yet here they are, shooting and stabbing and blowing one another up without reservation or inhibition.

Me—I know killers. I have known killers far worse than any of these Camorra. I think of what Richard Kuklinski would have done, how through guile and cunning he would have managed to get members of the Camorra where he wanted them, torture them in the most heinous ways imaginable, using methods he developed that involved ripping out the spine while people were still alive; that involved feeding people to feral rats while they were still alive; that involved tying people to trees and using a fillet knife to slice off long strips of skirt-steak-like flesh from their bodies, before he poured a box of fine kosher salt all over the open wounds. I wonder if anyone in the

Camorra will eventually read these words. Most of my books have been published in Italian so they just might. But the killer stalking me, I know, is far more dangerous and cunning than the Camorra could ever be.

Because of the government's residency requirements—in order to get IPLEX—we have to stay in the home of an elderly Neapolitan couple on Rua Francesca, just near the port. When we arrive back at the apartment, Laura washes me up and puts me to bed. Though I have an awful lot on my mind, I lie there thinking of my grandparents, their die-hard quest for a new life, the irrational absurdity of the Camorra's violence, how they kill one another—the grief they cause. These men have mothers, sisters . . . wives and children. I make a mental note to go to the funeral of a Camorra and see for myself how they express grief. They, like all Italians, will be overtly sorrowful, histrionic, and tearful. I figure with Laura and Kelsey at my side and me in a wheelchair, we will have no problem getting in.

Inexplicably, I start thinking of my childhood, wondering if this raptorial dragon seed was inside of me then. When I asked my doctors in New York about how the killer had found me, if it was something that you inherited, they all told me there was no rhyme or reason; that it could be readily likened to being struck by lightning. To add to my confusion, as a young boy I was amazingly athletic, was always the fastest runner in my class, extremely well coordinated. I began boxing when I was ten years old and put down whoever was in front of me. Lying here, my mind turns toward sudden, irrational violence—I wonder if the blows and hard knocks to my head over the years had opened the door to the killer; if my getting shot when I was sixteen, the trauma of the bullet tearing into my skull, had something to do with my getting ALS. More about this later. Lying here, I remember the first time in my life I saw abrupt, irrevocable violence—murder.

It began, innocently enough, in the Cropsey Avenue Park. There were children's silvery swings, seesaws, a sandbox, and sprinklers they turned on in the summer months. It was here that I first saw and came to know the legendary Jimmy Emma.

Jimmy was in his early teens, a thin, excessively muscular, blondheaded boy with a broken nose that veered off to the left. It would be because of Jimmy that I would actually witness a murder in cold blood.

Jimmy was by himself in a quiet corner of the playground doing endless push-ups with his shirt off. Shyly, I ambled over to him and he smiled and showed me how to do proper push-ups. As the long, lazy days passed that summer, I saw Jimmy more and more often and he was always exercising.

He seemed to be training for some great physical exertion, a championship fight, a marathon race that would never happen.

As well as show me how to do push-ups and chins on the monkey bars, Jimmy told me and the kids from my block all about street fighting, defending yourself. He showed us how to correctly make a fist, how to throw a punch, how to use leverage and proper balance for the maximum effect. He explained that in a street fight the object is to win, to walk away victorious, and you can do "whatever you have-ta." Kicking and biting and scratching were all allowed and advocated by Jimmy. "In street fights, there are no rules," he said, a thing I had known instinctively.

Jimmy seemed to genuinely like us kids. He never acted annoyed or as though we were bothering him. I would later find out that he had no brothers and perhaps that's why he warmed to us. In any event, we all came to respect and like Jimmy and were sure he could beat up anyone. We had running debates about his prowess in combat—that he could beat up this or that guy and we were all sure that he could even take on Superman, if it came to a fight between the two. Jimmy seemed to take a particular shine to me. I think it was because I was the smallest of our little group and wouldn't take any abuse from anyone. I had "moxie." There were many factions of kids in the park; that is to say, they hailed from different neighborhoods in Bensonhurst. For the most part, we all got along. Once in a while a bully would show up but Jimmy would set him straight right away. Jimmy didn't like bullies. Jimmy was a bully slayer. Though none of us ever saw him actually fight, we were all certain he could take on *anyone*. Jimmy had a fierce reputation and just a look from him was usually enough to keep potential adversaries at bay—walking away.

We finally did, however, get a chance to see Jimmy actually fight on a hot summer night when the dark came late and most all the neighborhood was out and moving about slowly because of the heat. Lightning bugs began to blink on and off. Some of my buddies and I from Bay 31 Street were playing tag in the park. In Brooklyn, when we played tag, we punched one another, not tagged each other. Ralph the parky wanted to close the playground and in his nasty way told us to leave, which we were doing, but apparently not fast enough for Ralph's liking so he kicked me in the ass very hard.

"Get going," he said. More than hurting me physically, he hurt my pride and I cursed him seven ways from Sunday, and he hauled off and slapped me. I was shocked, feeling the hot sting of his dirty hand on my face.

"Get lost, you little WOP," he said.

This, I would later come to realize, was why Ralph was so mean to us kids. We were, for the most part, the children of Italian immigrants who had come to this country looking for a better life but often ran into irrational prejudices and animosities that had nothing to do with anything we had done. Ralph was Irish and he didn't like Italians. As groups, the Irish and the Italians often vied for the same jobs, lived in the same neighborhoods, and pursued one another's women with lustful abandon. The hard-knuckled animus between the Italians and the Irish at the turn of the century was legendary.

WOPs . . . WOP means "without papers," and Italians coming from Italy with no papers were summarily deemed WOPs. At that point, when I was eight years old, I knew nothing yet about the ongoing feud between the Italians and the Irish; I didn't even yet know what WOP meant, but I was sure it was something disrespectful and terrible.

I heard Jimmy coming before I saw him, the fence rattling. He had apparently seen Ralph slap me and he was climbing over a ten-foot chain-link fence to get inside the playground proper. Ralph the parky saw Jimmy walking toward him and belligerently turned to face him, a slight smile on his pug-nosed face, chest out, shoulders back. Jimmy calmly walked straight toward Ralph, who was much larger than Jimmy, had at least a foot on him and a hundred pounds, but that didn't slow or dissuade Jimmy in any way.

"You wanna hit someone, hit me," Jimmy offered, a malevolent smirk playing on his broken-nosed face, looking up at Ralph, moving closer to him, as if a fearless bull.

"What's this to you?" Ralph demanded, disdainfully looking down at Jimmy.

"The kid's my friend," Jimmy said. Again, I would not realize this until years later, but what was about to happen occurred because my last name ended with a vowel and Jimmy's last name ended with a vowel. Though Jimmy did not look Italian with his blond hair and blue eyes, I would come to realize that Emma is an Italian last name.

"Take a fuckin' hike. Mind your own fuckin' business," Ralph said, and dismissively turned away from Jimmy.

Jimmy, however, went after Ralph, grabbed his shoulder, turned him around, and slapped him so hard a strawberry-colored Rorschach immediately formed on Ralph's Irish-pale face. Ralph swung at Jimmy, missed, and in the next instant Jimmy got Ralph on the ground and beat him to a bloody pulp. Blood was everywhere, gushing from Ralph's nose and mouth.

Standing, Jimmy said, "You ever touch any of these here kids again, you are going to the hospital for a long time—mick-motherfucker!"

And with that, Jimmy turned and calmly walked away with his easy, cat-like gait, moving closer with each step toward his incredibly violent destiny—murder most foul in broad daylight involving the Colombo crime family.

I had never seen anyone fight with such single-minded ferocity. Jimmy was my hero. He had vanquished Ralph the parky, who from that day on never bothered any of us. Ralph became as meek as a docile lamb.

I learned that humid summer evening in August 1957 that size doesn't matter; that the bigger they are, the harder they fall. That might is right. I was many years away from knowing, however, that the pen could be mightier than the sword.

My mind now back in Naples, lying there immobile and breathing with a machine, Laura sleeping lightly beside me, I hear still more gunshots—three consecutive ones. Wondering if someone has been shot, who that someone was, I silently drift into a welcoming sleep. In sleep, the disease has no access to me. In sleep, I am whole and healthy again, often walking, sometimes running. I don't dream as such anymore—what come to me now are more like three-dimensional hallucinations. Dreams have become peyote trips for me. In my dreams, moving along in the dappled light cast by giant oak and maple trees, I am jogging on the horse path around the Central Park reservoir, free and strong and sure-footed.

2. The Tyrrhenian Sea

To get to Ischia, you have to take a ferry that leaves from the port of Naples on the south side of the city. We arrive at the pier at ten o'clock the following morning with our special van, our luggage, and me in a wheelchair. I think that just about everyone who sees us comes to the conclusion that both Laura and Kelsey are my daughters. For the most part, the Italians are respectful and helpful. Without any of us asking them, Italian men gladly pick up my wheelchair and carry me onto the boat. It is a dated, double-decker ferry like you'd find anywhere in the world. The ferry can carry about thirty cars and several hundred passengers. The ride to Ischia is approximately one hour. To get there, we have to pass the famous island of Capri. In a sense, from a mile away or so, it seems that Capri is purposely hiding Ischia from the world, shielding it from the hurried, boisterous tourists who flock to Capri like bees to flowers in the early months of spring. The three of us are on the half deck as we pass Capri, making comments about its lagoons and the clarity of its water. I say nothing about what I know of Tiberius Caesar. This would only put a damper on the beautiful painting before us, though, in my mind, I cannot help but think of what Tiberius did. Why, I wonder, how, I wonder, had he become so deranged, such a monster; what was wrong inside of his head that would compel him to be aroused by the torture and death of prepubescent children? Was his brain hardwired that way? Had he been abused as a boy by one of the other Caesars? Certainly possible in ancient Rome. Even I, who know so much about killers and psychopaths from hands-on experience, talking to them, cannot put a face on Tiberius. In addition to the serial killers I have known personally, have interviewed personally, I have studied in great detail all the more infamous killers from our history as a species. There is a long list of mad sexual sadists from all over Europe, surely too numerous to name here, the most prominent of which would be Jack the Ripper.

I turn my wheelchair away from the island and my eyes invariably fall upon my fellow passengers—many of whom are my ethnic contemporaries, for the blood that runs in their veins runs in my own. My people are from this place—I am a Neapolitan. As I look at the men, how strong and well coordinated some of them appear, I remember what I was like before the killer grabbed me by the throat and began to squeeze the life out of me. I remember well running in Central Park during hurricanes and snow blizzards; I remember skiing with mad abandon the incredibly steep slopes of the Italian Alps at Cortina d'Ampezzo, the Swiss Alps at Verbier, the Austrian Alps at Ober Lech, and the indescribably beautiful Alps of Saint-Moritz, Switzerland. I remember, too, when I lifted weights, did curls with fifty-pound weights in each hand. Now, I struggle to pick up a spoon; a toothbrush is as heavy as a fifty-pound dumbbell. Though I have learned to accept my lot, seeing these men reminds me of what I once was.

The terrible pain and turmoil and chaos when first diagnosed, the "why me" phase, the depression phase, the suicidal phase are all in the past. Now, I look forward to the future. My life is about creating, not incriminations or pain or tears or questions about why the grim reaper chose to knock on my door.

You can smell Ischia soon after you see it, growing out of the horizon. It is an earthy, fertile odor that speaks of all the good that comes from the soil here. Unlike Capri, Ischia is an agricultural bonanza, green and lush. I cannot help but fantasize about Roman legions sailing here to enjoy the healing springs. We, Laura, Kelsey, and I, are now coming here for those same springs. Maybe, I hope, the healing waters will energize my muscles, soothe my bones and joints, and give strength to my legs. They cannot hold me. If I could manage to stand up, I would immediately fall over. Three times since I have been diagnosed, I fell down and was knocked out cold. It's a harrowing experience for, as I go down, I don't have the strength to grab something and stop myself, lessen the fall.

Ischia makes all three of us smile without anyone saying anything. The boat docks. Again, without being asked, Italian men effortlessly pick me up and put me on solid land. I am concerned about being able to get phone calls here. I am concerned about the Italian courts in Naples giving me the green light to get Iplex. Laura checks the phone reception and it is strong. We get in the van that Laura has arranged to pick us up and are taken to the hotel/residence we have booked. The hotel has a spring on the premises. But first, of course, we have to eat lunch. In Italy, you look forward to breakfast, lunch, and dinner in a way that, back home, you rarely do. Every which way you turn is the smell of something delicious—an unspoken celebration of food: meats fused with garlic, red wine, and rosemary; fish wrapped in different spices; marinara sauce cooked over low heat with basil and garlic; large, circular loaves of peasant bread baked in open hearths heated by wood—all these smells entice you and beg for your attention. Here, on Ischia, a symphony of mouthwatering odors serenades you.

Now that we have arrived on Ischia, my mind goes back to this book, writing—my one true passion in life. After much soul-searching, I decided to write about what I do, my entering prisons, my interviewing killers, juxtaposed against my having a fatal disease. Some days, writing this comes easily. Other days, it's very hard for it is profoundly personal, perhaps so personal that it could be unhealthy. This is not about purging myself, something cathartic. I don't think writers have any right to use the writing of a book as some kind of therapy. I always felt that was self-indulgent, rather self-centered. However, I feel what I have been doing, what has happened to me is a story that needs to be told, a rare journey into what having a fatal disease is like while spending time in the company of monsters.

Kelsey and I find a veranda at the hotel surrounded by a garden from which grows a variety of colorful flowers and plants, dwarfed by palm trees. From where we sit we can see the Tyrrhenian and the strong Neapolitan sun reflecting off it. Dictating what I would have normally written by hand is an inherently difficult task, something you must practice in order to get used to and, ultimately, master. With time, and with practice, I have learned to write as vividly by dictating as I once did by holding a pen in my hand and having the luxury of stopping and starting as I pleased, staring off into space, without somebody waiting for the next sentence, thought, image.

As with many things I took for granted when healthy, little by little—over a four-year period—the disease stole away my ability to write by hand. Holding a phone is now impossible, the holding of a book is gone, being able to master the folds you need to read the *New York Times*, using a fork, shaving are now all things of the past. One of the things I miss the most because of my illness is cooking. I grew to love cooking and became very good at it, but now I cannot use a knife; cannot sauté with a frying pan . . . can't even stand in front of a stove. Thankfully, after much anguish, I have learned to write fluidly and succinctly by speaking.

Kelsey says she has to use the restroom. She gets up and goes inside. Laura is in our room, freshening up. Even though I know Kelsey will be right back, I do not like being alone. I feel pinpricks of anxiety on the back of my neck.

My eyes move to the horizon. With quiet joy, I watch the sea meeting the sky, the contrast of different blues. I take a shallow breath, enjoying the smell of the ocean and the flowers I am surrounded by, the lovely terracotta tile all about the veranda. Sparrows noisily chatter in a thick fig tree to my left. I feel a little groggy. I have been taking lithium now for eleven months. The drug is prescribed to me not for any psychiatric disorder but because it is believed that lithium has a positive effect on rebuilding damaged motor neurons. It is failing motor neurons in both the brain and the upper aspects of the spine that cause amyotrophic lateral sclerosis. There was a study done on fifty Italian patients with ALS. The study concluded that lithium inhibited the disease. I don't like taking this drug. I have a tendency to inexplicably nod off at inopportune moments. I see vivid-fanciful images—as though I were standing still and watching a speeding train go by, people living their lives in it.

Other times, the images come to me as though on a merry-go-round, swirling images of people and places and things. Sometimes what I see makes sense; more often than not, there is no rhyme or rhythm to these images, though there is usually a feeling of dread and foreboding about them.

Sitting there on the veranda in my jazzed-up wheelchair, I feel my eyes getting heavy, slowly closing. I am not tired as such. I am excited and exuberant about being here. But my eyes become heavier and heavier still.

The chirping of the birds moves off to a faraway place between the twilight zone and consciousness. Here, in this limbo, I see different vignettes of my life spread out before me. Today I see myself walking on 86th Street with Gerard Pappa. When I was thirteen, fourteen years old, I regularly hung out with Pappa. He was five years my senior; I was kind of like his mascot. Later, Gerard Pappa would become a made man in the Genovese crime family, one of their premier assassins, would murder thirty-eight people. This was my mentor.

I first met Pappa at Sal's pool hall on Bensonhurst's 86th Street.

As most all the boys in the neighborhood, I was in awe of Pappa. He was a celebrated gladiator, admired and feared at the same time. For some reason, Pappa took a shine to me. I think this had to do with the fact that I had a reputation as a stand-up kid; that I dressed well, comported myself as though I were older, was comfortable in my own skin.

Even then, in the years 1963–65, Pappa was clearly destined to become La Cosa Nostra. He was without question the kind they wanted. He was as tough as rusted nails, had a nice appearance, was fearless and treacherous in the extreme. As well as being a notorious street fighter, Pappa had a charming side. Women were drawn to him, staring and swooning as he passed. In addition to what I had learned from Jimmy Emma, Pappa took the rudiments of street fighting to new levels for me.

"If you gotta bite somebody's nose right off their fucking face, do it. There's no such thing as dirty fighting," he said many times over.

My world still consisted of Bensonhurst, Brooklyn. Not knowing any better, I was inspired by his words. I still had no idea there was a whole other universe out there that had nothing to do with fighting, hurting people, being tough.

The thing that struck me most about Pappa was how nice he could be. He was always making jokes, quick to laugh, and I never saw him bully anyone. He said that if you were truly tough there was no need to act it, to push people around. All the many months I hung around Pappa, I never saw him pick a fight, though he would go on to become a premier Mafia assassin.

Coincidentally, Pappa's best friend was none other than Jimmy Emma, the guy who had beaten up Ralph the parky for me, my protector.

By now, Jimmy had grown into a muscle-bound monster. He, like Pappa, was renowned throughout the whole of Brooklyn as a badass guy. Indeed, these two were the fiercest street fighters in all of Brooklyn. They were destined to either kill each other in combat or become friends; they chose the latter. Pappa's uncle Vinnie Pappa was a member of the Genovese family, and that was how Pappa ended up in that borgata. Vinnie Pappa would become infamous for his central role in the much-touted French Connection heroin case. It was Vinnie Pappa who partnered up with French gangsters out of Marseilles and distributed amazingly pure heroin across the United States. The French Connection case wound up becoming the basis for an Oscar-winning film starring Gene Hackman named *The French Connection.*

Conversely, Jimmy Emma hated mafiosi and was not afraid to express his disdain—a recipe for disaster. He had become known throughout the neighborhood as a bona fide psychopath. Jimmy was the first of many psychopaths I would come to know well. It was perhaps because of Pappa and Jimmy Emma that I was able to readily enter and leave the netherworld of full-blown serial killers, sadistic Mafia hit men and bosses I would eventually write about.

As I said earlier, because of Jimmy, I actually witnessed a murder.

This is what went down: Jimmy and Pappa were in a bar called The Latin Quarter on New Utrecht Avenue in Brooklyn, drinking with their girlfriends, when a mob capo by the name of Coney Island Mimi started insulting one of the girls. Pappa and Jimmy took him to the back of the club and beat him mercilessly—stuck his head in the toilet bowl and beat him some more. This would cause the wrath of the whole Colombo family—indeed, all the Mafia. You cannot beat on a mafioso and not expect dire consequences.

A few days after this incident, I went to see Pappa because I wanted to borrow $500 to buy a pound of pot. I had it in my head to sell nickel bags from the pool hall and make a killing. By now, it was the mid-'60s and most everyone smoked grass, but there was no reliable supply in the neighborhood. Looking for Pappa, I went to Joe's Candy Store on 79th Street and New Utretcht Avenue, where he hung out, held court. Pappa was shylocking money, dealing drugs on a large scale, and working his way toward being made. Because I went back with Pappa, and I was once his protégé, I felt he would loan me the money without difficulty. I had no intention of making the dealing of drugs any kind of profession. I was only doing it because I wanted material things I couldn't afford. I was still going to school and any kind of part-time job I could have gotten would have generated little cash. I wanted better clothes, a fleece coat, perhaps a car—if I could have pulled that off.

That day, I was walking south on New Utrecht Avenue toward Joe's Candy Store. Trains going to and from the city rumbled overhead on the New Utrecht Avenue El. I first spotted Jimmy Emma. He was sitting in front of the candy store on the fender of his car, a big-ass pink Cadillac you could see a mile away. Pappa was also leaning up against the car. You would think that considering they had beaten up a capo in the Colombo crime family, they would be in hiding somewhere, but not these two. They were fearless. Glad to see Pappa, I began to walk faster when a dark car came barreling down New Utrecht Avenue from the opposite direction and three men wearing stockings over their faces, obstructing their features, jumped out of the car and started shooting at Jimmy and Pappa.

Pappa ran straight in my direction with the speed of a cheetah, north on New Utrecht Avenue, as two of the gunmen took rapid shots at him, missing him, pop-pop-pop-pop. I ducked behind a van. A bullet hit the van with a loud, metallic bing. Pappa, white like a ghost, seemed to fly past me. Jimmy ran into 79th Street, got about thirty feet into the block when they shot him down in a hail of bullets and killed him there in the street. The three gunmen got back in the car and it pulled away. It would later be revealed they were Carmine Persico, Coney Island Mimi, and Shorty Spero. They drove past me as they were taking off the stockings. A second car quickly fell in behind them. They turned onto a side street. The second car, I knew, would block the path of any police cars or curious citizens that may have given chase. This was done all neat, tidy, and professional. This was a typically executed Mafia hit. This was my introduction to murder.

Shocked to the core of my young being, I slowly, hesitantly, walked to where Jimmy was lying in the middle of the street. His mouth was agape. His unseeing blue eyes stared at a low-hung Brooklyn sky. A wide snake of glistening blood was coming from his lifeless body as though it had been tattooed on his skin and, now that he was dead, it was leaving his body. It was an unseasonably warm January day, though windy. The wind rippled across the blood and moved it unnaturally, as though it were quivering, had life. Above the elevated train headed toward Manhattan, roared overhead as bright orange sparks fell from the tracks. Onlookers, neighborhood people, children, old ladies, and old men cautiously gathered around the unmoving body of the once omnipotent Jimmy Emma—now dead, yet another victim of La Cosa Nostra.

Like forlorn wolves, the plaintive wails of sirens soon filled the air. As I walked away, I carried an unusual, unnatural weight on my shoulders.

That night, alone in my bed in my parents' home, I thought about Jimmy Emma—the first time I saw him, how he beat up Ralph the bully, how he also made sure none of us kids were bothered by the pedophiles who roamed the park like hungry sharks in the shallows where children swim. In a sense, I thought, when Jimmy was killed part of me died, part of what I believed in died. Part of the Brooklyn mantra died. "Might is always right." A bullet to the head wins any argument.

Jimmy Emma was laid out in D'Angelo's Funeral Parlor on Bath Avenue and Bay 19th Street. I felt compelled to see him and pay my respects. There were hundreds of people there, seemed the whole neighborhood had turned out. I stood at Jimmy's open casket and prayed for his soul, tried to tell God that Jimmy belonged in heaven; that he had a big heart; that he had protected us kids from bullies, from Ralph the mean parky. Many viewed Jimmy as a monster, a mean-spirited street fighter with no feelings for anyone or anything, but I knew better. I'd known Jimmy since I was a little boy and I had loved him. I never thought I'd ever see him dead; he was invincible, impervious to bullets. I stared at his thick, powerful hands, the knuckles broken, the skin scarred and pocked, and I cried for Jimmy. Seeing him there like that, dead, cold, lifeless, changed me, made me realize how fragile and volatile life really was; that the direction I was moving in was not the right one.

Eventually, Pappa and I drifted apart. He had taught me many lessons about the street, for which I will be forever grateful. Even to this day, I do not sit with my back to the entrance of a restaurant. Whenever I am hanging out on the street with a friend, I will always have my back to the wall because of him. Pappa made me aware of the vicious predators in this world not because he was a teacher as such but because he was a vicious predator himself. He also gave me something that would enable me, years down the road, to readily talk with killers as though I were one of them, enabling me to learn who they really are. Inadvertently, he gave me a tool that I would be able to use to discover the innermost secrets and workings of dedicated murderers. Because of Gerard Pappa, there is no dark street I am afraid to walk down. I can see trouble before it arrives.

I feel a tingle in my left hand. My eyes pop open. My head is all bent forward because I've been nodding off. The top of my vertebrae hurts. I slowly push my head back. Because of the weakened neck muscles, my head feels like it is a hundred pounds, a cannonball. I look left and see that Laura is slowly returning. I say nothing to her about where I've just been and what I've seen.

"Are you okay?" Laura asks.

"I'm fine," I say.

Kelsey joins Laura and me and the three of us go to experience the hot springs we have heard so much about. Luckily, Kelsey and Laura get along. My relationship with Kelsey is beyond what normally exists between an employer and an employee. She is an intricate, intimate part of my writing, my ability to write—the most important enterprise I've ever been involved in. Considering what I'm dealing with, if my wife and my voice, as it were, didn't get along, it could have disastrous consequences. But they do, and we all head over to the spa.

You can smell the natural spring from a block away. It is a strong, sulfuric stink. Black bubbles the size of half dollars float on the surface of the water. With the help of two men who work at the hotel, I am slowly lowered into the spring. It is hot, but amazingly soothing. Soon the three of us are soaking in these waters where, for hundreds of years, people from all over Europe have come for their healing powers. For the most part, I have given up praying and asking this, that, or the other God for help with the killer, and I am not about to ask the healing waters to get rid of the killer now. I just enjoy the soothing deep heat on my diminished muscles and my joints. I close my eyes, but thoughts of Jimmy, my seeing his murder, return without my permission or invitation.

The days here on Ischia go surprisingly fast, punctuated by one good meal after the other, my writing, spas, and massages in between. We patiently wait for word from the Italian courts. In that Italy is one big bureaucracy, fueled by three-hour lunches and short workweeks, we are prepared for a long stay. I keep busy by working with Kelsey on this book as well researching a true story involving the war on drugs and a psychotic capo in the Bonanno crime family.

Luckily we are able to get the *Herald Tribune* here and thus we keep abreast of what's going on in the world. Both Kelsey and Laura read the different papers to me, sitting by the pool. Here, brilliantly colored hummingbirds shoot to and fro all about the hotel. Some days the ocean surrounding us is calm and friendly; other days it is rough. This morning I saw a giant, ten-foot-long tuna fish, caught just hours before, on the back of a flatbed truck. It was a graceful, monstrous thing to behold. Its eyes were as large as softballs. It reminded me of days I went deep-sea fishing in Montauk, Long Island, and Key West, Florida. What great fun that was. I once caught a giant tuna and it was amazingly strong. That, going fishing with my friend Simon, is another thing that has gone by the wayside.

Soon, Kelsey, Laura, and I are again sitting at a dining table, our mouths collectively watering as we talk about what we would like to eat, smelling the delicious aromas issuing from the kitchen.

I'm going to begin with melon and parma prosciutto, I'm thinking, as a lightning bolt cracks open the Neapolitan sky and the sound of huge cannons rolls across the ocean, echoing and rumbling as it comes and goes, leaving me feeling small and vulnerable. We order our food. After the prosciutto and melon, we have grilled octopus served with a dark chocolate sauce. Silently, the waiter watches Laura cut a piece and feed it to me. Wordlessly, he tells me with his eyes that he is sorry. In turn, I say thank you with my eyes. The combination of seared octopus and chocolate is amazingly good.

IPLEX . . . my mind keeps going back to the drug. I'm hoping with all my heart and soul that we get it. Something has to stop this vampiric ghoul from slowly drawing away my life force.

Inevitably, for the hundredth time, I wonder how I got this disease. My mind races back and forth with this question as we eat this delicious food. When I was young, I suffered numerous blows to my head; as I got older, I used cocaine. Could either of those things, or perhaps the fact that I was shot in the head, have contributed to the motor neuron disease eating me up with the gusto with which the Italians around us take food? I know no one on either side of my huge family has had this disease.

When I was young, I was not especially close to my parents. As a boy, I was dyslexic, had ADHD, and school was difficult for me. Rather than understanding and treating my disabilities, my parents were angered and let down by how I did in school and so there was always a wall between us. Back then, in the 1950s, dyslexia was little understood, never treated, a monumental problem when you were a child trying to read, trying to keep up with the rest of the class. Funny how I ended up becoming a dedicated writer when the written word was my nemesis throughout my formative years. In that my father believed in corporal punishment, I ended up getting beatings, struck in the head, and, too, I was in many street fights and bangs to the head in Brooklyn's Bensonhurst were the norm. When I asked my doctors if any of these could have brought on the disease, they collectively said no.

The disconnect between myself and my parents carried over into my teens and the moment I had the opportunity to move out of their home, to move to New York City, I jumped at it. But now, as I said, I concern myself more with the future than with the past. Today, my parents are my best friends. Sometimes, when my mother looks at me, the state I'm in, she begins to cry. Seeing her cry, seeing her hurt so, hurts me more than anything else and I demand that she stop crying.

Still, I know she is a mother and I know what it must be like for a mother to see a child slowly withering away.

I force these thoughts from my head. My future now holds a dish of steak with marinara sauce and large, dark capers and an excellent glass of light Chianti pressed right on the island.

Soon, the dining room becomes crowded. I am sitting with my back to the wall facing the room. I count twenty-eight tables. I enjoy watching the Italians eat. There's a love of food, an obvious, harmonic synchronicity between the different tastes and their taste buds. There is no hurrying.

When we finish our meal, Carlo the waiter appears out of nowhere and quickly clears the table.

"Dolce?" he asks.

We decide to leave dessert up to him. He serves us fresh grilled figs with thin slices of parma prosciutto and a delicious cheese made from goat's milk. With this, we have a liqueur made from fresh licorice, which spreads a sensual warmth as it goes down, helping you digest. In that I am wheelchair-bound and can't get up and walk around to help myself digest, eating has become somewhat of a chore for me, though still a great pleasure. When we are ready to leave, as has become my custom, I say, "Let's go for a roll."

"Yeah, good idea," Kelsey says. "Let's roll." The rolling comes about as a result of my being in a wheelchair.

I follow them through the dining room to the exit, watching the diners stare at Laura and Kelsey as they move across the restaurant. Italian men look at attractive women the way they look at delicious food, laid out for the taking.

Outside, it is suddenly quiet; the smell of the sea is all about us. Because of the full moon, we can see that the tide is high. We make our way to the main road, which connects to the town, and quietly walk with the sea on our left and the moon on our right. There is little wind and that makes the smell of the sea that much more pungent. We sit at a café in town just near the water and order lemonade. Here the lemons are extraordinary feats of nature, some of them as large as grapefruits, amazingly tasty, vividly sweet and sour at the same time. The day has been long. We are tired and start to walk back to the hotel. I would love to rip off my clothes and dive in the water, enjoying the warm embrace of the Mediterranean Sea, but that ain't happening.

Laura and I say good night to Kelsey and return to our room.

Inside the room, Laura washes me up and brushes my teeth. We talk some about the food. Our conversation turns to IPLEX. Not getting it would be a devastating letdown and all things devastating I want to avoid, as she well knows. Aggravation, disappointment, confrontation are all things that people with ALS cannot deal with. All hasten the progression of the disease.

We find CNN on the television and avidly watch the coverage of the early presidential race, hoping Obama gets nominated and becomes president. Though I have nothing against Hillary Clinton, I feel Obama will do a better job. He isn't weighed down with the Clintons' dirty laundry. The thought of John McCain winning is anathema to me. Obama is a strong advocate for stem cell research, one of the few things that can help people with motor neuron afflictions. Parkinson's, multiple sclerosis, and Alzheimer's patients could all benefit measurably from the application of stem cells. When I think about how George Bush vetoed stem cell bills passed twice by both houses, it makes me sick to my stomach. To arbitrarily impose his religious beliefs upon the whole nation without consideration for the many different denominations that make up this wonderful country was a crying shame, a bona fide sin. I take a long, deep breath. My long, deep breaths these days are so shallow, my chest barely moves. Instead, I must use the breathing machine to facilitate a full breath. Laura changes the channel. I watch a giant sperm whale cut through a cobalt blue sea. I marvel at the majesty of the beast, the king of the seas effortlessly moving through the water.

For the most part, I sleep like a dead man. My eyes close and the next thing I know, Laura is standing over me, waking me. "It's time to get up," she says. "It's time to get up." I don't feel like I've slept at all. All of my bones and joints ache from sitting still in a wheelchair all day long without the benefit of muscle support.

"I don't want to get up," I tell her. This is a kind of ritual we go through each day. She prods me to get out of bed. I refuse. The fact is, I could sleep fifteen hours and still wake up exhausted. I'm told it is the nature of the disease. A good, restful night's sleep, among many other things, has been subtly stolen away from me.

I'm sleeping on my side. Laura gently rocks me. I don't want to get up, but ultimately Laura bribes me with the delicious espresso and honeydew melon they serve in the restaurant. I soon struggle out of bed and off to the restaurant we go. As we enter the dining area, we are greeted by the other guests.

"Bongiorno," we hear over and over again.

I take honeydew and toast and espresso, and as Laura is feeding me, her cell phone rings. It is my Italian attorney calling to tell us that, unfortunately, the Italian courts have turned down my request for IPLEX. I will not be getting IPLEX here in Italy. I thank him for all that he's done and hang up. All our efforts to get the drug have been for naught.

This does not surprise me. I have always known it was a long shot. We all had. But still, it was . . . disconcerting. A door was slammed in my face. In that Italy has socialized medicine, I thought it would be a real stretch for them to pay for a drug that costs over $150,000 a year. While in Ischia, I also find out that the Italian government has regularly been turning down Italian citizens with ALS. Still, I felt it worth a try, but now we are back to square one. I want to shout; I want to scream—I want to bang my head against the wall, but I don't have the luxury of any of that. We've done our best. Quiet and morose, we make plans to go back to the States and begin at the beginning. Kelsey and Laura hide their disappointment.

In our room, Laura quietly packs. I am sitting in my wheelchair on the terrace facing the sea. I close my eyes. The Mediterranean sun feels wonderful on my face, warm and soothing and comforting—an old, dear, trusted friend. Laura comes outside with two pink capsules, my daily dose of lithium. I take the two pills with a glass of Pellegrino. I don't like this drug but it is the only viable possibility and so I reluctantly take it twice a day.

As we are leaving Ischia and passing through Naples, I feel the only hope I had has been taken away for no good reason. Why, I can't help but wonder, can the Italians get an American-made drug while an American citizen cannot? Go figure. If I let it, it would make me bitter. It would make me angry. But I know better and try to avoid those emotions because if I don't, they'll inevitably turn on me and bite me in the ass. As the special van to accommodate my wheelchair climbs up above the Bay of Naples, its aged transmission straining, I stare at the beautiful wonder of this ancient city, again thinking about how my forbears left this place in search of better lives. As we move on, we pass sweet-smelling orchards filled with lemon, orange, and peach trees; there are also neat rows of gnarled olive trees most everywhere you look

Crack, crack, crack! come gunshots from across the city. Again, we all act as though we don't hear them, ride on in silence, leaving behind this beautiful though very dangerous metropolis.

"The bay is really beautiful," I say. Neither Kelsey nor Laura answers me. They are wrapped up in their own thoughts. Considerate of my feelings, neither of them expresses any disappointment about not getting the drug.

"It's a hell of a sight," I repeat, pursuing them for a response, trying to shake them out of their reverie.

"Yes," Laura says.

"Si," Kelsey agrees.

There is more than one way to skin a cat, I think.

We arrive at the Neapolitan airport. It is small and quaint, more like an airport from the 1950s. As we make our way through the terminal, the burnt, nut-like smell of espresso comes to us again. As we move, my eyes start lowering, my head drooping. It's the lithium. I decide to have an espresso. Espresso, not surprisingly, counteracts the lithium. A waiter clad in a white vest serves us three espressos while adroitly making paninis. I marvel at how Italians have turned a simple sandwich into a delicious meal.

Our flight to Rome, from which we'll fly to John F. Kennedy Airport, is announced. Courteously, an employee of the airport helps us to the gate. Here, too, at the airport, as in Naples proper, the threat of violence looms large and real. We pass machine gun–toting police, both men and women, sporting fashionable uniforms cut just so. It's hard not to notice them. These people, the Italians, are a good-looking lot. Their cheekbones are high, brows wide and pronounced, lips admirably full. What makes them particularly attractive, however, is how comfortable they are within their own skin, natural and fluid. Clothes adorn them with elegance. Yet their eyes are suspicious and wary, for here the Camorra is not a problem, but terrorism is a real concern. They watch keenly, fingers on the triggers of their guns, for those who would destroy just for the sake of destroying—for the sake of Allah.

Without incident, we make it through security and begin to board the plane. I'm helped into my seat by burly stewards. I have to be frank, it's terribly embarrassing to be carried onto the plane as though I'm a two-year-old child, my legs dangling listlessly, useless pieces of rubber, like a dummy in a ventriloquist's lap. But I smile and thank the flight attendants and am seated and strapped in. We don't realize until we're on the plane that Laura's camera is missing. There's nothing we can do about it. We write it off as lost. I'm bummed out about it, though, for we had good pictures of ourselves in Naples and on Ischia.

Soon we are above the great Bay of Naples. Off in the distance I can see Mount Vesuvius, a menacing though majestic constant in the

Neapolitan landscape, smoke lazily issuing from it. As difficult as this trip has been—after not getting the drug—I am not angry. In reality, I feel I have been put in touch with a creative optimism that hails from the very soil of Italy, of Naples, of my people, that will help see me through this nightmare. As we gain altitude, I can see Sorrento, Positano, and Amalfi beyond—some of the most beautiful real estate anywhere in the world. My dream is to get better and buy a place here with orange and peach, lemon and olive trees, with an outdoor, woodburning stove on the property. I envision myself going down to the sea every day and doing exercises in the shallow water, stretching my legs, making my legs stronger, drawing on the life-giving Mediterranean Sea. Surely, such a dream, such an aspiration, won't be taken away from me. I am going to get better. I am going to do this. All my life, everything I've ever really, really wanted, I've gotten—through perseverance, through blood and sweat and tears. Perhaps more than anything because I wouldn't accept no for an answer.

Slowly, my eyes again get heavy. I don't want to sleep. I want to stay up and think my thoughts. I want to admire the beautiful Tyrrhenian Sea and the Amalfi Drive, but I am tired and before I know it, my eyes begin to close, the drone of the plane lulling me to a place I've never been.

3. Plan B

We don't want to go back to New York, but I have to. It is fall and New York is prohibitively cold. Sufferers of ALS have a hard time dealing with cold weather. My hands cramp up; my feet swell and I am prone to respiratory problems. In that my diaphragm muscles are compromised, I cannot cough, cannot get rid of effluviums and bacteria that build up in the lungs as a matter of course. The best medicine for me is a warm climate.

Unfortunately, ALS is a rare, little understood disease. Most everyone afflicted with it goes through one, two, three neurologists and are all told the same thing—"I'm sorry, there's nothing we can do; we suggest that you put your affairs in order." Essentially, go home and die. Inevitably, you run into a kind of stoic indifference that is a farewell, a slow closing of the coffin, tolling of the bells. I have three noted neurologists overseeing my care, one of whom is Lew Rowland, the esteemed head of the neurological department at Columbia, and the sum of what he told me when he diagnosed me was: "Prepare to meet your maker."

In light of this brick wall we in the ALS community face, we have formed little cabals to help battle the disease. We liken ourselves to guerrilla fighters. As an example, my going to Italy, my trying to get IPLEX on my own, was a commando operation.

Two of the people who are part of our commando operation to beat this cursed disease are Steve and Barbara Byer out of Madison, Wisconsin. Their son, Ben, was diagnosed with ALS when he was twenty-seven years old, comparatively young to contract the disease. Steve relentlessly fought to try to help Ben. He traveled around the world, spoke to doctors and scientists and medicine men in China, Germany, throughout the United States, all to no avail. Steve is still on the cutting edge of all *possibilities*.

Unfortunately, before Steve was able to help him, Ben died several months ago of the disease. He was 110 pounds and six feet two when he passed on. Most all of the people I've known with ALS have died. Several of them have committed suicide. One minute, one day, one week, one month, I'm talking with them, talking with their husbands or wives, and the next thing I know we get a phone call or hear via e-mail that they are no more. This is another one of those things that could easily distract you, take you to a negative place you don't want to go. However, that is exactly the opposite of what must occur, what I must do. Thinking positive thoughts, staying busy, trying to keep the disease from enveloping you—your mind—and taking you to a place from which you can never come back.

Over the phone, little by little, Steve Byer and I have become very good friends. He can't get over my street savvy and how I come up with these plans to try to get what we need—in this case, IPLEX. It's been three years now since he and I, his wife, Barbara, and my wife, Laura, have been battling to get the drug. At sixty-eight, Steve has become a tireless force in the ALS community. Steve is now helping ALS patients all over the world by giving lectures at symposiums. In a way, I have become a surrogate son to him.

On the day that Laura and I first actually meet Steve and Barbara, it is still warm out and we are in the backyard of our apartment in Manhattan's West 80s. Steve is six foot two with gray hair tied in a ponytail and he is quick to smile and laugh considering all the tragedy, human grief, he deals with. Barbara has dark hair and vivid blue eyes, is demure and friendly, and is also unusually well informed when it comes to ALS, though not to the degree that Steve is. During lunch, they tell us that many people, people in high places, are now in the battle for IPLEX. Congressmen and senators are being petitioned. The drug company that makes IPLEX, Insmed, is being pressured from many different angles. More important, Steve says, the FDA, which has refused to approve the drug, will hopefully be accountable to a new administration—a democratic administration—more apt to give permission to the drug distributor on a "compassionate care" basis. Both Hillary Clinton and Barack Obama are progressive advocates for stem cell research. This sounds really good, but I've heard it all before. I have become cynical and wary. My optimism has been dashed so many times that it's hard to be up about it. Nevertheless, I enthusiastically go along with Steve and Barbara and Laura. How could I not?

"I'll write senators, I'll write congressmen," I offer.

"How long do you think it will take?" I ask Steve.

"Not long at all. A couple of weeks, maybe. But it's going to happen, Phil. It's going to happen."

"Great," I say. We talk for a while more, all of us sad and regretful that Ben will not have the benefit of the drug, that Ben is no longer with us.

All around the backyard are tall maple and elm trees. Leaves from the trees, as though they were dying butterflies, fall and silently come to rest on the table, the yard, and Steve's broad shoulders. Though the leaves are still green, tinged with browns and reds, they are dry and brittle. I look up. More leaves are falling. For me they are as clear a signal as drums resonating through a jungle, as smoke signals being sent by Indians—*get the hell out of town.*

I start to get tired. My eyes begin to close. I see a statuesque Indian with a magnificent headdress before me. My eyes open. I'm facing Steve.

"I'm sorry," I say.

"No, don't be silly. We understand."

And I know they do.

They soon leave. We hug and kiss good-bye. Seeing the Byers makes me sad because it brings home only too well the irrevocable, fatal consequences of ALS. Their pain is real and tangible. They just buried their son. Laura shows them out. I do a complete three-sixty in my wheelchair and look at the trees, their branches suddenly appearing like gnarled, arthritic fingers. I lean farther back in my wheelchair and I watch the last of the leaves fall, carpeting the ground. Some fall on my lifeless legs. I've always equated fall with death. I don't like the leaves on my legs and I try to brush them off, as though they have some sort of hidden meaning, an agenda, but cannot move my arms.

Dusk comes on quickly. Laura is inside talking to her sister Karen on the phone. Slowly, I guide my wheelchair back into the house. I turn on National Geographic. I doze in and out of polar bears chasing seals. I feel for the seals but can't help admiring the focused determination and hunting prowess of the grand polar bear.

"They have to eat," I think, and doze off. Laura moving about the house wakes me up. We discuss the tragedy of Ben's loss, how thin he was when he passed on. To die a sudden death of natural or even accidental causes is one thing, but to slowly die a little each day over a period of years is another thing entirely. We order in Chinese food. Patiently, Laura hand-feeds me. I hate having another person feed me. It makes me feel like I am some kind of hapless creature in a forgotten zoo somewhere. Laura puts a spare rib covered in duck sauce to my mouth. Jokingly, I growl and take a big bite out of it. Tonight, in just a little while, I'm going to watch a movie I've been wanting to see for a long time—*The Red Violin*, directed by Francois Girard. Laura puts it on for me. It opens in seventeenth-century Italy. I am stunned and taken aback by how truly brilliant the film is. I'll say no more about it here other than it takes place on five continents and in five languages. I'm so taken with the film that I find myself talking aloud to the TV, a thing I very rarely do. There is one scene toward the end that makes me cry like a baby. I really want to recommend the movie to Kelsey, but she's already in South Beach. She did not come back to New York with us because she had no reason to meet the Byers and we had that obligation and some other family business. I do not want to be here in New York. I do not want to see falling leaves. I complain to Laura about the cold. I complain to Laura about everything.

"We're leaving tomorrow, don't worry," she says.

Thank God, I think to myself, replaying the beach, the ocean and its soothing sounds in my mind. The waves have always been like a resonating, melodic heartbeat to me. I'm concerned about my heart. All this trouble breathing and shallow coughing spasms are putting an inordinate amount of strain on it. I get very little exercise. I work out as best I can, but what I do is minimal. I exercise my legs by Laura putting two-pound weights on my ankles and I move my legs up and down; unfortunately, this does scant little for my heart.

My mind turns back to the sun and the sea and the sand. Again, my eyelids become heavy. They begin closing. I can see horses galloping on the insides of my pink eyelids, wild horses out in the open, running with mad abandon—a thing I once knew well myself. I used to think of myself as a thoroughbred horse. In my sleep, I inadvertently hit my joystick and my wheelchair lurches forward, rudely awakening me.

The following day—*Halle-fucking-lujah*—we leave New York behind and head south. I'm anxious to get back to work on the book, angry that I've been away from it because of Kelsey's absence. A book becomes, for me, anyway, like a child. It needs to be nurtured and loved, carefully looked after. My New York masseuse, Evelyn Gomez, an attractive, almond-eyed Latina, comes over and gives me a massage. Sitting in a wheelchair all day plays havoc on the muscles, and the joys of massages are heaven-sent.

We are flying to Miami on JetBlue. All the staff is helpful. Rather than make me feel self-conscious and like an invalid, they are polite and friendly. I hate feeling like a burden. That bugs me. The flight down south is rough, plagued by much turbulence. I hold on to the armrests with the little strength I have. I think about how helpless I'd be if the plane went down. Can't stand or move to help myself, plus I'm tethered to a breathing machine. If the plane does go down, I think, let it all be over quickly.

DEATH . . . in death, you feel no pain. In death, you are whole and complete. The specter of death never really frightened me. Now I tend to think of death, the grim reaper, as something almost—well, comforting. The turbulence suddenly stops. We fly on uneventfully. We land perfectly. I'm safely home. I'm really looking forward to getting back to South Beach and begin work on this book.

4. Mako on a Truck

We are forced to land in Fort Lauderdale because JetBlue doesn't fly to Miami. When we disembark, Laura follows me in my motorized wheelchair to the front gate. Kelsey is already at the gate waiting for us. I feel like I haven't seen her in a long time and I hug her as well as I can considering the atrophy in my arms. I drive up the ramp into our van and we head south on I-95. It is late afternoon and the traffic is heavy. On my right, along the service road, are all types of stores, shops, and warehouses. A lot of them cater to the outdoors, sports, pool and outdoor furniture. I see shops that sell guns, rifles, and pistols. The first several years that Laura and I came down to South Beach, we went shooting at least once a week. I bought us each a 9mm automatic and we enjoyed practicing shooting with her cousin, Tatum. Tatum, a voluptuous blonde with a sardonic sense of humor who is a joy to have around, is a crack shot. She understands what a gun is really for—self-defense—and I have no doubt that both she and Laura would put a bullet between the eyes of a man who tried to assault them. Both Laura and Tatum are from Brooklyn, where you learn very young that it's a dog-eat-dog world.

"I really want to go shooting this week," I say optimistically.

"We'll go . . . we'll all go," Laura says, both of us knowing that I can no longer hold a handgun and point it correctly.

I have no particular love for Fort Lauderdale. Though there are many nice homes here, clubs and restaurants, it seems like one big sprawl of shopping centers coincidentally connected by the Intercoastal. I do not get the feeling of the tropics the way I do in South Beach.

Normally, I'd be in and out of these large sporting goods stores, but I fear those days are gone. I absently look left and I see a man in an old pick-up truck driving rather fast. I note he has something odd in the back of his open truck. As I look closer, I realize it's a mako shark, about eight feet long, quite dead, just lying there like it's on some kind of tour. This fish I know well. I went fishing for them in Montauk, Long Island, on numerous occasions, and I fished for Makos in Salinas, Ecuador, with my friend Simon.

Seeing the Mako reminds me of Simon and I naturally enough begin thinking of him. Simon and I both left Brooklyn at the same time, grew our hair long at the same time, did everything we shouldn't do—smoked marijuana, did acid and, coke, and endlessly pursued girls—at the same time, Luckily, each of us ended up with our feet on the ground and our heads on our shoulders, I a writer, he an accomplished sculptor and painter. His real name was Joe, but when he became a hairdresser, they renamed him Simon at Vidal Sassoon. The two of us looked a lot alike. We were the same height, coloring, weight, both of us Italian-Americans with a Brooklyn state of mind. That is to say neither of us would take any abuse from anyone. Often, people mixed us up for each other.

In 1967, Simon joined the army to fight in Vietnam. We argued heatedly about this. I thought he was nuts, but he was much further to the right than I was politically and he gleefully had himself strapped to the open door of a helicopter and manned a 50mm machine gun. From that position, my friend Simon shot to death, tore apart, scores of Vietcong. When he returned from Nam, he was not the same person. He was quiet, morose, and much more introspective; there, too, was a dangerous air about him, an unspoken dread that he would readily kill you if need be. He also had difficulty talking to women, getting close to them. Before Nam, he had been at ease with the opposite sex. I talk about him here because we drifted apart and he moved to South Beach in the early eighties, before it became fashionable. He bought himself a beat- up co-op apartment on Collins Avenue and Fifth Street, and there he painted his pictures and did sculptures. Simon was quite talented, but for some reason he kept missing the boat. He moved to the South Pacific, lived on Bali with another friend of ours, John De Coney. John had been Simon's boss at Sassoon and they both left Sassoon together. John opened up a salon, which had a long of list of celebrity clients—Truman Capote and Andy Warhol, George Plimpton and Gore Vidal, to name a few. Simon had met Liza Minnelli at Sassoon and he became her personal hairdresser, friend, and confidante—and lover. While Simon lived in Bali for several years, I lost contact with him. I heard he sometimes came back to South Beach and when I was there working on a book in 1991, I ran into my old buddy sitting at the News Café. We had a few lunches together. I returned to New York and soon he left South Beach and went to live in Brazil's Rio de Janeiro. Simon had married a beautiful Brazilian woman named Yada. He loved all things Brazilian—the food, the music, and the women. The marriage did not work out and after breaking up with Yada, Simon lived in the favelas just above Rio, a very tough slum area, but he managed to fit in and the Brazilian gangs left him alone. He learned to speak Portuguese fluently. In Brazil, he was making masks out of wood using a technique he had learned in Bali. The masks reflected every human emotion you could imagine, from absolute rage to gluttonous satisfaction. They were all colors, amazingly creative.

As the traffic slows and we come abreast of the open truck, I am able to get a better look at the mako shark and I remember a trip Simon and I made halfway around the world—to Salinas, Ecuador—for the sole purpose of going fishing. Simon had read about Salinas in some fishing magazine and he wouldn't shut up about it. From New York, it would take approximately fifteen hours for us to get there. We would have to fly to Quito, Ecuador, catch a plane to Guayaquil, rent a car, and then drive through a desert for some six hours. Yes, I liked fishing, but I didn't like fishing that much. But back then, in those days, I was a cocaine aficionado and I was thinking I might be able to see where and how cocaine was made. For me, the trip was not just about fishing, but it was a South American adventure, seeing a new culture, a world I knew scant little about.

We arrived in Quito as planned, flew to Guayaquil, rented a car, and drove across a searing hot desert. For hours, we saw no people, just tall, indifferent cactuses. I kept thinking we were going to drive off a cliff somewhere, have a breakdown, and die of heat prostration, but we managed to make it to Salinas, a little fishing village. We rented a boat named *Pilar* for the following morning to take us fishing. At seven A.M., we were on *Pilar* and heading out. It was a forty-foot boat captained by a friendly Ecuadorian who assured us we would catch whatever we were after. What we were after were not Mako sharks but black marlins. Of all the game fish in the sea, the black marlin is on the top of the list—royalty. This is the fish that Hemingway wrote about in *The Old Man and the Sea*. You could readily liken a black marlin to a train with a spear sticking out of its head. For Simon and me, catching a black marlin was a once-in-a-lifetime opportunity. The water here was teeming with fish. We saw giant, elegant, dream-like beluga whales and dolphins as we navigated the waters where black marlin ruled supreme.

The way you catch a marlin is by pulling a bait fish with a hook sticking out of its belly along at three or four knots. The marlin sees the fish, thinks it's real, and goes for it. Twice, we saw giant spears pop out of the water and strike at the bait fish, trying to catch it. It was an amazing sight, but neither time did we hook the fish. Then, out of nowhere, the captain's eyes widened and he pointed and yelled, "Mako! Mako!" We looked and there was this huge triangular fin of a shark coming up right behind us. At the sight of that dreaded fin, I could feel my stomach tighten, a tingle run up and down my spine. Since I was a kid I had an unusual fear of sharks. Their indifferent killing powers were something I appreciated even as a boy, long before I went fishing for them in Montauk, Long Island.

My God, I thought. *It's a monster.*

A mako is a sleek, torpedo-like killing machine. It is the fastest fish in the ocean—the cheetah of the sea. Its whole being is made up for speed, from its pointed nose to its streamlined body.

As I am looking at the truck now, at the mako shark in it, I remember how that mako back in the Ecuadorian waters went for the bait and took it. It was my turn up. Simon and I had flipped a coin for who would catch a fish first and I was up. I grabbed the fishing pole and sunk the hook into the mako and he went down; after four or five seconds, he came straight up like some kind of submarine missile and seemed to hang in the air, water dripping from him, the arc of a rainbow forming directly under him. When he went down, he did so with the elegance of a championship diver. I looked at Simon and he looked at me, smiles on each of our faces. The fish continued to go down, taking a lot of line, and it almost pulled me overboard. Simon would never let that happen. He would go down with me before he let me be pulled overboard. He grabbed me from behind and held on to my waist and made sure I didn't go over.

The third jump of the mako was a tremendous, Olympic feat. We figured he went about fifteen feet into the air. After about an hour and a half, the Ecuadorian sun blazing, we finally got it up alongside the boat. We had no intention of killing this grand fish. Though it was good for eating and the Ecuadorians of Salinas liked to consume it, I wasn't going to kill it. We tagged the giant mako and we let it go, though we measured it first and it was fifteen feet long. That is a monstrous mako. All this I remember now as we head toward South Beach and, looking at my hands, I quietly begin to cry, solitary tears sliding down my face, for—unless I reverse the progression of the disease— I will never go fishing again.

When the mako shark, a natural-born killer, was up alongside the boat, it looked at me and I looked down at it and it had teeth as long as a man's pointer finger, seven rows of them. Its eyes were devoid of feeling, big and black. I would later come to see and know black eyes like that in the face of men—killers.

After the fishing trip, Simon returned to New York City. I had heard a lot of wonderful things about Rio. Instead of going back to New York, I jumped on a plane, went to Rio for Carnivale, and had a blast—the music, the food, the women . . . just wonderful. In fact, I met a hot Brazilian lady in Rio named Cecilia Medeiros Lima. She lived in Copacabana just across the street from the beach. I was supposed to stay in Rio six days, but I stayed there a full month. Cecelia, an extremely shapely brunette, wound up moving to New York and we lived together for three years. During the three years I traveled to Rio ten more times and grew to love this hot, steamy, sexy city by the sea.

Over the ensuing months and years, Simon and I grew apart. He was living in both Bali and Rio, painting and making his masks. Life, for my dear friend, was good. Then, as with me, a curveball suddenly disrupted his life.

While Simon was living in Brazil, he was diagnosed with a virulent lung cancer and was told that there was nothing they could do for him. Hoping he could get some kind of care, attention, medication, he returned to South Beach, the place I am coincidentally going to right now. He checked into the Miami Veteran's Hospital. I would learn from his brother Dennis that Simon was in great pain. They gave him a lot of morphine. For the most part, Simon was out of it. Dennis stayed by his side and all Simon was concerned about was, "How do I look? How do I look, Dennis? Am I cool? Am I cool?"

What he was asking was if he was going out like a man. That was his only concern. I learned all this later on, after the fact.

"Good. You look good, Joe," Dennis told him, as Simon drifted away on an opium-induced cloud that took him to a place with no pain, no suffering, no cares, where he died.

But all through life, my friend Simon did what the hell he wanted, danced to his own beat. Ultimately, Simon went out with grace. Not one "Why me?" He had made a life for himself in two of the most beautiful places in the world, painted and sculpted and didn't give a flying hoot about what anyone thought of him. As we now draw near South Beach, I shake my head and wipe tears from my face. Neither Kelsey nor Laura sees my tears. I say nothing about them.

We now get off 395 and make our way east on Fifth Street. It's funny, every time I come back to this place, I feel like I'm here for the first time. It's always new, always a pleasant surprise. I wish my friend were still alive to share this place with me, its bounty of tropical beauty. I take a long, deep breath. I hope you're having fun wherever you are, Si'. Looks like we soon might be hanging out again, I think, amused but not laughing.

5. South Beach

The weather is glorious in Miami, eighty-four degrees, sunny, clear blue skies. I feel fortunate to have the wherewithal to choose where I live during this dire time. By the time we arrive in Miami, it is late afternoon. I am especially comfortable in South Beach, very fond of its distinct European ambiance. Many Europeans have come here to open businesses, restaurants, boutiques, art galleries, and the like. On just about every block, there is an excellent Italian restaurant actually owned and run by Italians. In South Beach, the appeal of dining and lunching al fresco is large. Born and raised in New York, it was something I hadn't enjoyed much. I'm a natural-born people watcher and dining outside gives you the luxury of both eating leisurely and watching people as they go about their lives. Men and women from every corner of the globe flock to South Beach for vacation, sun, business, and pleasure.

Laura, Kelsey, and I are all looking forward to a good meal. As we make our way through South Beach proper, I can't help but think of Naples. My being there had a profound effect on me because it was not only an attempt to save my life, but it was also the place from which my grandparents left in search of a new life in America, the proverbial streets paved with gold—the elusive American dream. A dream the Italians were able to grasp, hold tenaciously and refused to let go of. Look at me: I've published some nine books, bought property in Manhattan without any formal education to speak of. I've made movie deals and a very good living. Where else but in America could such things happen?

As we take a left from Fifth onto Washington and head north, a motorcycle in front of us backfires and I remember the crack of the gunshots in Naples. Inevitably, without wanting to, I remember when I was shot in the head, a sensation I will never forget.

If you can imagine getting hit directly in the face with a baseball bat, then you have some idea of what it feels like to get shot in the head. The shooting was over a stupid argument with the guys I hung out with on Bay Parkway and a rough-and-tumble gang of youths who hung out over on Avenue X.

That momentous evening, we piled into my friend Roger's car and went over to Avenue X looking for the guy who had ripped off a friend of ours. There were five of us, six of them. Outnumbered, stupidly, boldly, we filed out of the car and attacked them with fists and feet of fury. This was common fare in that neighborhood in those days. It became something else entirely when I got one of them down on the street and began pummeling him. Out of nowhere, a friend of his ran up and, without so much as a how-do-you-do, pointed a pistol at me, pulled the trigger, and fired. There was a deafening explosion. A tongue of orange flame leaped out at me from the barrel. The world began swirling. I felt like I was being lifted up and carried away to a foreign, hostile place. Without me knowing it, the whites of my eyes filled with blood. I lost consciousness. When I came to, I was in the hospital. The bullet wound had been cleaned when I was unconscious. There was a large bandage on my forehead. Distraught, my parents were there. In chorus, they demanded to know what happened; I told them a guy in a car shot me as the car sped past me.

"Shot you? Why?" my father asked. "What are you doing? What are you up to?"

"I was just standing there and he shot me. I think they thought I was somebody else." I was always an efficient, adept liar—a natural-born storyteller. After all, what *is* good writing, fiction, the penning of a novel, but stringing a bunch of lies together and making them believable?

At the hospital, several doctors told me how I lucky I was that I didn't lose an eye . . . that the bullet hadn't penetrated deeper into my brain. No doubt, one of them speculated, the ammunition had been old and didn't have its normal punch.

For weeks, I had to convalesce. I looked very strange in the mirror because the whites of my eyes were blood red. I had no desire to go hang out with my friends. What I did with all this downtime was sleep and read without hurry. Perhaps for the first time, I allowed myself to appreciate what the authors were trying to explain and show. Before I knew it I felt as though I were in the story traveling to faraway places. I became . . . well, enthralled. Enthralled at the magic of the written word, enthralled by the fact that words, sentences, paragraphs, *books* were all different elements of a magic carpet that could take you anywhere in time—back in history or way into the future. It is, I think, somewhat ironic that my first in-depth experience with books, literature, was a direct result of being shot in the head, that I would wind up writing about people being shot in the head—and everywhere else.

So, Kelsey, Laura, and I have an early dinner at Sardinia, a local Italian restaurant we like. The owner, Pietro, is a friend of mine from New York. He used to manage a restaurant on Columbus Avenue called Pappardella. Pietro has a rather hard exterior, does not often smile, but in truth he's a nice man, a gracious host. Pietro was born and raised on the scenic Italian island of Sardinia. Of course, we have Sardinian pasta and salads. He sends us over a round of drinks. When Pietro looks at me, I can see a sadness in his eyes for he knew me well when I was healthy and vigorous. He says nothing of my illness, though it's a hard thing to ignore with the breathing tube sticking out of my mouth.

After dinner, we get back in the van and drop Kelsey off. She is staying on Euclid and 7th in a quiet, three-story building with a huge front yard bursting with flowers canopied by palm trees with large leaves. Most all the houses in this neighborhood are art deco, candied warm pastel greens and pinks, soft tans and yellows. It is a very pleasant place to live. Kelsey has grown fond of the area and that makes me happy, for if she's not content, the process of birthing a book to her would be impeded. As I said, the writing of a book, especially in its early stages, particularly a memoir, is a sensitive, personal enterprise and the rapport between the person talking and the person getting what's said down on paper must be strong.

We hug Kelsey and drop her off. Laura and I go on to the building where we live, several blocks away on Ocean Drive, right on the beach. I am in a despicably bad mood, but I keep it to myself, or at least try to. I should be in a good mood. I said this already but I love being in South Beach. I look forward to waking up every morning and getting outside. I look forward to all the outdoor cafés. Yet here I sit with a storm cloud over my head.

We get into the elevator and silently ride up to our floor. Our apartment is a large one-bedroom with a terrace facing the ocean. I cannot describe the joy I derive from being in South Beach, close to the ocean like this. The air is permeated by the sea, clean and fresh. There is no pollution. As Laura begins to unpack, I watch a movie. Since I was diagnosed with ALS, I have been watching two or three films a day. In that I'm wheelchair-bound and prohibited from freely moving about, I find movies a great relief. I look at movies now the way I first looked at books when I started reading—they are a way to learn, see new worlds, experience different cultures, get outside yourself, travel far and wide without leaving your couch. Good film is essentially a first-class ticket to wherever the hell you want to go. No strings attached, no promises to keep.

Tonight, I am watching the wonderful classic *The Good Earth*, based on a book written by the late, great Pearl S. Buck and starring Paul Muni. It is a wonderful though sorrowful depiction of how the Chinese suffered at the hands of the Japanese prior to World War II. Riveted, I am drawn into the film, drawn into the pain and heartaches of Wang Lung, and I am no longer in South Beach. I am no longer suffering from ALS. I am in China. It is 1934. Several times during the film, my eyes get heavy. It is not because I'm tired. This has more to do with the lithium. I shake my head and cry as I watch the end of the film.

Laura has fallen asleep on the couch. I gently wake her. I then slowly and carefully manipulate the wheelchair next to the bed. Laura straps a thick canvas belt around my waist and stands in front of me, bends, and places my arms around her neck. Keeping my knees between her two knees, she grabs the canvas belt, picks me up on the count of three, pivots, and puts me down on the bed. She helps me put my head where the pillows are. I cannot get into a comfortable position by myself. When she first sits me on the bed, if I'm not supported, I quickly fall, and with the weight of my upper body, it is a hard, potentially dangerous fall. An unsupported fall could conceivably snap my neck. In that the right side of my diaphragm is completely gone, I find it easier to breathe when I sleep on the right side.

Still using the breathing machine, I try to find a comfortable position in which I can support my head and not wake up with all kinds of cramps. A saving grace is the nearby ocean, for I can hear waves gently breaking on the shoreline. It is a melodic, sweet sound that I have loved since I was a boy. It lulls me off to a sound sleep, to a dark place that could be readily likened to a cave deep in the earth. All is black. All is quiet.

"Shhhh . . . shhhh," goes the sound of the sea.

In the cave, there are creatures furtively scurrying. I hear them. I'm frightened. There are bats, I realize. There is the odor of death, strong and pungent in my nostrils. I wonder if it's guano, or the smell of decomposing bodies. The smell of human death and the stink of bat droppings are shockingly similar. In my quest to write about murder accurately, I have visited both the Los Angeles and New York City morgues, a college of death, and I will never, ever forget the rancid stink of human corpses.

Laura is gently shaking me. I open my eyes. The sun is shining. The smell of the ocean is strong. I don't know where I've been. I don't know where I am. The Florida sun streams through the shutters in the bedroom. There are golden wisps of hair around her head.

"What time is it?" I say.

"Nearly eleven," she says.

"Why did you let me sleep so late? I have a lot of work to do. Where's K?"

"She's inside," she says.

"Oh, okay, help me up," I say.

Laura uncovers me, takes both my ankles and swings them off the bed. She then takes my hands and, on the count of three, pulls me up, a new day before me.

6. Waves

It is a glorious day, a sweet breeze off the ocean, not even a hint of a cloud in the sky. We live just near the Savoy Hotel at Fifth Street. The Savoy is a two-story, all-white structure, reminiscent of an era gone by. It looks like an elegant Southern plantation from the last century. Over the many months that we have stayed in South Beach, we have become good friends with the manager and all the people who work at the hotel. They have shown us tremendous empathy and friendship. Fact is, most everybody with whom we come into contact is kind and generous and offers a helping hand before I ask.

Here, I feel at home, at ease. Here, I don't feel as though I'm an outcast, some kind of freak. Here, I am a hardworking writer who happens to be in a wheelchair. At the Savoy, most everyone knows I'm a writer and has even read most of my books. One can readily say I am the Savoy's artist-in-residence.

Kelsey, Laura, and I move through the palm-tree-studded grounds of the Savoy to the beach. The Boucher brothers run all the concessions on the oceanfront, from South Beach north all the way to Virginia Beach. They provide umbrellas and lounges and towels. When they learned of my plight, that I actually wrote on the beach every day, they were kind enough to let their employees use golf carts to take me from the back of the Savoy out onto the beach proper—a place I really should not be right now considering my condition, my lack of mobility. Getting on the beach with my wheelchair is impossible because the sand would screw up the motor.

Here comes our friend Wilson driving the golf cart. He's one of the strongest men I've ever met. Black as ebony, originally from Trinidad,

Wilson smiles as he effortlessly picks me up, puts me in the golf cart, and takes me on to the beach. Kelsey and Laura follow. It is a big difference between enjoying the beach and ocean and having to sit by the pool. On the beach, I am like everyone else. In theory, I should be hospitalized now. In theory, I shouldn't be out and about like this, writing books, going to the beach. But until I absolutely cannot get up, I am coming to the beach and I am doing everything else I can. That doesn't mean that I'm planning to go to Disneyland or deep-sea fishing, but just this nice enterprise of coming onto the pure white beach, quiet and serene, in contact with nature and writing my books, for me is a golden luxury.

"Are you okay, man?" Wilson asks as he gently places me on the lounge as though I were a fragile child.

"I'm fine, thanks to you, Wilson."

"Nothing, man . . . nothing," he says.

On the beach, we meet the beach attendant, our friend Sergio. Sergio works for the Boucher brothers. He mans the concession service at the Savoy. He is from Argentina and has a strong accent and a large white smile. He has the ways of a little boy about him that, inevitably, ingratiate you to him. He is an eccentric good friend who has always gone out of his way to help me get on and off the lounge, make sure my lounge is in a good place, etc. In that I can't get up and walk away from a noisy group of people or someone throwing a ball or playing paddleball, Sergio is my protector. Also, he knows that I write about various heavy, serious subjects, that my books have been published in his native language, Spanish . . . as well as many other languages. Here, I am kind of thought of as a celebrity, which to me is absurd. In any event, I am pleased to see my friend and I hug him. He has set up lounges for us and after ordering iced cappuccinos, Kelsey and I begin what you're reading now. We get comfortable. Sergio knows when to make himself scarce and returns to his little cabana. He wears all white and is quite tan. I am facing the water. Kelsey is sitting across from me on a lounge wearing big, round sunglasses, facing me with the computer in her lap. On my right, Laura is reading a magazine. My mind goes over what I'm going to write, say, put down on paper. So much has happened; where to begin? As always, I will focus on an event, some relevant detail, and I will let the story tell itself. Somewhere inside of me, it's already written. I just have to grab the thread, pull it and weave it into words.

The Miami sun is strong, hot and piercing. I can only take an hour or two without an umbrella even though I'm dark-skinned. There is no wind. The water is calm and friendly. I close my eyes. The sun feels wonderful. It soothes my joints. I'm so glad to be out of the wheelchair. I'm clearing my head, about to start writing, feeling and thinking about the dilemma my life has become. When I open my eyes, there is a commotion down by the shoreline. Screaming, people are running from the water.

"Shark! Shark!"

Kelsey and Laura stand up. I want to stand up, but of course I can't. Most everyone runs down toward the water. I make out the triangular dorsal fin of a shark in the shallows, moving toward the shore swiftly. I'm stunned because I just saw a mako on the truck and was thinking of sharks, my trip to Salinas. Suddenly, shockingly, a huge shark bursts from the water's edge pursuing a panic-stricken, foot-long red snapper onto the beach. The shark is about six feet long. A few women scream but people still run down to see it. Of all the things in the world, I have to see a shark up on the beach. I've always been fascinated by sharks. One of the few phobias I've had in life is sharks. I have rarely gone in water above my mid-thigh and now here's this big shark flopping around the shoreline. The lifeguard starts blowing his whistle. More people come running. Laura and Kelsey abandon me to go see the shark.

"Fuck!" I say, looking at my stick-like, useless legs. *This is ridiculous. So unfair.* Soon many more people have come to see the shark. They surround the fish and I can't even see it. I am told, however, that it shook its way back into the water and disappeared, leaving the hapless snapper on the beach, people's mouths agape. Kelsey and Laura return. It's crazy, but I'm angry at them—angry that they were able to see this *National Geographic* moment and I wasn't.

My mind returns to sharks, perfect predators; perfect killers. I begin thinking of not only predators from the seas and jungles, but human predators. I remember well the first serial killer I ever met, became intimately acquainted with—Richard Ramirez, aka The Night Stalker. Ramirez terrified Los Angeles County for fourteen months, entered homes in the middle of the night and killed and raped at will. Lying on this beautiful beach, Kelsey listening to me and typing as I speak, I very vividly remember Richard Ramirez's eyes. They were big and black and flat—like the eyes of a shark. All you got back from them was your own reflection. When looking at them, it was like looking at two black pool balls. No depth, no soul, no feeling.

For thirty-three days, I interviewed Ramirez from eight in the morning until two in the afternoon, just he and I alone in a stone-walled room at San Quentin's death row. San Quentin is an archaic, frightening place where, since 1898, the state of California has executed its condemned—421 men to date, first by hanging, then the gas chamber, and, finally, lethal injection. While at San Quentin, I had the rare opportunity to actually see an execution, and I jumped at it. As you approached the prison and entered E-Block, you got the feeling you were walking into an insane asylum. However, once inside, you got the very distinct feeling you were walking into a morgue—a place of death.

When I arrived at E-Block—death row—word was sent to his tier to bring him down. As I sat there waiting for him, I finalized questions in my mind. I had no paper, no pencil. Those luxuries were not allowed inside San Quentin. My intention was not to necessarily talk with him about the crimes he had been convicted of. Rather, what I wanted to know was what had truly motivated him, what drove him—how he got the insatiable need to kill human beings with the ferocity of a hungry shark.

As I sat there, I put together my strategy to get him to talk, open up. I knew one thing for sure: I would not be accusatory. I would not point my finger at him. My object, to the extent that it's possible with such an individual, was to befriend him. Far off to my right, I heard a heavy door open and slam closed, then a second door open and slam closed. I heard the rattling of thick chains moving across the floor. Suddenly, the door to the room I was in opened and Ramirez was standing there, all chained up in his evil glory. He was larger than I had imagined, tall and handsome in a brooding, dark way; his cheek-bones were excessively high, his lips full. He kind of looked like a Latin Mick Jagger. Aside from those malevolent shark eyes of his, one could not help but be drawn to his hands. Now they rested in front of him as though they were two birds of prey satiated and restful after having gorged themselves. As we talked, he often used his hands for punctuation and animation and I couldn't help but think of the terrible things those hands had done while holding hammers and pipes, tire irons and knives, guns and machetes and wire and rope to kill most foully—suddenly and without cause. I wanted to grab his right hand. I wanted to yell at the hand, "WHY? WHY!!?"

Instead, I smiled and started telling him about Brooklyn, about my seeing Jimmy Emma shot, about the Mafia constantly around me while I was growing up. Not surprisingly, he warmed to this. He began to view me as an outlaw who, coincidentally, wrote. For the first few hours, we talked about me. Inevitably, the conversation turned to him and thus, the real interview began. Ramirez had been born and raised in El Paso, Texas. Even then, as I sat opposite him, his speech had a distinct Texan twang. A former policeman in Juarez, Mexico, Richard's father had been a strict disciplinarian and beat him throughout his formative years for both real and imagined infractions. He had three brothers and one sister and a devoted mother. Born and raised a devout Catholic, he told me he became a Satanist when he was sixteen.

"Why," I ask, "did your head go that way? What drew you in that direction?"

He said, "I was having all kinds of bad thoughts involving rape and murder—all things to do with death. When I discovered *The Satanic Bible* written by Anton LaVey, I realized there was another way, another route, another path, dig? For them, what is sinful to a Catholic is not a sin."

As the Night Stalker talked, I realized he was far brighter than one would have thought. He talked about human sacrifice as a means to an end—not a crime. He had studied, he told me, how the Aztec and Mayan cultures regularly practiced human sacrifice. How the Mayans would kill upward of five thousand people a month, men and women and children—though mostly the young. He told me how he was trained by a cousin, who was a Vietnam veteran, to expertly use weapons and, diabolically, how to become invisible at night. All his crimes, I knew, had been committed in the dead of night, between twelve and three A.M.

"Black shoes, black socks, black pants, black shirt, with a black hat pulled down low," he said. "You could be standing right next to somebody and if you were wearing all black at night, they won't see you."

As I sat there listening, staring at him, I got chills at the thought of Ramirez dressed all in black with a knife in one hand and his erect penis in the other. This was a man, I knew, who was an extreme sexual sadist. All the females he had come into contact with he had raped repeatedly. Age was no barrier. He had raped a ninety-two-year-old woman, an unspeakable crime. As we discussed it, I got a bad taste in my mouth. I wanted to stand up and point my finger at him and say, "WHAT THE FUCK WERE YOU THINKING, MAN? HOW COULD YOU?" But I stayed seated and said, "I see."

When it finally came to discussing the actual crimes he was convicted of, that was a sticky wicket. His lawyers were appealing his conviction and he had a chance to win. This was something that was, I knew, a difficult thing to get around. But I had known for sure, before I even went in the prison, that I could find a way to get him to talk, admit the truth, give me details; for the first time tell the world what the Night Stalker was really about.

Bang, bang, bang, on the door.

"That's it!" a guard called out in some kind of strange Southern twang. I had been there from eight to two, some six hours, but it felt like much longer.

I stood up. We shook hands.

"I'll see you tomorrow."

"I'll see you tomorrow, Fe-el," he said.

When I walked out of the prison's main gate, there were no cabs. I had found a hotel seven miles from the prison and I walked all the way back. The area where San Quentin is located is one of the most beautiful locales in all of northern California. It is right on the water's edge of a huge bay called the Bay of Skulls. The famous Fisherman's Wharf of San Francisco is a mere ten minutes from San Quentin by boat. As I made my way back to the hotel, I walked along the bay, studying the Richmond Bridge as I went, mulling over what Richard had told me, mulling over this unique place of incarceration and death called San Quentin— a place where the worst of our kind were housed, put to death.

When I arrived back at my room, I changed into shorts and running shoes and stretched. I then ran the seven miles back to the prison, turning the day over in my mind. While running, large doses of oxygen flooding my brain, I could see myself sitting with Ramirez, hearing his answers, his large black eyes an unsettling sight. I knew I was on to something very illuminating, that I had entered a world of murder and mayhem that few were privy to, and I wondered how the hell to start this dark story of rape and murder. I was intent upon getting rid of whatever negativity, hurt, pain, and suffering I took from what he said by running. Neutralize it. I would not use alcohol or drugs or any mind-altering substances to dilute what he told me—confuse it, numb it. As I ran, I thought of Truman Capote. He wrote the classic *In Cold Blood* and became deeply involved with Richard Hickock and Perry Smith, the two murderers who killed the four members of the Clutter family. I thought now of Truman because he became an out-of-control alcoholic who pretty much drank his talent away. The genius that he was, he spent a lot of time walking into walls and falling down when he should have been writing and he died years before his time. Still, he became a celebrated household name. I am certainly not comparing myself to Capote. I just knew the pitfalls of working intimately with the dark side of human nature and would avoid them at all cost.

It's not just writers who suffer from looking into the abyss. It is also people in law enforcement, detectives who work homicide, the crimes against children unit, the rape unit. They are forced to confront, on a daily basis, the dregs of society. We know that the suicide rate among law enforcement individuals is unusually high.

As Nietzsche once said, "And if thou gaze long into an abyss, the abyss will also gaze into thee."

On the way back to the hotel, I felt strong and refreshed. I sat down and made notes, thinking that I knew how to get him to talk, the key to getting the truth. But, I wondered, did I really want to know the truth? With that thought in my mind, I lay down and drifted far away from Marin County, San Quentin Prison.

As the sun rose that morning, so did I. There was a small, excellent luncheonette around the block from where I was staying called Le Croissant. It was run with great care by a middle-aged couple and their teenage son. They had amazingly good pastries and breakfasts I was an early customer and had bran muffins with raisins as large as grapes. As I was sitting there, cops came in. They were having their morning meal before they went on duty. It was six A.M. The eggs there were delicious. As I tell Kelsey this, I can see it so vividly. I'm not sure if it is all because everything was so exceptional in this place or because I again had quit smoking about two weeks earlier, but the food was just marvelous. This time I had vowed to never pick up a cigarette again and I never have.

As I was sitting there drinking a wonderful cappuccino, mulling over my day with Ramirez, in walked George Lucas. I soon found out that his studio was a mere two blocks away. I passed it several times a day as I went to the prison and returned from it and then jogged past it later on. I thought of the make-believe monsters Lucas had so adeptly created, how I was sitting with a real live monster.

Day two. San Quentin. Same scenario. Now when Richard entered I said, "I know how we can do this."

"Yeah?"

"What I'd like to do is talk about you as if you're not yourself."

"Say what?" he asked.

"What I'm saying is, you are no longer 'you,' you are 'he.' What I'm saying is this: tell me what happened, but don't say, 'I saw' or, 'I did.' Say 'He did' or 'He saw.'"

"Oh, that's a good idea. So I'm not admitting anything?"

"You're not admitting anything," I said, "He did it. Not you."

He bought into it hook, line, and sinker. And I had a list of the nineteen crimes he had been convicted of in my head and little by little we went through the list and Richard told me what he did and him did and he did and him did. He was very comfortable talking in this third person and it flowed from him like a torrent of foul water coming from a sewer faster and faster still, and the faster it came, the more foul it was. As it turned out, Richard was hypoglycemic and after several hours of this, he started dozing off on me, put his head down on his folded arms like young kids do during rest period in school. When I realized he was hypoglycemic, I started bringing in Nestlé candy bars from the machine just outside. I gave him the chocolate, he took a few bites, became all animated again, and, with the help of Nestlé chocolate bars, I got the Night Stalker to tell me all.

Ostensibly, he was from the same mold that Jack the Ripper, Ted Bundy, John Wayne Gacy, and Jeffrey Dahmer were; they all were intrinsically linked. Hurting people, scaring people, beating people, torturing people was, to their ilk, an aphrodisiac. Murder—to a serial killer—is sustenance, food to a starving man, water to someone dying of thirst. That's the sum of it.

Why . . . ?

We talked about Richard's childhood. There were indications that he had been sexually abused by a teacher. His father beat him excessively; he had severe traumas to the head; his brothers all had very bad tempers. All of them had been arrested. But only Richard went to a point where murder became what he enjoyed most in life.

When Richard reluctantly told me about his cousin Mike, it became rather clear why he, Richard, was in San Quentin's death row. Long story short: Richard's cousin Mike Valez was a highly decorated Vietnam veteran, a homicidal maniac who thrived in a war setting. He took to killing Vietnamese like a duck to water. He not only gleefully shot to death Vietcong but he abducted Vietnamese women and girls from small villages, took them into the jungle, bound them to trees, and raped, mutilated, and murdered them, keeping ears and other body parts as trophies. He also took Polaroid photographs of his victims posed obscenely both in life and death. When Mike returned from Vietnam—a highly decorated hero—he had a box filled with photographs of his victims, the carnage he wrought.

When Richard was eleven years old, Mike regaled his young cousin with what he had done. He showed the boy the Polaroid photographs. They had an exceedingly deleterious effect on the boy. Then when Richard was just twelve years old, his cousin Mike got into a domestic dispute with his wife, Jessie. The argument ended when Mike put a gun to Jessie's head and shot her to death in cold blood, right in front of the young Richard. Mind you, Richard did not tell this to me as any kind of excuse. He very reluctantly shared what Mike had done, what he had seen. I literally had to badger him to get him to divulge what had occurred. I do not here offer this as any kind of rhyme or rhythm as to why Ramirez turned out the way he did, though I verified it with Richard's family and the El Paso police department. What Richard had told me was true. You did not have to be Sigmund Freud to deduce that Richard's cousin Mike showed the boy a path in life that would lead to murder and mayhem, unspeakable rape, and paralyze with fear a community of 13 million people.

I could smell him. I had heard, over and over, from people in law enforcement and forensic psychologists, that serial killers had a particular odor. Not a smell of B.O., but something else. It is a fusion, a combination of wet leather and hazelnuts. When the door behind Richard was open and the air rushed in, I could smell this odor issuing from him. *Why*, I wondered, *do they have this in common?* Surely it had to do with a glandular commonality, an overactive or underactive gland that helped produce this odor and that these men had in common. Toward the end of the interviews, which had lasted for over one hundred hours, I asked Richard this question: How can a woman avoid a person like you . . . avoid a serial killer?

He gave me this long, baleful stare.

"Or rather, him?" I said.

"They can't," he said. "Once a serial killer's got somebody in focus, that's it. What a woman can do is be more aware, though. Walk with her eyes up. Walk as though she's not the only person in the world. They need to know who's behind them when they're getting in their car, going into their house. It's like this: when you go swimming in water where you know there are sharks, you're aware, you take precautions, but if you go out too deep, no matter what, they'll get you."

With this, my initial interviews with Richard were coming to an end. He was all upset when I arrived at the prison the following morning. He had been in the yard earlier and two death row inmates had gotten into a fight. When ordered by the guards to stop, they refused and kept battling each other, punching each other. Richard was just near them, standing up against the wall, minding his own business.

"The motherfucking guard shot one of them in the head without any warning and his head exploded. Look," he said, showing me his sneakers, on which was a strange, gray matter. It was on his legs, on his shoulder. It was the man's brains.

On that note, I sat down with the Night Stalker and did my last interview. When I left, we parted as two men who knew each other well, but not friends. I shook that large, bony, malevolent hand of his and slowly left San Quentin's E-Block.

I left E-block and pensively walked toward San Quentin's front gate. A cold front had come in. The sky was low and dark and mean, stacked with swirling gunpowder-gray clouds. Strong winds whipped the Bay of Skulls, causing white-crested waves to hurry across the large expanse of the water. I zipped up my jacket and pulled up my collar. When I got outside the prison gates, I turned around and stared at this foreboding, unforgiving place of death for the last time. It was now time to go to work, to write my book, a blood-and-sweat task that would take me three long years. When I finally walked away from San Quentin, I knew I would never forget its sights and smells, the dread that permeated the place.

I don't know whether or not I should add this, but it is relevant and, to be candid, something I'm proud of:

Best True Crime Books: Truth Stranger—and Scarier—Than Fiction
By book examiner Michelle Kerns
    If you'd like to peer into the dark heart of true crime, you can't do better than this list of the 50 best true crime novels ever written.
    50 best true crime books:

1. **In Cold Blood: A True Account of a Multiple Murder and Its Consequences**—*Truman Capote*
    The granddaddy of the modern true crime genre, In Cold Blood's detailed account of the murder of the Clutter family in 1959 rural Kansas is as good today as it was in 1965. Not only is it an admirable true crime book, it is non-fiction writing at its best. I included it in my list of 20 best non-fiction books for people who think they hate to read non-fiction.

2. **The Night Stalker: The Life and Crimes of Richard Ramirez**—*Philip Carlo*
    The satanic motivations of the rapist and murderer the "Night Stalker" are discussed in chilling detail in this book.

3. **Confessions of Son of Sam**—*David Abrahamsen*
    Classic scare-yourself-silly reading.

4. **A Rip in Heaven: A Memoir of Murder and Its Aftermath**—*Jeanine Cummins*
    Highly emotional account of the 1991 rape and murder of Robin and Julie Kerry and the attempted murder of their cousin, Tom Cummins, who, for some time after the crime, remained wrongfully targeted as the prime suspect by the police.

5. **Murder in the Family**—*Burl Barer*
    Details the 1987 Anchorage, Alaska murders of a mother, Nancy Newman, and her two daughters by the 23-year-old nephew of Nancy's husband.

I thought, for those more interested in my Q &A with Ramirez, I would include the below—

Carlo: Speaking of spirituality, let's talk about Satanism. There's been a lot in the press, Richard, about your devotion to and your affiliation with Satan. Can you tell me a bit about what Satan means to you?

Ramirez: What Satan means to me . . . Satan is a stabilizing force in my life. It gives me a reason to be; it gives me . . . an excuse to rationalize. There is a part of me that believes he really does exist. I have my doubts, but all do, about many things.

Carlo: When did you first turn away from Christianity—as I know you were brought up a Christian—and turn to Satanism?

Ramirez: From 1970—well, throughout my childhood and up to the time I was eighteen years old, I believed in God. Seventeen, eighteen years old. Then, for two or three years, I became sort of like an Atheist—I didn't believe in anything. When I reached the age of twenty, twenty-one, thereabouts, I met a guy in jail and he told me about Satan and I picked it up from there. (Richard had been arrested for stealing a car.) I read books and I studied and I examined who I was and what my feelings were. Also, my actions. Just like Hezbollah and different terrorist organizations—it is a driving force that motivates them to do things and they believe in it whole-heartedly. It had the same effect on my life.

Carlo: You were seen in court once with a pentagram inside your hand and you held it up and showed it to the press and the audience. Why did you do that? Did you feel that it would protect you, or were you just making a statement that you were in alliance with the Devil?

Ramirez: Yes, it was a statement that I was in alliance with the evil that is inherent in human nature. And that was who I was.

Carlo: Richard, tell us about the Marquis de Sade. I know that since you've been incarcerated, which is about eight years, you've been reading an awful lot and one of the things you've read is the Marquis de Sade.

Ramirez: De Sade had a large . . . uh . . . a large . . . somewhat large following in his time. He had a philosophy, a way of thinking that was contrary to what people of his time thought and eventually he paid the price for it. They placed him in an insane asylum, where he died. His belief was that there was pleasure in painful sex. He wrote many stories, short stories; one of my favorites was Justine. He talked about the governments and how they were oppressors. Hypocritical. Takers away—they took away rights that belonged to individuals.

Carlo: *Sexual rights, sexual freedoms?*

Ramirez: *Yes.*

Carlo: *But essentially de Sade was a sadist, right?*

Ramirez: *Yes, yes. He liked to inflict pain.*

Carlo: *Right. Do you feel he was ahead of his time in a sense? Do you feel he knew something about human nature—and explored it—that other people seemed to deny?*

Ramirez: *Well, I believe that—as time goes by, mankind will find new and different ways of living. He may have been ahead of his time, or maybe he just came about at the right time with his ways of thinking.*

Carlo: *I believe they had the death penalty in the time period de Sade was alive.*

Ramirez: *I think it was the guillotine.*

Carlo: *The guillotine.*

Ramirez: *I think all this took place in or about France.*

Carlo: *They did not give him a death sentence for his practices, but they indeed locked him up for the entirety of his natural life, but—*

Ramirez: *Because of the stories he wrote.*

Carlo: *The phenomenon of serial killers—is it a sexual thing, too, Richard? Is sex an intricate part of the crimes?*

Ramirez: *Sex? For some serial killers, sure. For some it is the very act of killing another human being that is sexual to them. It's a bloodlust, I guess you could say.*

Carlo: *Do you think a person who becomes like that is responsive to a bloodlust because of a genetic propensity or because of environmental influences, or both?*

Ramirez: *Yes. Serial killers and most killers in general have a dead conscience.*

Carlo: *When you say a dead conscience, that means they don't respond—*

Ramirez: *No morals, no scruples, no conscience. Some of them don't even care if they live or die themselves and they are just the walking dead.*

Carlo: *The first really noted serial killer was Jack the Ripper.*

Ramirez: *Yeah.*

Carlo: *He killed seven prostitutes in London in the 1800s.*

Ramirez: *Yes.*

Carlo: *I think there were other serial killers loose and participating in those types of activities but they just never got the press that Jack got.*

Ramirez: Jack the Ripper created an aura around himself, or maybe the media did.

Carlo: The press . . .

Ramirez: But it was one of mystique and . . . a sinister character who was never identified. I remember in my childhood reading about him and I was intrigued by the way this killer, Jack the Ripper, was depicted. Wears a black cloak—

Carlo: Right—

Ramirez: —Fog—

Carlo: —Right—

Ramirez: —Nighttime—most of the time, the media tends to, if not glorify, but . . . paint him in a way that is very sinister and diabolical and to some of us, that is appealing. Certainly, it was to me.

Carlo: Why do you think it was particularly appealing to you? It seems appealing to everybody . . .

Ramirez: Well, not everybody.

Now, back on South Beach, the lovely white sand, the teal blue Atlantic on my left, a clear blue sky the color of Paul Newman's eyes above, I remember Ramirez's smell—what he said about sharks. How . . . well, cryptic, I think. I don't know if this is a good or a bad omen. It's somewhat disconcerting. The heat, the Florida sun, is too much and I ask Kelsey to get Sergio to stick some umbrellas in the sand for us. This is kind of a ritual that we have. It becomes too hot and I call for an umbrella. When I was younger, I used to be able to sit in the sun all day long without a problem but now after two hours, I start feeling uncomfortable. I look at the water. It beckons me. *Shhh . . . shhh.* Oh, how I want to get up and run to you, submerge myself in you.

"Water! Ice-cold water!" A black fellow we have come to know shouts out as he comes down the beach toward us. He has scant little more than what is on his back, yet he is always smiling and out there selling his bottles of ice-cold water. I buy one for each of us and he continues down the beach, shouting, "Water! Ice-cold water!"

Sergio gets the umbrella in place. The shade is cooling and much welcomed. I ask Kelsey to go get a bucket of salt water and pour it over my head. Sergio has a few buckets near his cabana. Dutifully, understandingly, Kelsey walks down to the water's edge, shapely, beautiful, both men and women watching her as she goes, unaware of anyone's attention. Turquoise waves wrap themselves around Kelsey's waist as she slowly moves into the water. She returns with her hair wet, all slicked back, carrying a full bucket of sea water.

"The water's great," she says, smiling.

"Lay it on me!" I say.

She slowly pours the ice-cold water on my head. It is clean and cold and refreshing—most welcome. As always when we do this, we are careful not to get any water on her computer or on my breathing machine, which is discreetly ensconced behind me and under the chair. What I like about this particular beach, right in the middle of South Beach's hubbub, is that there are very few people here; those on this beach are mostly guests of the Savoy. The public, for the most part, stays away.

I am indexing and organizing my thoughts, looking for a place from which to continue to tell the story. My eyes move again to the water. I'm drawn to the sea like it is some kind of powerful magnet. I love, when writing, to be able to focus on the horizon. When focusing on the horizon, you can see all the possibilities of life, all the different types of weather, lightning bolts, strong winds, blue skies, and calm seas, reflecting, in a sense, the full spectrum of human emotions. One day there is a hurricane with thirty-foot swells; next day it's calm and the ocean is like the water in a bathtub. I think, in a sense, watching the horizon encourages imagination, encourages the mind to reach out without inhibition. Sitting there, my eyes again move to my legs. They are absurdly thin. At this juncture, I cannot move them at all. With the lack of movement, both my feet have become swollen. They need to be massaged regularly. If it's not one thing, it's another, a cacophony of dilemmas both big and small. This is the world of ALS I've found myself an unwitting citizen of. I remember well the day I first realized something was out of sync, wrong. I have been avoiding writing about this because it is terribly hurtful and brings me back to the day when I first realized my life was altered forever.

7. Most Insidious

The proverbial tolling of the bells began like this: I was coming back from an interview with Richard Kuklinski, aka the Ice Man, at Trenton State Prison. It was the latter part of February 2005, a blistering cold day. While I was making my way through Penn Station, I noticed that my left foot was sort of flopping on the hard, marble floor. It was strange. I stopped near a doughnut shop. People hurried around me. The announcements of trains coming and going resonated loudly, rudely. I leaned up against the wall and looked down at my foot. There was something oddly out of sync about it. I was thinking it surely had to do with my running too much, with my injuring my foot and not realizing it—not tending to it. I didn't pay much attention.

However, the foot continued to get . . . stiffer, less flexible. Strange.

I had plans to travel to Mykonos, Greece, for the summer and write *The Ice Man.* I was going to Mykonos, one of the most beautiful islands in all of the Mediterranean, to write without interruption or distraction. Precious luxuries to any author. I had already gotten the first few chapters of the first draft done. I was looking forward to the inherent beauty, peace and quiet, and perfect weather on Mykonos. I had been spending summers there for the last eight years. For me, it had become in my mind a kind of life-giving ritual. I did not realize how serious the problem with my foot would become, that the grim reaper was diabolically plotting to make me his own, that he had already sunk his filthy talons deep inside of me.

When I returned to New York City, I planned to go to a doctor.

Innocently, rather naively, having no idea what was in store for me, I boarded a wide-bodied 747 and flew to Athens, where I caught a smaller, propeller-driven plane to Mykonos. I was staying at the Mykonos Grand Hotel, an exceptionally well run, beautiful establishment that was built smack on the Aegean Sea. The view was magnificent. The Aegean is indescribably majestic, clean and clear and blue like the eye of a dove. It has an unusually high salt content. You can readily float on the water. There is one gorgeous beach after another on Mykonos, fine sand, impeccably clean and safe. There are outdoor restaurants on the beach that serve food directly from wood-burning grills. I knew most of the people who owned these restaurants, and when they saw me coming, they smiled and I got hugs and kisses on the cheek.

"Carlo, ah, you are back! Welcome! Welcome!"

Relatively speaking, Mykonos is inexpensive compared to other hot spots in the Mediterranean . . . Sardinia, the South of France, Ischia, Ibiza, Marbella.

Every day I went to Agrari beach at nine-thirty or so. At that early morning hour, the beach was just about empty. At Agrari, you could rent a comfortable lounge and an umbrella. This was where I did my work. Agrari happens to be a nude beach and I could lie there undisturbed in the sun or in the shade and write to my heart's content.

Naked, every half hour or so, I dove in the water and went for a swim, feeling incredibly free, in touch with the elements, my mind, body, and spirit. The swimming, I figured, would be good for my left foot. Around noon, people began showing up. My work day was finished at 1:00; I would write about four hours straight every day. I had learned early on never to write to exhaustion, to stop while you're going strong. After a day's work, I had a light, nutritious lunch at a family-owned restaurant right on the beach. Most often, I had a little wine with lunch. After lunch, I went back to my hotel and had a nap. Like this, I worked every day until it was time to return to New York. When I was ready to leave, *The Ice Man* was written. I believed *The Ice Man* would be a great book. I believed I had hit the mark with it. Yet I had no idea it would be as well received as it was all around the world, that it would become a bestseller in multiple countries and reach the venerable *New York Times* bestseller list; become a major motion picture.

By the time I returned to New York from Greece, it was the middle of September. I had lost weight and the limp had become somewhat more pronounced. Still thinking I had some kind of running injury, I went to see my chiropractor.

. . . I must stop writing here. The thought of telling what was to come, what I've been through, is upsetting to me. I tell Kelsey to take a break. She gets up and walks toward the ocean for a swim. I take a long deep breath, watching gentle waves break on the beach, Kelsey walking toward the water's edge. Though now I do not hear the melodic sound of the waves. I hear in my head those terrible words.

There is little wind today and the heat is intense. I look for Sergio to move our umbrella but he's nowhere to be found. He doesn't like when we move the umbrellas on our own; that is invading his domain. Our friend with the cold water comes by and we buy a couple of bottles and I drink half of it and pour the other half on my head.

"Where is Sergio?" I ask Laura.

"Do you want me to go find him?" she asks.

"Yeah, please do. I'm burning here"

Laura gets up and walks toward the hotel. Again, I take a long deep breath, close my eyes. I drift off somewhere, not sure exactly where I end up, but I distinctly hear the sound of horses' hoofs running faster and faster, see their muscles rippling. Somebody pulls my toe. I pop out of my reverie. A smiling Sergio is there with my umbrella. He sinks the umbrella's point in the sand and opens it. The shade feels good, soothes and embraces me with cool fingers.

"Much better. Thank you," I say.

Strangely enough, Laura never uses the umbrella nor sunblock and she never gets burnt. This is surprising because Laura has light-colored eyes. All the time I tell her she should use sunblock, but she's the type of woman who, if you tell her to do something and it sounds like an order, she'll do the exact opposite. The best thing to do with Laura would be to tell her not to use sunblock and she'd probably use it.

Kelsey returns and we are soon up and running. I am now ready to tell what I couldn't before.

"Ready?" I ask.

"Yep," Kelsey says.

So, shortly after I got back from Mykonos, I went to see Dr. DeAndrade, the chiropractor. Dr. DeAndrade prescribed a set of orthotics for me, though she said that my problem might be neurological, that I should consult a neurologist. I went to see my personal doctor, Dr. Alpert. He examined me and said I had "neurological issues" and suggested that I see his wife, who, coincidentally, was a neurologist. From his office, I went straight to his wife's office at Mount Sinai Hospital. As Dr. Polinsky examined me, her grave demeanor alone told me something serious was afoot. After examining my left leg, she turned her attention to my hands. Strange, I thought. She pointed out that I had atrophy of the muscles just behind each of my thumbs.

"What does that mean?" I asked, surprised I hadn't noticed this before.

"To be frank with you, it could be any one of several afflictions, including brain trauma. Have you had any brain trauma lately?"

"No, not at all," I said.

"I'm going to order a series of tests and we'll find out what the problem is."

"You can't tell me now?"

"I can't definitively tell you now, no. All I can tell you with certainty is that it is neurological."

Dr. Polinsky first sent me for a CAT scan at Mount Sinai and it was normal; nothing was wrong with my brain. Great, I thought. I next went for an EMG at the Hospital for Joint Diseases on Second Avenue and 17th Street. This test involves sticking a long, thin needle, which is connected to a computer, into each of the major muscle groups. You are then asked to flex the muscles slightly and the computer gives you a readout on the integrity of the muscle. The doctor administering the test became more and more serious-faced. I kept asking him what the problem was. He kept saying he would let me know when the test was completed. As he administered the test, several more doctors entered the room and finally there were seven of them circled around me, one of whom was the chief of neurology at the facility. Their faces were expressionless. I was worried. It was raining outside and strong gusts of wind blew against the windows. As I looked at the windows, I imagined tears hurrying down the glass.

Finally, the head of the department, Dr. Kopinski, slid his chair up to where I was sitting and said, "Mr. Carlo," his words slow and heavy and deliberate, "you have a very, very serious motor neuron disease. It might . . . it might be cancer of the spine. If it is, you are lucky because we can treat that—but the other . . . the other we cannot treat."

My mind raced with the implications of what he had just told me. I'm lucky if I have cancer of the spine? I thought. I felt beat up, put upon, weighed down all at the same time. The room swirled. I stood up and put my arms around him, hugged him, and thanked him for his candor and honesty.

Surely, I was thinking, I can deal with this—however fucking insidious it is. I soon put on my raincoat, bid them all farewell, and slowly went downstairs by myself. A cold, brisk, needle-like rain was falling. I had never felt so alone. I looked for a cab. There weren't any. By now, I had a distinct limp. My gait was a kind of herky-jerky amble. Like this, I slowly made my way up Second Avenue looking for a cab, the doctor's words ringing in my head like giant, brass knells, deafeningly loud. *For whom the bell tolls? The bell tolls for me.* Fuck. This had to be a mistake. I had no idea what a neurological disease did, what it was about, what its nature was. I still didn't know how bad—what a malevolent killer—it really was, though I would soon find out.

8. Life Change

The grim reaper was suddenly walking behind me, stalking me.

9. Death Sentence

Still, as bad as things appeared, they would get far, far worse.
To be definitively diagnosed, I next went to the sprawling Columbia University Hospital complex on 168th Street and Fort Washington Avenue by myself.

Dr. Polinsky wanted me to have two opinions and I was going to see one of the two doctors she strongly suggested—Dr. Lewis Rowland, the head of Columbia's neurological department. Dr. Rowland was ninety-one years old, spry and surprisingly lucid considering his age. Dr. Polinsky had told me that Rowland did not have a good bedside manner, but I was not prepared for just how bad it was. When he finished examining me, he took me to his office and sat me down at his desk, all dire and morose. After reading the EMG report, he gave me a long, solemn look and told me I had amyotrophic lateral sclerosis, commonly known as ALS or Lou Gehrig's Disease. In the most melodramatic terms, he told me I had three to five years to live. He said I wouldn't be able to walk, talk, use my hands—that ultimately I wouldn't be able to breathe, for the disease would waste away my diaphragm muscles. There was suddenly nothing else in the world but Doctor Rowland, his desk, the wall behind him, and me. I was numb, numb as though I were frozen. Dr. Rowland was dismayed when I told him that I lived alone, that I wasn't married, I had no children to help care for me. As he spoke, I felt as though I were slowly being lowered into a deep grave in a foul swamp. There were worms, leeches, maggots consuming me. It's hard to describe what you feel when a doctor of his stature tells you that you have a fatal disease. Speechless, I looked at his wizened face and asked myself what had I done to deserve this? Why?

Dr. Rowland went on to say it had nothing to do with genetics. "It strikes as randomly as lightning." He told me, too, there was no cure, no medicine, no kind of treatment—NO NOTHING.

"In short," he said, "it's the worst disease of modern times."

As he talked, his words became drowned out by the rushing sound of tumultuous surf in my head. He suggested I go to the ninth floor, where they would teach me about diet and home care and therapy. When I left Dr. Rowland that day, I was not the same man I had been. The Philip Carlo who had hopefully arrived at Columbia was no more. He was dead and buried and gone.

It was raining again. There was a gray, swirling storm blowing in off the turbulent expanse of the Hudson River, which Columbia is just east of. I couldn't find a fucking cab. I finally managed to get a gypsy cab on Broadway, several blocks away. I went home and sat down at my desk. I was in a form of shock, but I knew I had to speak with my father. Though as a youth I had not been close with my dad, he has become my best friend, more like my brother than my father. My dad has outlived all his family, seven brothers and three sisters. I didn't want to, but I had to tell him what I'd just been told. I called him up and, trying to be strong, trying to be a man, I told him what Dr. Rowland had said. He was shocked. He didn't believe it. He said it had to be a mistake. He kept saying, "No one in our family has this!"

I, for the most part, stayed stoic. I did cry for a bit, though not with the raging hysteria I felt swirling around inside of me.

Killers—I wondered if my delving into the minds of the horrific killers I had written books about, my entering death rows had played into this—done something to my brain. I decided one thing had nothing to do with the other; surely shining light in dark places would not cause one to be cursed with Lou Gehrig's Disease. I thought about my future, my career, my writing. No matter what, I resolved without a second thought, I'd write and write and write and write until the day I died. I would not be a victim. I would not succumb to this disease . . . this curse, the grim reaper.

As I sit here now on the beach with Kelsey, telling this, I remember next going to see Dr. Mark Sivak. As brutal and indifferent as Dr. Lew Rowland was, Dr. Mark Sivak at Mount Sinai would prove to be gentle and caring. He would become a friend, an ally in my war against ALS.

Initially Dr. Sivak refused to diagnose me with Lou Gehrig's Disease. It is the most heinous death sentence a doctor can give so he kept his lips sealed until he was sure. Dr. Sivak wanted me to have another brain scan, a spinal tap, and various blood tests before definitely saying I had amyotrophic lateral sclerosis. Having a glimmer of hope now, thinking I may have been misdiagnosed, I went through the battery of tests at Mount Sinai suggested by Dr. Sivak. These tests were administered over a period of several weeks. During these weeks, I continued riding my bike around Central Park, but running had become arduous, difficult. It felt as though large weights were attached to my muscles. The atrophy was inexorably weakening me and I was barely able to do half a lap around the reservoir, whereas I once did three laps without effort every single day, rain or snow or sleet or hail. Because I wasn't picking my feet up high enough, I found myself tripping over rocks and bumps on the horse path.

Still, I had made up my mind to live my life regardless of what curveballs were thrown at me. Where, exactly, I got the balls to look at this disease and say, "Go fuck yourself," I'm not quite sure. I did feel amazing depression at first, went through the "why me" phase. But what I decided I would do is live every day I had to the fullest. If you looked at me, I didn't appear sick at all. I had color from riding my bike in the sunshine. I still had some bounce in my step. But I had gone from 170 pounds of solid muscle to 150. The 20 pounds I lost were all muscle. Though it seemed I was slowly melting away, I continued to write every day. I forgot the disease. I got out of myself.

The results of the tests Dr. Sivak had ordered came back—it was too good to be true. I hadn't been misdiagnosed. Dr. Sivak confirmed I had Lou Gehrig's Disease. Even now, some four and a half years later, as I say these words, as Kelsey writes them down, I feel a pang of anxiety that a man walking to the guillotine might feel, but it is fleeting. I will not allow it to set up shop and make itself at home . . . in my head, in my soul.

   Writing this tires me. I feel my eyes closing. The work combined with the strong Florida sun has made me weary. We have Wilson's phone number and we call him to come pick me up in his golf cart and take me back to my wheelchair, which we left at the Savoy Hotel. I am unusually silent. Wilson soon appears with the golf cart and a broad smile on his face. He picks me up and puts me in the cart. Off we go.

10. Hollywood Comes Knocking

The following day is glorious. The sky is a rich pastel blue. A sweet breeze issues off the ocean. After a breakfast of toast and fruit, a few phone calls, a few e-mails, Kelsey, Laura, and I make our way back to the office. Today I ask Sergio to arrange our lounges as close to the water as possible. Why exactly I don't know, but the closer I am to the sea, the better I feel. It's as though it has some kind of cosmic control over me. Its smell, its sounds inspire.

Kelsey and I were working on this book when I got a phone call from my film agent telling me a big Hollywood mogul, Lorenzo di Bonaventura, wanted to option my book *The Ice Man* and make it into a memorable feature film. I have always felt *The Ice Man* would make a terrific movie and has elements never before seen couched within one of the most interesting, compelling, terrifying murder stories of all time. As time went by and it developed, I learned that di Bonaventura wanted to cast an actor named Channing Tatum as Richard Kuklinski, which I adamantly disagreed with. Tatum is a pretty boy from *Step Up*, a dance film, and, more recently, *G.I. Joe*, and does not remotely have the depth or sense of danger that was inherently Richard Kuklinski's. When di Bonaventura's option on the book was up, he said nothing about it expiring and suddenly—thankfully—I had the film rights back. Several weeks later, he tried to reacquire the film rights, but I refused to option the book to him again. All this, my refusing to deal with di Bonaventura, made it into the *New York Post*'s Page Six and soon was a big story around Hollywood, how a mere author turned down a Hollywood mogul, a rare thing these days. In any event, it was this incident, or rather series of incidents, that caused the actor Mickey Rourke to contact me through a mutual friend. We make plans to meet the following day. HBO did three sixty-minute documentaries on the Ice Man and Mickey has seen all three of them, he tells me. He was blown away and is hell-bent on playing Richard in the film. At this juncture, all I know about Mickey Rourke is that he is a hell of an actor who got caught up with drugs and drinking, as many excessively creative people do. I've seen just about every film he's been in over the years and I'm sure he'll portray the Ice Man brilliantly. I view him as a combination of Brando and James Dean.

Several days later, Mickey and I sit down in a small, quiet restaurant. He is a bigger man than I thought, more muscular, taller, and broader, has on a black vest and a black hat. After ordering coffee, he says, "I just love the book. It would make an amazing film. I've read it twice already. What a character."

All things I am pleased to hear but all things I've always felt, for I spent over two hundred hours with Kuklinski at Trenton State Maximum Security Prison. For a writer like me, who thoroughly researches every aspect of the story, I appreciate hearing this. I have always believed in my heart Kuklinski was a uniquely diabolical killer who on the one hand could be ice-cold and on the other hand be a warm and loving father and husband. In the morning, Kuklinski could be ripping the spine out of a man while he was still alive; then, later that same day, bring toys to his sick daughter in the hospital. At six foot six and 320 pounds, he was a very dangerous man who killed over two hundred people during his . . . I was going to say career, but I think reign of terror would be more appropriate.

I was quite candid and honest with Mickey about how I managed to get Richard Kuklinski to tell me all, *bare his soul*, about the many hours I sat down with him at Trenton State Prison and, little by little, got Richard's trust and ultimately became his . . . confidant. Everything I said, every word, intrigued Mickey. Several times over, he said, "This is gonna to be my *Raging Bull*."

I went on, told him how Richard's wife, Barbara, made peanut butter and jelly sandwiches in the morning, put them in a paper bag, and off to work he went, his work being—filling murder contracts; how he slept on the floor of a hospital ward where his eight-year-old daughter was being treated for a bladder infection; how he bought candy and toys for all the children on the ward; how he rented a garage in Bergen County, New Jersey, for the sole purpose of taking marks there to be tortured and killed—he bolted a metal chair to the garage floor, bound his victims with duct tape, paralyzed them by ripping out the lower aspects of their spines with his bare hands and proceeding to cut off body parts while they watched; how he gleefully hosted Saturday pool party barbecues for his children and all the other kids on the block, doting over them as though he were mother hen. There was a shockingly long litany of murder methods Richard had perfected, and I told Mickey about all of them without any editing, watching as his mouth hung open. When I finally finished, he said, "Holy fucking shit."

"Indeed," I said.

I tell Mick how when Richard first entered the room where I did my interviews with him, the guards made us sit close, knee-to-knee. I was always amazed at how he dwarfed me. After two months of my interviewing him like this, he one day said to me, "Phil . . . you know I've grown to like you. But I want you to know something. If you ever fuck me or lie to me, I'll kill you."

That coming from him was a startling revelation. I looked at him and he was deadly serious. To try to lighten the moment, I said, "Well, Richard, you know I'm not so easy to kill. I'm very fast."

He smiled at me, just his lips moving, his eyes staying cold and steady on me. He raised his huge ham-hock hand, clenched it into a fist, and, in the blink of an eye, brought it down with disarming speed and stopped just before he struck my leg, slightly above the knee. I was amazed by how fast he was.

He said, "My friend, I just broke your knee, and you ain't going nowhere. I could pick you up and break you over my knee like a pretzel." And he was right. I tell Mickey, "His speed was such that I had no chance. I knew for sure that he had more than enough power to easily break my leg."

Mickey says, "Fucking chilling."

"It was."

Mickey tells me he'd like to produce it with me and of course I agree. In the end, however, a sharp producer named Matty Beckerman calls me and he ends up underwriting the film, with a slated budget of $25 million. Beckerman brought on board screenwriter David

McKenna—the writer of the movies *American History X*, *S.W.A.T.*, and *Get Carter*. Everyone is in agreement that the film will be shot in the actual locations where the story played out. This I look forward to in a big way. This is, in a sense, the best medicine I could have. I plan to walk on the red carpet the opening night of the film—or rather roll.

"By the way," I tell Mickey, "I have all the outtakes from the HBO interviews Richard did."

"I'd love to see them."

"I'll get them to you."

We shake hands. He embraces me strongly, kisses me on the cheek, and makes for his car. He's a warm, gracious man and I look forward to working with him. I go back to our apartment, thinking about Richard . . . the Ice Man. I'll never forget the day he told me about the time he saw his six-year-old brother beaten to death by his father, Stanley Kuklinski. Richard was four years old when this unspeakable act occurred. It happened in 1937, at a time when funerals were still held in the home. The four-year-old Richard stood at his brother Florian's open coffin saying to himself, *"Florian, don't leave me; don't leave me alone with Daddy. Florian, please don't leave me."*

Richard was so utterly frightened of his father that he urinated in his pants at just the sound of his father's voice. Richard did not tell me this willingly. I had to coax and pull it out of him for over a week. Thus, I learned how the Ice Man became so cold.

I stare into space and remember well the things Richard told me. I think about the time he was hired to kill a rapist right here in South Beach. It was a brutal, barbaric murder, something I will never forget. In that it is a bird's-eye view of exactly how a Mafia hit goes down, I thought I'd share it with you here. Roy DeMeo was an out-of-control, homicidal maniac in the Gambino crime family. According to the FBI and the U.S. Department of Justice, DeMeo murdered and butchered over two hundred people in the back of a bar he had in Canarsie, Brooklyn, called the Gemini Lounge. Several books were written about this individual, delineating how truly bad he was. It was Roy DeMeo who gave Kuklinski the piece of work I am about to describe:

Richard was beeped by DeMeo and went to meet him at the diner near the Tappan Zee Bridge.

"Hey, Rich," DeMeo greeted him, and they warmly hugged and kissed, these two, oversized, stone-cold killer. They began to walk around the parking lot.

DeMeo said, "I gotta a special piece a work for you. This Cuban cocksucker down in Miami beat up and raped the fourteen-year-old daughter of an associate of ours. She couldn't pick him out in a lineup because he wore a fuckin' bandanna, but we know who he is; he works as a maintenance guy in the complex where they have a place. It's called the Castaway right in Miami, on Collins Avenue. Richie, you go see him and make sure he fuckin' suffers . . . really suffers! You understand?"

"My pleasure," Richard said, and he meant it.

"This is from our associate," Roy said, and slipped Richard an envelope with twenty thousand dollars in it. Mob guys make trainloads of money, and twenty thousand dollars was a mere drop in the bucket, though it was enough for Richard to leave for Miami the following day. Now he did not stop for lunch or stay at a nice hotel on the way down. He drove straight through. When he bought gas and oil he paid with cash. Even if he had a credit card he would not use it, because he wanted no record of this trip. There was no photo of the mark, but DeMeo told him the kind of car he drove and that he parked it in the designated area for hotel employees; he even gave the license-plate number.

The only people Richard hated more than bullies were rapists. As he drove he thought about how he'd feel if one of his girls were attacked that way . . . the rage and hatred he'd know. As cold and indifferent as Richard could be to human suffering, he had a great empathy for a young woman who had been raped. This killing was a piece of work he'd enjoy. This was a piece of work he'd gladly have done for free.

As always, Richard was careful about not speeding, even though he was in a hurry—indeed looked forward to doing the job. He had with him a .38 loaded with hollow-point rounds and a razor-sharp hunting knife with a curved blade and a hardwood handle. The handle had four notches on it—Richard liked to notch his knives when he used them to kill someone. He explained, I didn't know how I picked up the habit, but I always liked to notch my knives. Like gunfighters used to. Over the years I had dozens of knives I used to kill. Some of them had ten to fifteen notches on them. Then I'd just get rid of them.

Richard planned to use a knife for this particular job. He very much enjoyed, he says, killing with a knife because it was so personal; you had to be close to the victim. He liked to see life leave the eyes of those he killed; especially a rapist. This would be . . . fun.

The Castaway was a sprawling three-story condo complex on Collins Avenue, near 163rd Street, on both the ocean side of Collins and the street side. Richard checked into a hotel near the place, had a nice lunch, and drove to the parking lot, looking for the mark's car. It wasn't there. Richard quickly found out there were two shifts, 8:00 A.M. to 4:00 P.M., then 4:00 P.M. to midnight. It was now the middle of winter, 1974, and the parking lot was full. He would have to be careful, he knew, about being seen taking the mark.

He left, returned at 3:30 P.M., and waited. He didn't have to wait long, for the mark soon pulled into the lot and parked, not a care in the world, singing to himself. He drove a beat-up red Chevy. The license plate matched. Richard smiled when he saw the guy, a tall, skinny Latin with a thick, greasy head of black hair combed straight back. Richard quickly saw how the job should be done and left.

Now it was only a matter of time.

At eleven-thirty that night, Richard was back in the parking lot of the Castaway. Just across the street was a hangout for young people called Nebas, and a huge crowd of kids were mingling. Richard parked his van as close to the mark's car as possible, got out of it, walked to the red Chevy, gave it a flat, then calmly returned to the van. This was a tried and proven method Richard would use many times over. He already knew where he'd take the mark once he snatched him—a desolate stand of palms about half an hour north of the hotel, right by the ocean.

Near midnight, the mark came bopping over to his car. He spotted the flat, cursed out loud, and opened his trunk. As he bent to pull the spare out, Richard stole up behind him and the put the .38 in his lower back.

"My friend, I need you to come with me," he said, his voice faraway and detached, as if it were coming from a machine, a telephone recording. Richard let him see the gun now, took his skinny arm and marched him to the van, put him inside, handcuffed him, put a sock in his mouth, and taped his mouth shut with heavy-duty gray duct tape. Richard calmly got behind the wheel and pulled out of the lot. The whole thing took less than two minutes. As Richard drove north on Collins, he talked to the mark.

"My friend," he said, "I want you to know that I've been sent by friends of the girl you beat up and raped."

With that the mark began to moan and flop around like a fish suddenly out of water.

"If you don't stop making a fuss, I'm going to hurt you."

The mark became still, silent. What was so unsettling about what Richard said was not so much the words. It was the cold, detached way he said them, each word like the cut of a jagged knife.

"So, my friend, I want you to know that you have to suffer before I kill you. They paid me well for that, but truth is I'd gladly do this for free. I want you to know that."

"Hmm! Hmm!" the mark mumbled, panic-stricken.

"If you believe in God, my friend, you better start praying because you've reached the end of the line. The train is going to soon stop and it's time to get off."

Richard was purposely tormenting the mark, letting the caustic words be the last words he heard in this life.

"Did you really think you could do such a thing and go about your business like nothing happened? Well, my friend, you picked the wrong girl this time."

Richard turned right, shut off the lights, and made his way onto a rough road that went all the way down to the beach. There was a nearly full moon in a velvet black sky. The moonlight, white and clean and lovely, reflected off the calm sea, laying a glistening lunar highway on the still surface of the water. Richard stopped, sat, and listened. All was quiet and still. No sound but the gentle lapping of small waves on the fine white sand of the beach.

Richard put on blue plastic gloves, pulled the rapist from the van, dragged him to a wide, particularly curved palm, and tied him to the tree with yellow nylon rope. Now the mark was in a frenzied panic. Richard showed him the gleaming curved blade, the moonlight reflecting ominously on the razor-sharp steel.

"So, my friend, let's get started."

And with that Richard roughly pulled down the mark's pants, took tight hold of both of his testicles, and pulled so hard he literally tore them off the mark—

White-hot pain exploded where his testicles had just been. His eyes burst open. Richard showed him his balls.

"How's that feel?" he asked, smiling. "My friend."

Richard gave time for the shock to wear off a bit and for the pain to set in.

"Nice night, isn't it?" he asked. "Look at the moon, how pretty."

Now he used the knife; he grabbed hold of the mark's penis—"This is what got you in all the trouble, you don't need it anymore"—and easily cut if off. He showed it to the rapist as blood gushed from the sudden fleshy stump Richard had created. He went back to the van and put the severed member in a Ziploc sandwich bag he'd brought for this purpose.

He returned to the mark, ripped all his clothes off him, and began slowly slicing away fillets of flesh—kind of like pieces of skirt steak, making sure to show him the pieces he was methodically taking away, smiling as he worked.

The mark was soon a monstrous sight, terrible to see in the pale silver light of the Miami moon. Richard again returned to the van. He had brought along a large container of fine kosher salt and he now poured the salt all over the exposed flesh. The salt would bring, Richard knew, a whole new symphony of pain. He gave time for the salt to work.

Now Richard forced the blade into the mark's lower abdomen and slowly pulled it up with his superhuman strength. The mark's guts spilled forth and were suddenly just hanging there like a nervous cluster of blue-red snakes.

Richard cut him free, put a life preserver on him, grabbed his ankle, and dragged him down to the water's edge, talking as he went: "My friend, I know the tide's going out now, I checked, and you're going out with it. I put the life vest on you because I don't want you to drown. I'll bet you my last dollar that the sharks'll find you in no time. I hear there are big nasty tiger sharks here." And with that Richard swung him up and around and tossed him into the water and watched him drift out. Then he turned and went back to the van, retrieved what he had cut from the mark, threw it all in the ocean, and returned to his hotel, where he had a nice sandwich—his favorite, turkey and mayo on rye.

This was Richard Leonard Kuklinski, born and raised on the mean streets of Jersey City, New Jersey.

When I get back to the house, Laura tells me Kelsey's on the beach and asks what I thought of Mickey. I tell her I was very impressed by him, the questions he asked, his heartfelt enthusiasm for playing the Ice Man.

"I think he'll do a great job. I think he's going to win an Oscar."

Laura excuses herself to take a phone call from her sister. Laura, like most women, is a great phone talker. I think she finds solace in phone calls and a way to escape the blatant hardships of our lives. The fact that I'm so ill—terminally sick—has a huge effect on Laura's psyche, I'm sure. For the most part, she is helpful, but the strain of my condition takes both a physical and a mental toll of both of us. Caretakers of the terminally ill truly are a put-upon lot, but I can do little about this one way or another. It is what it is. Laura tells me she's going to take a shower. I wheel myself out on the terrace and stare at the beach, the turquoise ocean and slow-moving white cottony clouds.

The bell rings. It's my therapist, Sharon. I'm lucky, for here in Florida I have a therapist who comes twice a week. She's an attractive, buxom blonde, and she pulls and stretches me and, holding me, giving me support, makes me stand. Though I quiver as though I'm standing in an earthquake, I still manage to stay upright. It feels fantastic.

What is so insidious about ALS is the fact that it slowly kills the muscles throughout your body, which ultimately forces you to remain sedentary, which further compounds the loss of muscles. It's like throwing gas on a fire. Being immobile makes everything worse, adds to the problem, an insidious, vicious cycle. As I sit here, I'm looking out the sliding glass doors to the terrace and the ocean beyond. If I could just get down to the water's edge and move my legs up and down, it would be very helpful, it would stimulate the muscles, stimulate the nerve endings. But now my legs are like two rubber bands. If I try to stand without assistance, I go right down; another milestone of loss. Sharon hugs and kisses me good-bye, shouts so long to Laura, and off she goes.

Laura comes out of the bathroom. She likes taking long showers. Naked, she is quite a beautiful woman in the bright light of day streaming through the terrace doors. As always, impetuous and in a hurry, I want to get down to the beach. We began calling the beach the office last year. I wrote my most recent book, *Gaspipe*, there, and the year before, I wrote several chapters of *The Ice Man*. I don't just mean figuratively—I mean actually sat on the beach, wrote with my hands until my hands were no more, and then began working with Kelsey. With me, as with most people with fatal diseases, most everything must be done now. There is an inherent imperativeness to things. I'm intolerant with tardiness, I'm intolerant with the wasting of time. Laura loads up a beach bag with fruit and reading material and off we go, get in the elevator.

For the most part, in our building people are respectful of the fact that I am in a wheelchair, and they make room for us, hold doors for us, and the like. When we get out to the street, the Florida sun is hot and white and I am forced to put on my sunglasses. I have become used to the fact that I am wheelchair-bound but people often stare at me, some quite rudely, though I have managed to become used to that, too. In fact, I see a lot more people stare at Laura with her Bardot looks than the spectacle. We take a right into the Savoy and go to the rear of the hotel where we see our friend, Wilson, who again takes us out onto the beach in a golf cart, and soon I'm comfortable in the "office." Kelsey's been here a couple of hours by herself and she already has a good tan. It's become a bit windy today, the ocean rougher, but it's still champagne-popping glorious to be out in the fresh sea air.

Wanting to ward off the pallor people with ALS often have, get a tan, I tell Sergio, "I don't want an umbrella, thank you."

As is our custom, Sergio complains about various people on the beach who have been rude to him and we all listen as if he's discussing important world events. To him, I suppose, they are important matters but to us they're comical . . . somewhat absurd.

"See her?" he says. "She has this radio and she's playing it very loud. She's disturbing lots of people. I told her to lower the radio and she told me no. And you see her? Yesterday she left with one of the towels. She stole it!"

Gravely, we look at the woman he's indicating. A French couple walk onto the beach and wave for Sergio to bring them an umbrella. As he walks away, up pulls Raf in a golf cart. Raf is also a good friend. He too works for the Boucher brothers, managing all the different concessions they have on South Beach. He is a blue-eyed, baby-faced, upbeat Brit. He and I have one thing particularly in common—he is a big fan of ultimate fighting, as I am. We excitedly tell Raf about the shark we all saw. He was not there the day the shark came up on the beach, and we give him all the colorful details. He tells us, surprisingly, he's never seen a shark on the beach.

"That's because you're not looking," I tell him. "Raf, you're too busy ogling the girls to look at the ocean."

He laughs. He is summoned to another beach over his walkie-talkie.

"See you later, mate," he says, and off he goes in his golf cart.

I turn to Kelsey and say, "Are you ready?"

Just before we are about to begin, a disgruntled Sergio returns.

"I don't know if I'm going to be here next year. I don't think so," he says out of nowhere. He's been saying this for the last few years. We tell him how much we will miss him.

"Kelsey, are you ready?" I say. That is a signal for him to make himself scarce.

"So where are we going to begin?" Kelsey asks.

Part of the inherent problem with writing a book is where the hell you begin after you've stopped. I ask Kelsey to read me the last couple of pages we did. She does. I think about what she reads. My mind starts going back to the story, but I remember I told Mickey Rourke I would get him the HBO tapes, which are back in New York. I call my friend Mike to find them in the basement and ship them to us here. The tapes are quite extraordinary because they show the Ice Man in a relaxed mode, his real persona. Kuklinski talks about the weather, politics, murder in great detail, and is not answering questions posed to him about his crimes, as such. They will be invaluable to a method actor, I know. I got them from senior HBO producer Gaby Monet— a very nice lady and a dear friend.

Early on, when I first started researching the Ice Man case, I thought it imperative that I meet the producer of the three documentaries HBO had done on Richard Kuklinski. Each of them was highly acclaimed, seen by over 150 million people, praised by the *New York Times*. They showed us a slice of life, a candid dark side of human nature we'd never seen before. I found out that the producer was a woman named Gaby Monet. I phoned her up at HBO and she, somewhat reluctantly, agreed to meet with me. We had lunch in a restaurant on 46th Street called Un Deux Trois. Gaby was a petite, attractive woman with dark hair and large, dark, intelligent eyes. She was fragile and very ladylike; much in contrast to what you'd expect from the producer of a documentary on one of the most prolific murderers of modern times. I told her how I'd seen one of the documentaries, became interested, wrote to Richard, and he agreed to work with me. She told me she thought that a good book on Richard, a definitive study of his life and crimes, was much needed. Our lunch was cordial and friendly. I gave her a copy of *The Night Stalker* and a copy of *Stolen Flower*. Gaby explained to me that since she first met Richard, he had been calling her every day collect from Trenton State Prison. She had developed a unique friendship with him. When she spoke of him, she did so in glowing terms. The Richard she had come to know was not the hired assassin. He was, as she put it, "a gentle giant." As I spoke with her, I realized that she was genuinely fond of him. This piqued my interest further and made the case that much more interesting. The fact that an intelligent woman like her could think well of him was telling and compelling and made the case that much more three dimensional, I thought. As I started researching the book in earnest, I became more and more friendly with Gaby. We took to having lunch once a week to discuss not only Kuklinski but the world at large. The many documentaries she produced for HBO are amazingly good. I watched them all and was truly impressed.

When I was diagnosed with ALS, I had a scheduled lunch with Gaby the next day. On the dreadful afternoon I arrived home from Columbia after having just seen Dr. Lew Rowland, she called to confirm our lunch. Not wanting to, angry at myself, I began crying when I told her what I had learned that day. It just poured out of me. She was amazingly sympathetic and suggested I meet Valerie Estess as soon as possible, that Valerie was on the front lines of trying to find a cure for the disease. Gaby told me HBO did a documentary called *Three Sisters Looking for a Cure*. It told the story of Jenifer Estess, who contracted ALS and, after a protracted battle to find a cure, succumbed to the disease in 2003. Devastated by the loss of their sister, Valerie and Meredith went on to start a nonprofit organization— Project ALS. The two sisters managed to raise over $57 million to help find a cure for the disease, which they donated to Columbia, Harvard, and Johns Hopkins University hospitals.

"Phil," Gaby told me, "I'm so, so sorry. I feel just terrible."

I told Gaby I couldn't meet her the following day for lunch. She understood. I was . . . for want of a better word, distraught. A few days later, I called Valerie Estess. Gaby had called in advance. Valerie agreed to meet with me and I went to her downtown office. She was an attractive blonde, athletic and well-coordinated, who looked more like a dedicated surfer than someone fighting the grim reaper that is ALS. I was hoping that she would have some kind of good news; that she knew of a breakthrough; that there was something just around the corner that will help. She told me there was nothing, sadly shaking her head, but said that they were working hard on two fronts.

One, finding a drug that will help and two, perhaps more important, using stem cell application to regenerate the dying motor neurons that characterize ALS. I asked Valerie what she knew about IPLEX. She said she had heard mixed things about the drug. Some people, she said, seemed to benefit while others did not. Overall, she was upbeat and very optimistic and I left believing there was hope, thinking that this woman who had the unorthodox courage and the ability to think outside of the box might very well hit the bull's-eye and find a cure.

Over the ensuing weeks and months, Valerie and I became good friends and lunched often, but there was no good news, no definitive remedy for the disease. Still, I have hope and faith in her.

However, in my most recent meeting with, Valerie she told me that scientists Project ALS had funded had just discovered how to make motor neurons from small samples of ALS patients' skin. First, she said, the samples are collected, then scientists introduce a few growth factors into a petri dish, and the skin cells turn into embryonic-like stem cells, with the ability to become any cell type in the body. This was hopeful, she said, because scientists for the first time would be able to directly treat, in a laboratory setting, the cause of ALS—the failing motor neurons. When I asked her how long it would be before there would be some kind of treatment that could help, she gave me a long, baleful poker stare.

"One . . . maybe two years," she said. "There's really no telling, but we are working as fast as we can." This was, unfortunately, nothing I could hang my hat on, take to the bank, I know. But I still have faith and confidence in Valerie that she may pull a rabbit out of a hat, that rabbit, unfortunately, being my life.

11. The Fireman

For any writer's work, be it a book, poem, magazine story, to be made into a major motion picture is winning the lottery. Today, taking into account the way the book market is, publishers pay scant little compared to what studios will pay when they really want a property. In theory, I should be overjoyed; here I have a major star, a controversial, interesting artist wanting to put his heart and soul into playing the Ice Man, but I'm afraid I don't feel overjoyed.

Instead, what I feel is a contemplative wariness. If I allow myself to feel joy, to feel like I want to jump up and click my heels—if I could—I would be setting myself up for a letdown. I know from being in the writing business for many years that things don't always pan out the way they should or could or would. It is this that prevents me from feeling the elation that comes with hitting a home run. When you are burdened with the overwhelming weight of ALS, a letdown is like an anchor being thrown overboard; disappointment equals a turn for the worse. This is not a contrivance or dramatization or a figment of my imagination. Each of my doctors has told me to avoid aggravation, strife. Steve Byer also warned me about getting upset. Aggravation has a degenerative effect on the weakened motor neurons. So, therefore, I must stay detached.

Still, Mickey Rourke's warmth and enthusiasm are overwhelming and I feel this is really going to happen, not because I want it to but because he wants it to and it is an amazing story. I really do believe that this complicated, dark role, his playing The Ice Man, will at the least get him nominated for an Oscar.

For the most part, I try to be upbeat and have sunshine about me, not dark clouds, but that it is far easier said than done. Sometimes I am somber and morose when I should be joyful and happy. This has more to do with the disease than with me. Laura does her best to try to help, but occasionally I am impatient and a ballbuster, which of course makes Laura's job that much more difficult. I try to explain to her that my impetuousness, short fuse, is the disease, not me, but it's impossible. This, after a while, sounds like no more than a shallow excuse for bad behavior, a jive-ass mantra that resonates as tin repetition, rather than the truth—but my telling her this is, in fact, my reaching out, my trying to close the gap between us because of the inevitable friction and arguments, considering how hapless I am, considering that we spend all day and all night, every day and night, together. Under the best of circumstances, I know, any couple thrust together for twenty-four hours a day will start to go at each other.

"Get me this!"

"Get me that!"

"I need this."

"Laura! Laura! I GOTTA PEE!"

All this weighs heavy on Laura, I know. It's inevitable, human nature.

How dare she resent my calling her all the time! I sometimes think. But for the most part, I feel great empathy, great sympathy, for her. The caregivers of those with terminal diseases should be made saints—they essentially have a one-way ticket to nowhere. After all, in the end, what happens? A death, a burial. A huge gap, a silent void in the caregiver's life. And the last memories—what are they about— heartache and difficulties . . . the loss of a loved one, a broken heart. Where there was once conversation, there is now only silence.

Life can be a cruel thing. Inevitably, people with ALS turn inward, look for solace and comfort inside ourselves, rather than the outside world. We know that nobody can know what it's like to watch your body slowly die over a period of days, weeks, months, years.

"You don't know what it's like!" I often tell Laura. She says, "I do! I see it every day!"

But what she sees is only the outward manifestation. She cannot know what it's like to feel the loss of the ability to pick up a tissue, the ability to brush your teeth, the ability to scratch your face or blow your nose. I used to love eating soup, especially coconut shrimp soup with ginger and lemongrass, but if I try to eat soup now, I end up wearing it, not eating it.

Another thing is my being a spectacle.

I don't mind being in the company of family and friends, but I don't like being around strangers. Even some family functions I avoid—weddings, birthdays.

Sometimes around Laura's family I feel like a burden—the excessive weight of her chores becomes apparent quickly to them. *What kind of life is this for a young woman?* they must be thinking. It's a given. In my mind, what makes my presence onerous is the fact that when I'm sitting at the dining table, I have to have the ventilator tube in my mouth. This automatically connotes to them that I can't breathe on my own, that if I didn't have this machine, I theoretically couldn't live. I hate the ventilator. When we go out, I have to have it with me at all times, this crazy, stupid thing I need to breathe.

When we go down Ocean Drive, many people stare at me and they think I must have emphysema, was a heavy smoker, and got sick. But I don't have emphysema. I have this ridiculous ventilator because my diaphragm muscles are shrinking, failing me. Sometimes, at these times, I feel like I am already dead. After all, if a man can't breathe of his own volition, isn't he dead? But the irony of it all is that when I'm here on South Beach, I'm all tan and healthy-looking. Laura bought me a dozen bright Tommy Bahama shirts and they work well on somebody couched in a wheelchair. That's another thing I've grown to hate—the wheelchair, but the wheelchair has become a trusted friend that gets me to where I want to go.

Still, I regularly make jokes and silly faces and try to make Laura laugh, though considering what she's faced with every day, all the different needs I have, laughter is sometimes a rare commodity. Laura has a somewhat stoic, introspective personality sometimes, a tough Brooklyn edge. Other times, she's all bubbly and effervescent.

I want to get the hell out of the house. When it's nice weather outside, sun shining, birds chirping, being inside makes me feel claustrophobic.

"Are you ready?" I keep asking Laura.

We finally leave the apartment and make our way downstairs onto the beach—the office. I have much to say; it's been bottled up inside me all day.

I begin writing, that is, dictating to Kelsey, who is on my left. Laura is on my right. I take a long, deep breath and look at Laura. I admire her handsome profile, the arch of her brows, the sweet ridges of her cheekbones, her full lips. She is a radiant, intensely beautiful woman. She has to be, I think, the most attractive caregiver that ever was. She is contentedly reading. I don't say anything to disturb her. I assume it's a gossip magazine. When we first met, she'd wake up early to read Page Six every morning, and I could never understand it. We'd get in fights about it. I guess to some degree it is her escape from the truth of what our lives have become.

Now, lying on the beach in front of the Savoy Hotel, palm trees gently swaying in the breeze directly off the ocean, the Miami sun is hot though pleasant on my skin. Again, without asking my permission, my eyelids begin to close. I suddenly open them and Kelsey is staring at me with questions on her face.

"It's the lithium. It's my blood sugar," I say. We begin again. I suddenly wake up with her staring at me again. Fuck! I order a cappuccino. Again I doze off, go to that limbo between sleep and consciousness, and when I wake up, I'm covered in sweat. Kelsey is gone. Laura tells me she went down to the water. I'm glad she has gone swimming. I see Kelsey as an extension of myself and so I am happy she's in the glorious, wonderful water of Miami when I cannot be. I look down toward the ocean and think of all the oceans of my life, all the seas I've been in. The oceans of Greece, Mexico, and South America; also the waters off Saint John, Saint Croix, Saint Thomas, and a dozen other places. What I always did was run down toward the water like a ten-year-old boy playing hooky and dive in with no inhibition. My God, I miss the rush of the water suddenly engulfing me.

Maybe, when I get the IPLEX—if I get the IPLEX—I'll be able to do that again. I mean, I'm not going to be able to dive in right away, but if I could just get down to the water's edge with some help, I could sit there and be content as a bug in a rug.

I look up toward the building where we're staying and there they are, these six cobalt gray pelicans I see every day—silently, effortlessly gliding by—as though they're going to and from work. Giant birds with the faces of old men who have outlived their years but refuse to accept it. How outright ugly they are on the one hand, but how graceful they are when they fly.

Kelsey comes back and readies herself. She makes certain to dry her hair so as not to get water on the computer. I have Sergio set up umbrellas. It's funny . . . as cursed as my body is now, my brain has never been sharper. I write clearly and simply and there's little I can't recall. I remember the little tendrils of insect-like hairs protruding from Dr. Lew Rowland's nose as he told me I should go home and die; I remember Dr. Mark Sivak's face nearly bunching into tears, the slightest of creases on each side of his mouth, when he told me I did have Lou Gehrig's Disease; I remember like it was yesterday my limping up Second Avenue. I bring myself back, back to the beach, back to the moment.

And so Kelsey and I begin. It goes well. It always goes well. This thing, this story inside me, is hell-bent on getting out. It's as though there's a giant insect with claws and razor-sharp teeth biting and gnawing and clawing its way out of my body.

As I talk, as I tell the story, as I move my lips and tongue, Kelsey's fingers adroitly move over the keys of her computer. She doesn't miss a word. Anybody who sees us marvels at how quickly she can get down what I'm saying—and more important, accurately.

As we are winding down, my film agent, Jerry Kalajian, calls from Los Angeles. We discuss the movie deal with Mickey Rourke. When I hang up, we decide to wrap up for the day. We are tired, as we are every day. It's a funny thing. I don't think people realize just how exhausting writing can be. It's as though you are digging ditches. I suggest we go to the News Café for a snack. Both Kelsey and Laura think it's a good idea. We soon get off the beach with Wilson's help and start walking up Ocean Drive. Everywhere you look are bikini-clad people, many beautiful women, and neat and clean and geometrically perfect art deco buildings, one after the other, all in pastel colors. They remind me of an era gone by, a time of elegance and the good life. In that Ocean Drive runs parallel to the beach, it really is an ideal location, palm trees languidly swaying in breezes. Just opposite this glorious beach and the palm trees are outdoor restaurants. Some of these are tourist traps but tourist traps don't last long. Here, the competition between the restaurants is stiff. The quality of the restaurants has therefore become better and better. You excel, or you fail. When you look at Ocean Drive, the restaurants and boutiques, bars and gelaterias, you don't see the fact that the economy is in a bad state. Just the opposite. Here all the shops and restaurants are crowded; here, money is being freely spent and people are laughing and drinking and having a good time. Even though I'm afflicted with ALS, my limbs paralyzed, I very much enjoy being in this place, this Mecca of recreation and fun and good cheer, vacation and beach, though what we're doing here is none of that. We are here working diligently. I am writing a book, a very serious enterprise. I have the best of both worlds. If it wasn't for my being in a wheelchair, my hands twisted and still in front of me, I'd be sitting pretty.

The News Café is a large outdoor affair at Eighth Street and Ocean with waiters hurrying about under tall, stately palm trees. They serve good food twenty-four hours a day with a smile and no attitude. Here you can have breakfast at 5:00 P.M. and dinner at 9:00 A.M. The News Café draws an eclectic clientele. As we take a table and sit, many different languages are being spoken all around us. South Beach is popular with Europeans and with the weak dollar, they've flocked here in droves . . . Germans and Swiss, French and Dutch, and many Italians. In that it's the end of the day and our work is done, we order piña coladas. The café is known for its tropical drinks. We also order a big bowl of strawberries the size of lemons. Sitting here, we eat our strawberries and drink our drinks and watch the world go by. News Café is excellent for people watching, especially the legions of women. Here there are world-class beauties clad in bathing suits that could be easily blown off by a strong wind. Dressed in many different colored sarongs, they strut their stuff. We three have become comfortable enough with one another that conversation isn't necessarily necessary. We each have our own thoughts and our own minds. There is actually a news vendor at the News Café and Kelsey goes off to get the *Post* and the *New York Times*. Sitting there, we look at the newspapers, discuss the day, and talk about Mickey Rourke. We are all in agreement that Mickey would make a great Ice Man. I knew Kuklinski well and I am looking forward to sitting with Mickey and describing Kuklinski's nuances and idiosyncrasies. I think about how his daughter Merrick told me that when she was eight years old and hospitalized for days on end, her father was at the hospital constantly; her father slept on the floor; her father would bring toys for her and the other children on the ward. It is this interesting difference, these radically different two worlds, that will make for a memorable performance from Mickey.

As the sun sets, warm shadows appear on Ocean Drive but it is still hot and pleasant. Walking around in just a bathing suit is quite comfortable. Finished, we head back to our apartment while Kelsey takes a right on Seventh Street and returns to her place on Euclid Avenue. Just south of Fifth Street, there are very few restaurants and hotels and it is unusually quiet and tranquil. It is my favorite place. It is why we come here.

When Laura and I get upstairs, we have a message from a production company in the UK that is doing a story on the Mafia . . . specifically on Anthony Casso, the former head of the Lucchese New York crime family. As I said, I wrote a book about this particular mafioso. I was initially drawn to him and his story for several reasons. I was intimately acquainted with Anthony; he was our next-door neighbor for six years when I was growing up in Brooklyn.

During his infamous career in the Mafia, Anthony was responsible for killing over fifty people and devising dozens of schemes in which the family made hundreds of millions of dollars—union infiltration, drug dealing, amazingly esoteric robberies of bank vaults. When he was eventually captured, he decided to become an informer rather than face the music. While the Cassos were living next door to us, his wife, Lillian, and my mother became friends. My parents and the Cassos vacationed together. They often had dinner together. Though truth be told, Anthony was a very dangerous man, he was always a gentleman in our home; you really couldn't ever judge a book by its cover. In our home, he seemed like a gentle lamb when in truth he was a fierce lion, muscular and cunning and hidden in jungle foliage. He loved his wife. He loved his children. He was obviously dedicated to them. He was also obviously dedicated to La Cosa Nostra. I remember watching from our kitchen shady men delivering brown paper bags to Anthony's home day and night. Anthony was a short, stocky, handsome man with thick black hair combed straight back and piercing dark eyes. When Anthony looked at you, it was outright scary. His eyes were just like the Night Stalker's eyes: flat, black, cold—reminiscent of the mako shark I'd seen in Salinas, Ecuador. I think of Stephen Hawking, the brilliant scientist who also suffers from ALS, how he described in great detail the black hole that exists in outer space. With Ramirez and Casso, the black hole lives in their eyes. Though from two radically different worlds, both Casso and Ramirez had the eyes of a killer.

"What about Kuklinski?" people ask me. "Don't his eyes have that black void?" They didn't—au contraire. What the Ice Man had was the flip side of what Anthony and Ramirez had—his eyes were a translucent blue, as cold as ice. When you looked at Kuklinski, there was no black void as such; what you were staring at was Arctic-cold, frigid indifference.

When the Cassos moved from Bensonhurst to Mill Basin, my parents slowly lost contact with them. Through guile and cunning and sheer brutality, Anthony quickly rose up the ranks of the Mafia and ultimately became the head of the Lucchese family, one of the most vicious Mafia families of all time. Ultimately, one of the attributes that leaned toward Anthony's meteoric rise in La Cosa Nostra was that he was truly a stone-cold killer. Anthony was a killer of killers. In 1991, he was indicted in the famous "Windows Case" and went on the lam. When, in 1993, he was captured at a secluded house in New Jersey, I followed the case avidly. I wrote Anthony several letters but did not hear back from him. That was because the government was hiding him, but I didn't yet know that. I ultimately became involved in the *Ice Man* project. Upon my completing that book, I looked around for something new—an epic story that spanned years. Every few months, I read stories in the *Times* regarding Anthony and came to realize that he was far more dangerous, plugged in, powerful than I had ever imagined. He was the mob guy, as an example, who hired NYPD detectives Stephen Caracappa and Louis Eppolito—the so-called "Mafia Cops," who killed eight people at the behest of Anthony. I again wrote Anthony, this time at the Federal House of Detention in lower Manhattan and now, I hit fertile pay dirt. He not only responded, but he agreed to cooperate with me in the writing of an in-depth book on his life and crimes. More important, perhaps, he would share with me his intimate knowledge of the Mafia. This would be like talking to Einstein about physics. It was now the latter part of 2005. I had already been diagnosed with ALS and was slowly losing the muscular integrity of my body. It seemed every day I lost something more and I was absolutely intent upon keeping my mind on anything but my illness.

This project, the Anthony Casso story, seemed made to order. It began at the turn of the century in Sicily and evolved like some criminal Shakespearean drama that played out on the very mean streets of

South Brooklyn, Bensonhurst, and spread its insidious tentacles around the world. It would be the first time ever that the head of a Mafia family told all. Over the next ten months or so, I interviewed Casso extensively by way of telephone and hundreds of lengthy letters that he wrote to me, answering my many questions in great detail. He was a natural-born storyteller and surprisingly articulate considering he only had a tenth-grade education. While interviewing him, I learned about the inner workings, names and dates and times and places, of Mafia Commission meetings attended by John Gotti, Sammy "The Bull" Gravano, Vincent "The Chin" Gigante, Benny "Eggs" Mangano—notorious mafiosi all. The Bonanno family had been banned from meetings because they openly dealt in drugs, Casso said. Likewise, the Colombo family was barred from attending meetings because they were warring amongst themselves—the Vic Orena faction of the Colombo family on one side and the Persico faction of the family on the other side.

At the Commission meetings, important decisions were made: who lived and who died; who got what part of this or that construction site; exactly how the Mafia infiltrated and controlled unions across the country; how they brought heroin through Afghanistan and Sicily and Marseilles and Canada and, ultimately, to the States. As the head of a family, Anthony had access to secret information about La Cosa Nostra. I learned, also, the truth behind the Mafia's role in John and Bobby Kennedy's murders, fascinating stuff. Joseph Kennedy, the father of Bobby and John Kennedy, had been a very successful, ruthless bootlegger. In that role, he interacted on a large scale with mafiosi all over the East Coast. When John Kennedy was running for president, his father went and spoke to Sam Giancana, a Chicago crime boss, and asked him to help his son win Illinois' many electoral votes. Giancana delivered the goods. John Kennedy won Illinois and, ultimately, won the presidency. Bobby Kennedy hated his father's involvement with organized crime, what his father had done, and had an intense dislike for the Mafia. When Bobby was appointed attorney general by his brother, he went after the Mafia with an excessive zeal, vengeance, and during Senate subcommittee meetings, he intensely grilled various mafiosi, premier of which was New Orleans crime boss Carlos Marcello . . . a very dangerous, cunning Sicilian. Long story short—the Mafia decided to kill Bobby Kennedy. He was a thorn in their side. He was trouble. However, they realized that if they killed

Bobby, his brother would come after them with the full might of the United States government behind him. He would spare no resource, they knew. So they decided to kill John Kennedy instead to "cut the head off the body." Thus, President John F. Kennedy was killed in Dallas, Texas, on November 22, 1963. When Bobby Kennedy was later running for president, the mob realized he might actually win, and they knew they had to do away with him. And so Bobby Kennedy was murdered at the Ambassador Hotel in Los Angeles on June 6, 1968, shot down by Sirhan Sirhan, a shill for the Mafia.

"Nobody kills better than the Italians," famed Irish mobster Owney Madden correctly summed it up.

Casso also told me about J. Edgar Hoover's penchant for wearing women's clothing and how the Genovese family, in conjunction with Meyer Lansky and premier Mafia wolf Lucky Luciano, managed to get a photo of Hoover dressed as a woman at a gay party at the Hotel Nacional in Havana, Cuba, hosted by Roy Cohn. Roy Cohn, the homosexual attorney, set up J. Edgar Hoover for this photo. Interestingly, Roy Cohn was the right-hand man of the infamous Joe McCarthy. Hoover wore a red dress and a big, wide-brimmed hat. What a sight he must have been with that bulldog face dressed up as a woman. If that photo were ever blown up, it would have been the largest-selling poster in the history of the world. In any event, because of that photograph, J. Edgar Hoover vehemently denied even the existence of a Mafia until pretty much the day he died.

As I became deeply immersed in actually writing *Gaspipe*, it did nothing to assuage or slow my disease. Still, when I woke up in the morning, the first thoughts I had were about my book, my work, how I would portray the hundreds of scenes—the dramatic highs and lows—that naturally took place within the confines of its pages. I was engaged. I was busy.

However, the reality of ALS was brutally brought home when I tried to stand up and get out of bed. Initial atrophy in my left foot had now spread throughout my body. Walking had become difficult. I had a severe limp. My bicep, pectoral, and deltoid muscles had diminished significantly. My once muscular boxer's body of 168 pounds had turned into 140-pound shell of what it had been, for the most part devoid of muscle definition. I avoided looking in the mirror for the image that came back to me was shocking and depressing—something that I just didn't want to see.

However, I did not get into writing about the mob because it was commercially viable. I write about crime because I have a natural affinity to it, understanding of it; I was born and raised with mafiosi all around me and from the reading of many books I learned character development and how to make those worlds come alive, stand up, and walk about in front of you . . . haunt you at night. For me, it was never *bang bang, you're dead*. For me, it was always and still is the ongoing predatory aspect of what they're doing—their cunning. It was the cunning that drew me as a writer to that world. I believe it's that cunning, ongoing pathology that makes the public at large interested. What I just said can very well be applied to the world of serial killers as well.

I'm aching. Sitting still in this cursed wheelchair all day long causes my body to turn into a symphony of aches and pains. Thank God my masseuse, Virginia, is coming soon. When she arrives, I am very happy to see her. Virginia is a vivacious Brazilian who is as strong as any man. She has long, curly hair and a large, attractive smile. She is one of those gifted masseuses who, after five minutes, can reach deep inside the body, its muscles and bones and joints, and work you in the most unique way. One of the few, more beneficial treatments people with ALS can have is a long, deep massage. In that I can't get up and walk and use the muscles, the atrophy becomes more acute, is perpetuated, and massage is perhaps the only thing that can bring blood and oxygen to the muscles, stimulating them almost as though they are active, as though you are walking, exercising.

Naked, I lie down on the table with Virginia's help just near the terrace doors with the fresh ocean air blowing in and the sound of the sea whispering only to me. She begins on my back, going deeper and deeper. It feels so good. I've been sitting in a wheelchair now for some eleven hours, my spine and back becoming stiffer and stiffer. Now, Virginia's strong hands make me feel euphoric as she stimulates nerve endings and blood flow, relaxes the tightened muscles.

Slowly, I doze off. I hate dozing off when she massages me because I miss out on the joy of it. When she turns me over, I'm awake and try to stay that way. As Virginia works, she closes her eyes and seems to disappear, but those hands of hers; those hands of hers work and knead and knot and pull and slap the muscles. It's almost as though Virginia is really trying to make them come back to life, pour her energy into them. When she's finished with me, I feel loose and limber, my neck not filled with knots and pain. You do not feel pain with ALS as such. What becomes painful is the inherent lack of movement, sitting in the same position sixteen, seventeen hours a day—every day. The joints and muscles stiffen. The spine twists in odd ways. And headaches. You inevitably get headaches because when breathing with a respirator it is difficult to expel carbon dioxide and with the buildup of carbon dioxide, there are headaches, muscle aches, and joint pain. It is one big vicious cycle.

My caregivers back in New York have given me a box, which they call a comfort box. In it is lorazepam, haloperidol, bisacodyl suppositories, and morphine. Theoretically they are trying to make me more comfortable in these last days of my life and the morphine is supposed to get me through the day and night. I have not taken one pill or any morphine. For me, the taking of any of these drugs, especially the morphine, would be admitting my own demise. Plus I want a clear head. I want to know what's going on around me. It would mean becoming comfortable with the concept of death—embracing it. It would be numbing my senses, my sensibilities. Without these things, I would be living in the dark void I described earlier—that black hole.

When Virginia leaves, I return to my favorite pastime—watching movies we rent from Netflix. We are lucky that there are so many films to choose from. This has opened a whole new universe of film to me, in every genre, every language, classics and the most recent films. As a professional storyteller, I doubly get involved in films, paying particular note to how the story unfolds; what gets the viewer involved, what makes for a good performance. If I have learned anything from being an obsessive film enthusiast, it's that you must always keep readers or viewers in mind—make sure they remain involved, love the good guys, hate the bad guys. There should never be ambiguity, mixed signals. That's why I think people take to my books the way they do; the bad guys are so, so bad, and the good guys are so very good. To a degree, Richard Kuklinski was an exception. He indeed had a good side, was a loving father and devoted husband, but by the same token, when he was bad, few, if any, could match his icy sadism.

In any event, tonight I watch *The Black Stallion* with Kelly Reno, a marvelous story of a black thoroughbred horse lost at sea when a ship goes down in a storm and how it, the stallion, and a teenage boy, also washed overboard, ultimately become friends on an empty island. It was directed by Carroll Ballard out of the San Francisco school of directors and I'm in awe of how impeccably he presents the story, making you the camera. There is no camera. You become the conduit between the action and what your brain perceives. It is so intimate, it is yours and yours alone, you feel. The other members of the incredibly talented cabal of San Francisco filmmakers include Francis Ford Coppola, Phil Kaufman, George Lucas, Peter Bogdanovich, Saul Zaentz, and Clint Eastwood—more commonly known as the Fog City Mavericks. These dedicated artists still think of films as genuine art forms and approach filmmaking with that mindset; they use little if any special effects—Lucas being the exception—or gratuitous violence or sex. I say all this because on the very near horizon, I will be deeply involved in turning *The Ice Man* into a film, and I plan to make it something I'm proud to have my name on.

Near 1:30 A.M., a sour-faced, crabby Laura wants me to go to sleep. I have this whole thing about asserting my individuality, my freedom, late at night. It's one of the few prerogatives I have left. I don't want to go to sleep. I could stay up watching movies all night, but that would be unreasonable. Still, when I watch my films and she wants me to go to bed, I say, "You go to sleep, I'm watching a film." It becomes a big pain in the ass.

Ultimately, Laura often falls asleep inside and I watch my movies and then I slowly roll up to the bed after she's been sleeping for a while and wake her and she's angry. However, that usually passes quickly and she gets me into bed with the help of a lifting belt cinched tight around my waist. Still in my chair, I lean forward and put my arms around her neck, she leans forward and grabs the belt. We count to three and up I go; she slowly pivots and places me down. Tonight, however, as I'm going from the wheelchair to the bed, she loses her grip and I hit the ground, butt first. People with ALS dread falls. We have no capacity to stop ourselves, to grab something as we're going down, so the falls are unusually hard—and can be fatal. That combined with the lack of muscularity makes for potential tragedy. We know several people who have died as a result of falls.

Anyway, I'm sitting on my keester at two-thirty in the morning. Huffing and puffing, sweating, Laura is trying to pick me up, but she can't. She's getting frustrated and I'm getting frustrated and none of this makes any sense. Plus, breathing is harder when I'm stressed or straining. Near 3:30, I suggest we call the police, which seems like a ridiculous thing to do, but we both know it's the right thing to do, our only option, so she dials 911 and tells them that her husband has ALS, that he's fallen on the floor, that she can't get him up.

"Is he bleeding?" they ask.

"No."

"Is he breathing with a machine?" they ask.

"Yes."

"Are you alone?" they ask.

"Yes," she says.

She's told the fire department will be right over. I'm thinking that this is a bit of overkill. Here I am, this skinny, very tan, Italian-looking bald guy who has ALS sitting on the floor at four in the morning; I don't need firemen! I just need help getting in the freaking bed! But within fifteen minutes they arrive, three of them sporting huge, bright yellow rubber outfits, one bigger than the other, clearly serious men accustomed to putting out raging infernos. They walk in the room and at first they don't even see me because I'm sitting on the floor. Bemused, comically, I watch them search the room.

"Here I am, guys!" I say, and their eyes finally come to rest on me. "Thanks for coming," I say, feeling very lame.

Effortlessly, two of them pick me up. One holds me by my ankles and the other holds me under my arms. "Ally-oop!"

It's almost embarrassing how easily they do it, but they are nice about it and we thank them. "Don't mention it," they say.

"Anytime," the largest of them adds.

Ah, to be in a comfortable bed and off my butt, off the hard floor. It's funny how you don't appreciate the simple luxury of getting up of your own volition until you cannot. Laura's tired. I'm tired. We are both disgusted. She shuts the light. In the sudden darkness I stare at a ceiling I cannot see. Images of bats flutter in the black space above me. I still have the strength to turn myself on my side and I slowly do that now. It feels so good to take the pressure off my buttock and back muscles. On average, I'm in the wheelchair fifteen to seventeen hours every day. The immobility is taking its toll on me, compounding my dilemma. I take a long, deep breath. For some inexplicable reason, the smell of cotton candy the way it was made in Coney Island when I was a boy comes to me. With that I leave this world as sleep envelops me and takes me away on sweet, cotton candy–like clouds.

Sleep has become a little death, for me. No dreams. No life outside the black void you experience when you're sleeping and you have ALS. I think it has to do with the fact that brain motor neurons are dying and with them dies the conventional aspects of sleep—the REM and the non-REM modes are deeply affected, I believe.

Always, the next thing I see is Laura standing over me.

"Are you ready to get up?" she asks.

"No," I say, but still, she starts preparing to pick me up. As I lie there, I again begin thinking about IPLEX.

I'm convinced now, perhaps because it is so difficult to get, that it will help me, bring back at least some of the Philip I once was. Laura hoists me out of bed. Using the special belt around my waist, she picks me up and puts me in the wheelchair, my skinny arms wrapped around her neck. Like this, sleep still all about my face, I wheel into the living room, which is ridiculously bright with Florida sunshine. The apartment has white walls, and that amplifies the brightness. Laura tells me that Kelsey went to Starbucks and will be here soon.

Laura cuts up a big, golden yellow pineapple, juicy and sweet and well worth waking up for. Thankfully, I still eat well. Down here in South Beach, the fruit is exceptional. A bright, smiling, very tan Kelsey wearing bright green culottes walks in. She is carrying three coffees, one of which is my double macchiato. As is our custom, I begin dictating e-mails to Kelsey as I eat breakfast. I look through the terrace doors. The day is gorgeous. I want to get the hell outside. Always in the back of my mind, perhaps more subconsciously than consciously, my demise looms on the near horizon and I want to be sure I get down on paper everything I have to say, tell this story properly. I'm hot. My motor's running. I want to get in the race!

Laura struggles to pull on my bathing suit. In that I'm in a wheelchair and not standing, lifting my butt is a strenuous chore for both of us. She brushes my teeth and shaves me and washes me down with alcohol and hot water. As she works on me, I crack jokes about everybody. I have this kind of clown persona that I've developed since becoming sick. Oddly enough, considering what I write about, I have a keen sense of humor. It's just how I see the world. Laura packs our beach bag and off we go. Laura's wearing a big, beat-up straw hat and a green sarong you can see through. When we get outside, it is unusually hot. The street and the sidewalks are just about empty. The heat is so intense I feel as though I'm near a pizza oven. Kelsey tells us about a guy in Starbucks who is always flirting with her.

"How could he not? You're adorable," I say. She blushes slightly.

We move along to the Savoy Hotel and are soon back on the beach, enjoying the sand, the waves, a tropical sky on which large silk-like wisps of white clouds hang immobile, as still as the pastel art deco buildings lining the beach. Though I cannot move my feet at all, the hot sand feels good . . . soothing. "Are you ready?" I say to Kelsey.

"I was born ready."

"Ooo, that's rather hot," I say.

"Cut it. Let's go!" she says. We both laugh.

We begin.

For the most part, Kelsey is a pleasure to work with. She is anxious to please and has a sharp, keen intelligence. She wants to be sure that the work is right—that she gets what I say accurately—down pat. We both know the slightest error in a word can throw off a sentence, thought, scene, the true meaning of something. There are some days when Kelsey is not such a pleasure to work with. I think, to an obscure degree, she feels this work is below her, that she should be doing more, but I think that has more to do with the fact that nobody is good to work with all the time and she has every right to feel the way she feels—however it is—for whatever reason. All things considered, she's a pleasure to work with and I trust her implicitly. To me, in my mind, trust is more important than anything. Nobody's perfect. God knows, I certainly am not. One day, I'm sure, Kelsey will write a brilliant book, a book read by many people from all over the world. I can't help but think of Harper Lee; how she assisted Truman Capote in the writing of In Cold Blood and subsequently went on to write one of the most important books in all literature.

Today Kelsey is smiling and happy and has on a new white bathing suit she bought. Both Laura and she are bathing suit aficionados.

Soon, Kelsey and I disappear from the beach, South Beach, greater Miami, and both of us wholeheartedly enter the story. I am so engrossed in the writing of this book that when I look up, I'm surprised I'm here rather than in the story.

When I first began writing, I would write for four to five hours straight without stopping, to exhaustion. It didn't take me long to realize that was not the way to go and now what I do is take a break every half hour or so. It's like the brain is a muscle. In the way you should not overwork a body muscle or it gets sore, gets charley horses, you should not overwork the brain. A little break every half hour or so refreshes and energizes and helps a writer see, in his or her mind's eye, things clearly. This is not a new concept for writers. In fact, when I read Hemingway's *A Moveable Feast*, he talked about taking breaks every half an hour or so and his words rang true, loud and clear. Kelsey goes for a swim. I would love to join her, but at the moment, that's an impossibility. Unfortunately, I am forced to sit there—immobile, unmoving. At this point, I cannot even wiggle my toes. But still I am a part of a constant celebration of the great outdoors. The sea, the sun, the wind, the palm trees, the smell of suntan lotion permeating the air, all embrace me at the same time—a tropical cacophony that brings a smile to my face without my being aware of it. I could very well be in a dank hospital bed with robotic people caring for me, not able to write, but here I am in the great outdoors, doing my thing, writing my tenth book with an eleventh book on the docket, *The Prince of Cocaine: The High Times and Bloody Crimes of a Colombian Drug Lord.*

Me . . . I have nothing to complain about.

On my right, I watch people clad in shorts and bathing suits jog, run, and bike. These are all things that I once loved to do, that were an intricate part of my life. I imagine, envision, myself running on the beach where the sand is firm wearing just my bathing suit and sneakers, cruising along at an easy pace. Years ago, in 1994 or so, I came to Miami to research the story of a missing child and I remember well running every day from 39th Street, where I was staying, to First Street and back, all along this very beach. That was fifteen years ago. The distance is approximately eight miles and I did it rather effortlessly. To think of myself that way, so incredibly fit, compared to me now, is sobering to say the least.

But I know this is really the kind of thing that I should not think about because it will cast me into the abyss of anger and self-pity and blah, blah, blah. I'm tickled pink to be outdoors, on a beautiful beach, in the office. I leave it at that. The Philip who ran those eight miles all those many years ago lived another life not remotely connected to my life now. To separate the two is kind of like separating Siamese twins after birth, but separate them I must, and I do.

Kelsey returns. We resume working. Today, Laura's cousins Tatum and Ariel join us. The three cousins are close. Both Ari and Tatum are attractive women. When the Garofalo cousins are together, they talk nonstop. Kelsey and I move a little farther away so as not to disturb them and so they don't disturb us. We continue and it goes on like this all day long.

Near five or so, when the shadows are getting long, it's time to stop, and stop we do. Kelsey and I join the others. They go for a swim. I sit there watching them in the water. I suddenly have a craving for pizza. Just two blocks away there is a fantastic pizza place called Fratelli La Bufala. It is owned and run by Italians from Italy . . . imported ones, not domestic ones. Ah, viva Italia, I think. They have a wood-heated oven and the pizza is exceptionally delicious, well done and crispy. They serve it with only fresh bufala mozzarella straight from Italy. We go there a few times a week. When I suggest pizza to everybody, they agree and off we go. As we make our way to the pizza place, me bumping along in my wheelchair, the phone rings. It is Stephen Byer calling to tell us that he has good news. It is a long, convoluted story, but to make it short and readily understandable, Steve has formed a coalition of sorts to demand IPLEX of not only the company that makes it but the FDA. Through heavy, substantial political pressure, letters we and our family and friends have written to senators and congressmen, and an actual march of people who have ALS—their friends and family—on Washington, the FDA and the company that makes the drug, Insmed, have agreed to dole it out to a select group of people. This group of people has to have applied to the company for the drug several months ago. Thanks to Steve Byer, I was first on that list and, Steve is telling me now, all the ducks are lined up.

"You're going to get the drug," he says. "It's just a matter of time."

How much time barely matters, I'm so touched, but I ask. Time is a factor. The disease is not going to slow or go away.

"Days, maybe a week," he says.

With this, I begin crying there on the street. I tell Laura, and she begins crying, too. Laura very rarely cries. She has a stoic, hard exterior most of the time, frighteningly so, sometimes, but there we are, both of us crying. We've been through so much to get this drug. When we found out it was not available in the United States but might be available in Italy, we contacted my friend Robert De Niro and asked if he could perhaps pull some strings in Italy and help. Bob was nice enough to call the president of Italy himself and ask for help on my behalf. They said they'd see what they could do. Ultimately, because of the conflicting politics and miles of red tape in Italy, we couldn't get the drug through Bob's request, nor could we get the drug by going there and knocking on doors. Now this good news from Steve, but I've been let down so many times with the getting or not getting of IPLEX that I will not feel any kind of elation until the drug is in my hands. Still, I'll never forget how Bob tried to help me get the drug. It's interesting—his modesty—because when that was happening his assistant, my dear friend Robin Chambers, asked me to make sure not to say anything about how Bob lent a helping hand. I'm writing this now because I do want people to know what a fine man, good friend, Bob De Niro truly is. How I got to know Bob intimately is a story unto itself, which I will get into later on. Meanwhile, I wait for the UPS guy to ring the bell with IPLEX in hand.

PART TWO
High Hopes

12. Old Friend

Some six days later, we are told that my first supply of IPLEX is being sent out to us. Hallelujah! But we have to find a local pharmacy with a freezer that will accept it on my behalf, Steve Byer says. They cannot ship it directly to us. Laura and I find a pharmacy in South Beach that agrees to accept the drug for us. Mind you, this is a drug that costs $13,000 a month and I am getting it for free. I feel blessed. Still, I have this wary nature when it comes to the disease and I want to see it—my getting better—before I go up on the roof and begin banging pots and pans. But it is a momentous occasion, light at the end of a dark tunnel strewn with destroyed bodies, lives, families. We are hopeful.

Today is an unusually sunny day. There are no clouds in the sky at all. Laura walks and I roll to the pharmacy to make sure that they understand how important it is that the drug be kept refrigerated. I take a copy of *The Ice Man* with us and sign it for the owner. He is pleased—only too happy to help us. When Laura and I start back toward home, we make our way along Ocean Drive. Here, below Fifth Street, there are few restaurants and hotels, quiet and residential. Often the most action is palm trees swinging to and fro as though they were dancing to reggae music. We move side by side, me in my wheelchair, Laura in her beach thongs.

Laura, like me, is overjoyed that we're finally getting the drug. But I think, also like me, she has a certain amount of trepidation. We both know of a study that was done of eight people with ALS who had been taking IPLEX in this country before the drug was pulled. Three of the subjects had a notable positive response, and the other five less of a response. It seems the drug affected different people in different ways. Still, I will remain optimistic and reasonably hopeful; I have no choice, really. I look up at Laura as I move alongside her. She has a magnificent profile, is a truly beautiful woman. Her hair is golden, and with the sunlight above her, it looks like there is a halo about her head, long threads of hair like corn silk in the strong sun. I remember when I first met her. It was a bumpy, tragic road that brought the two of us together, which involved my book *The Ice Man*, an old friend I hadn't seen in fifty years, union manipulation, construction takeover, the Gambino crime family . . . John Gotti and Sammy the Bull Gravano. It also involved a diabolical murder on a quiet Brooklyn street on one of those warm summer nights when the dark comes late.

I met Laura by calling the underboss of the Gambino crime family a scumbag on national radio.

Throughout the months I was researching *Gaspipe*, I was also promoting *The Ice Man*. The book was a hit and I was doing radio shows all over the country, sometimes ten to fifteen of them a day. *The Ice Man* garnered so much media attention that I did *Larry King Live* with Mrs. Kuklinski and Richard's two daughters; because of this, *The Ice Man* became a *New York Times* bestseller. While doing a popular show called *The Radio Chick Show*, hosted by Leslie Gold, the subject of Sammy Gravano came up. Kuklinski had killed an NYPD detective at the behest of Gravano and I wrote about the murder in detail in *The Ice Man*.

Gravano, like me, came from Bensonhurst. I knew him well as a young boy, saw him in street fights. For those of you not familiar with this mafioso, he was John Gotti's second-in-command of the Gambino family. He was a tough piece of work. As a youth, he had been a member of a street gang that my old mentor Gerard Pappa was head of—the Rampers.

As an adult, Gravano had pled guilty to killing nineteen men and got an amazing sweetheart deal from the federal government that allowed him to get his freedom after he testified against John Gotti and a long list of mafiosi. One of the nineteen people he admitted to murdering was Eddie Garofalo, Laura's father. Eddie was the older brother of my best friend from grade school, Emmanuel. Gravano had killed Eddie because he was muscling in on Eddie's construction business and he, Eddie, resisted. I had seen Eddie's two daughters on different television shows excoriating the government for allowing Gravano to go free after killing their father . . . and for allowing Gravano to get $850,000 from HarperCollins for his life story. I was struck by how much they looked like my childhood friend Emmanuel. With their high Slavic cheekbones, broad foreheads, and green eyes, they were both extremely attractive. My heart went out to them. Not only had their father been murdered but his killer had gone free and allowed to keep some $11 million in illegal proceeds. Gravano had thumbed his nose at not only the rule of law, but the basic tenets of common decency . . . this all had been supported by the government. That day I talked about this incident in detail on *The Radio Chick Show* and, several times, I called Gravano a "scumbag" on the air.

The following day I got an e-mail out of nowhere that said, "Please call me, Manny," and there was a phone number. I called the number and, lo and behold, it was my grade school friend Emmanuel. I gave him my condolences over the loss of his brother. I hadn't heard from him or seen him in some forty-seven years. I told him that I had seen his two nieces on television. He asked me if I'd like to meet them. I said yes and within a week I was sitting at a table in a restaurant called Vento in New York's Meatpacking District, opposite the Garofalo sisters, Karen and Laura, both of them strikingly beautiful women. I told them, too, how bad I felt about the loss of their father. The more I talked to them, the more I realized they had a unique, compelling story to tell, and I instinctively started urging them to write a book about what had happened, what they'd been through. I knew that with their story, intelligence, poise, and good looks, they'd be any book publicist's dream come true. They seemed to warm to the idea. I myself wasn't interested in writing the story as such. I was then busy with the Casso book and I had other projects on my plate.

By then, August 8, 2006, the disease had progressed measurably. I had a distinct limp. The atrophy of my left foot had moved up my leg and there was nothing I could do to stop it. I was actually watching my body be eaten up by the disease. The muscles in my hands had diminished further, but, overall, looking at me, you would have no idea I was suffering from a fatal disease. Of course, I said nothing to my old friend Emmanuel, nor to his nieces.

Over the coming weeks, it became apparent that the younger of the two sisters, Laura, was more open to the idea of a book than

Karen. At the time, Laura was thirty-two and Karen was forty. Laura was seventeen years old when her father was murdered. Karen was twenty-five. Because of the age difference, Karen was closer to the incident than Laura was and I think that's why Karen had a lot of difficulty coming to grips with and articulating the events surrounding her father's killing. Laura, on the other hand, had records, trial transcripts, piles of newspaper accounts, and a quiet, seething outrage about what had occurred that would, I believed, enable her to write a book. As I interacted with Laura, worked with her on the book project, we became closer and closer.

When the issue of my limp first came up, I told Laura I had a torn meniscus and that's why I was limping. It's not as though I was lying. I didn't want to burden her with the truth. At that point, I wasn't sharing with anyone that I had been diagnosed with the most brutal disease of modern times. Doctors had told me that ALS is worse than cancer and leprosy combined. Ultimately, after the disease ravages your muscles, it ruins the inside of the body, atrophies your diaphragm, and steals your ability to breathe. The muscles you use to chew and swallow become ineffective. The muscles that support your head become weak and your head feels as though it is a bowling ball and it is very hard to support. The muscles you use to speak also die, leaving you a vegetable that cannot articulate, that cannot eat. It gets worse—ALS also wastes the sphincter and bladder muscles. This causes a whole host of problems too upsetting and numerous to delineate here.

Ultimately, as days went by and Laura and I became closer, I decided to tell her about my having the disease. I warned her not to look up ALS on the Internet because it always said, in the first line describing the disease, that it is fatal.

Rather than my dwelling on the disease, I concerned myself with writing—keeping busy, engaged, involved; I concerned myself with understanding the culture, the walk and talk of the Mafia—specifically Anthony Casso.

Rather than Laura shunning me, she and I became closer and, without my asking her, she made it her cause to help find a cure, some remedy for Lou Gehrig's Disease. So far, the only possibility of help has been IPLEX—the reason we eventually went to Italy. Of course, too, there is stem cell research, which my friend Valerie Estess is helping to fund. In addition to Valerie, I know, there were people all over the world trying to use the application of stem cells to fight a host of neurological diseases, as well as cancer. Prior to us learning about IPLEX, there were only vague promises, hopes, dreams, all things I would not allow myself to buy into, for to be let down would perpetuate my decline.

Back then, I was living in a triplex apartment that I had built and loved dearly. I couldn't live there any longer because it had become impossible to deal with stairs. I managed to take over the ground-floor apartment in my building, which had a huge garden—a true blessing. I was able to get outside all day and enjoy the fresh air, the chirping of birds, the sun and, more important, work undisturbed. With my friend Mike's help, we planted tomatoes and zucchini and basil. Yes . . . I was being stalked by the grim reaper, a cold-blooded murderer, but I was going to make myself as comfortable as possible and prepare to do battle, with fresh tomatoes at my side.

My family did what they could, but there was scant little anyone could do for me. Sure, on a daily basis, there were simple things like washing my face and brushing my teeth. But those were all left for Laura. All through the insidious decline I was experiencing because of the disease, Laura stayed by my side. Having a fatal disease can cause people to bond together much more rapidly than under normal circumstances. Everything is life and death, amplified and made all the more dire. Laura and I ended up getting married on a blistery cold day. My dear friend and agent Matt Bialer was my best man. Her best friend Roxanne Rizzo stood with her. We wed at City Hall. By now I was wheelchair-bound and not walking.

Back to this sunny, hot day in Miami's South Beach, as Laura and I continue along Ocean Drive, silent as we go, my mind goes back to George Bush. We all know that with stem cell research, there is the possibility that people like me, the millions suffering from motor neuron diseases, could be helped by stem cells. Inevitably, I start thinking about how Bush unabashedly, without apology or reservation—defiantly—stopped the federal government's support of stem cell research.

Stem cell research and, ultimately, its application, holds great hope for people with motor neuron diseases—Lou Gehrig's Disease, MS,

Parkinson's, Alzheimer's disease can all be slowed and perhaps even stopped with stem cell applications. As far as I'm concerned—and a large majority of the country—Bush proved to be a bona fide fool, a miscreant who stood in the way of good science and common sense for so-called religious reasons. Bush twice vetoed a bill that both the Senate and House passed after much tumultuous debate advocating that the federal government underwrite stem cell research. He not only vetoed the bills but he punished any hospital that did stem cell research while receiving federal funds. We, those suffering from terminal diseases, lost eight precious years that might well have been the time during which the scientific community found a way to perfect stem cell treatments. Bush—he should have been tarred and feathered and run out of Washington as far as I'm concerned. I absolutely hate the man not for any of the help I didn't receive, but for all the elderly and the young who may have had a shot at life had he not torn up the stem cell bill. My skin crawls when I think of that ridiculous smirk he had.

Personally, I had become somewhat ambivalent about a cure. I kept running into brick walls and it became too hurtful and distracting, which only made matters worse, my health suffer more. Back then, Laura had made it her job to find a way to stop the disease and she was often online communicating with doctors and ALS advocates from all over the world. Dutifully, I went to see my three neurologists, Drs. Rowland and Mitsumoto at Columbia and Dr. Sivak at Mount Sinai, but when I asked them if there was anything promising on the horizon, all I received were sad, baleful stares and a "No. I'm sorry."

That was the sum of it.

IPLEX is my only hope.

Now that IPLEX is truly on its way, I am nervous, I am hopeful, I am frightened—all at the same time.

By the time we reach the Savoy on Ocean Drive, it is near four. A little late in the day to go to the office, but it is a nice day and we soon find ourselves back on the beach. I worked with Kelsey earlier and we now go over what we did. I make it my business to never exhaust either of us. We have done a day's work and I am going to leave it at that. One of the things I used to really like doing on the beach was reading. I could stay all day on the beach reading a good book with ease. But now that simple thing, a book on the beach, is an impossibility for me. At this juncture, my hands have become so weak I can't hold a book. I can't even turn a page—not even a page in a thin paperback book. I'm not bitching here. I'm talking about the realities of ALS. Though not being able to hold a book is a major loss for me, rather than dwell on that, I think about writing books. I just try to adapt. That's all I can do; that's all anyone in my position can do, but there seems to be some evil irony at work here. I struggled all my life to learn how to write, and now I can't even pick up and read the books I've written. Go figure. Maybe I'll look into audiobooks.

I close my eyes and think of Sol. I only met Sol on the phone. When I first spoke to him, he was seventy-nine years old and suffering from ALS. He lived with one of three sons on a rotating basis. I contacted Sol because he had gotten a new surgical procedure in which electrodes were implanted in his diaphragm muscle and these electrodes were stimulated by a battery pack about the size of a Band-Aid box worn around the waist. When the disease reaches the diaphragm muscle, it's pretty much the beginning of the end. The diaphragm muscle becomes weaker and weaker until it does not have the strength and wherewithal to move the lungs at all, thus stealing away the ability to breathe. It doesn't stop there. With the lack of breath, you cannot cough or sneeze. Because a person afflicted with ALS cannot cough, he or she doesn't have the ability to cough up phlegm and phlegm builds up in the lungs, creating an ideal situation for bacteria and, ultimately, pneumonia.

I was seriously contemplating getting the diaphragm electrode operation but before I did so, I had to go to Ohio and it was cold and it would be logistically difficult. Plus I wanted to speak to someone who had the operation and so I was put in touch with Sol. The procedure had been developed by an innovative doctor out in Ohio named Ray Onders. I had several phone calls with Dr. Onders and he was an unusually warm, very bright individual who had a tremendous grasp of how people with ALS suffer, of how people with ALS die.

When I first spoke to Sol, I said, "My God . . . what a terrible, horrible disease this is."

He said, "Get over all that. It is what it is. Make the best of what you have." And I was struck by his stoic optimism and the fact that he didn't seem to let the disease affect him at all. He told me that he went to physical therapy several times a week, that he got into a pool and that light exercise is a good thing. Ultimately, Sol and I became friends of a sort—we had this horrible malady in common, each of us fighting the grim reaper tooth and nail. I took away a good lesson from speaking to Sol, combining it with what I already knew. I resolved to make the best of the time I had left. I would never, ever think of the disease. I wouldn't let thoughts of the disease, what it could do, what it might do, affect my state of mind. I would be productive and creative and enjoy whatever time I had left.

ALS . . . fuck ALS.

Philip Carlo at one month old being held by his father, Dante Carlo, Brooklyn, New York.

A young, overly serious Philip Carlo about to gallop off into his future.

A seven-year-old Philip Carlo with parents Nina and Dante.

Philip Carlo at age 19, shortly after leaving the mean streets of Brooklyn and moving to New York.

The author at age 24 pulling a sailfish out of the Bay of Acapulco.
At peace with the world, Carlo has no idea ALS has taken root inside his body.

The author with his pal, actor
Joe Pesci, on a terrace overlooking the
lush green of New York's Central Park.

Carlo at 36 with his friend, heavyweight
champion of the world Mike Tyson,
at the book party for *Stolen Flower*.

Carlo writing *The Ice Man* in Mykonos, Greece
in 2003.

Carlo with convicted serial killer Richard Ramirez, aka the Night Stalker, at San Quentin's Death Row during the time Carlo was writing *The Night Stalker: The Life and Crimes of One of America's Deadliest Killers*. Standing next to one of the most infamous serial killers of all time, Carlo has no idea a much more insidious killer is slowly coming to life inside of him.

Philip Carlo with friend Robert De Niro in Tribeca, New York City.

Carlo and good friends, the actors Danny Aiello and Tony Sirico, at the famous literary haunt Elaine's Restaurant, New York City. Writers as varied as Hemingway, Capote, Gay Talese, and Gore Vidal all hung out at Elaine's.

Carlo on the Italian island of Sardinia, there writing his book *Smiling Wolf*, oblivious to the grim reaper now lurking just behind him.

Philip Carlo on the glorious Greek island of Mykonos, where he wrote some of his book *Predators and Prayers*, circa 2003, some two years before the grotesque face of the grim reaper showed itself. Note Carlo's pectoral muscles just before the onset of the disease.

Philip Carlo interviewing Richard Kuklinski, the most prolific contract killer of modern times, at Trenton State Maximum Security Prison in New Jersey. Note the enormity of Kuklinski at 6 ft 6 in. and 320 lb. This photo was taken some two months before ALS began to ravage the author's body. Here Carlo is a successful author, at peace with himself, deeply immersed in the world of writing, having no idea that the grim reaper is stalking him, about to swing his scythe.

A headshot of Carlo during the summer of 2005 in Mykonos, Greece. At this point, Carlo has a slight limp he is attributing to jogging too much.

Carlo with his wife, Laura, South Beach, Miami, 2006. At this point, Carlo has been diagnosed with ALS. After much soul-searching and "why me?", Carlo resolved to get on with his life, not lie down and slowly die. Carlo was working on his book *Gaspipe: Confessions of a Mafia Boss*.

Carlo working with his assistant, Kelsey, in his garden apartment, New York City, circa 2007. Though Carlo can still walk, he needs a cane to do so. Note the muscle loss caused by ALS.

Carlo with dear friend, actor Tony Danza, and from left clockwise: Karen Scala, Katie Danza, Tracy Danza, and Laura Carlo.

The grim reaper has announced his presence. It is now 2008 and Philip Carlo has lost the strength in all four limbs and cannot walk at all. Here he is in his South Beach home dictating a book to Kelsey.

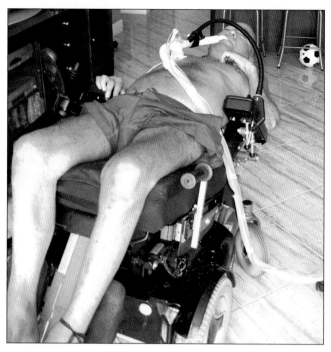

Carlo getting physical therapy with Sharon Wiegers, 2008.
Note the ravages of ALS.

Now, though really stricken with ALS, Carlo is out and about in a boat in
Miami with his wife Laura, sister-in-law Karen, friend Megan, and cousin Tatum.
Note the muscle loss in the author's neck causing his head to tilt; 2009.

Philip Carlo and Kelsey working hard at "the office." Note the breathing tube in Carlo's lap. The bandage on his chest is where the diaphragm pacer is connected.

Carlo working with Kelsey on this book, with Miami Beach and the ocean in the background. "No matter what, life must go on," says Carlo.

Carlo in his Manhattan home with his leopard blanket, 2009.

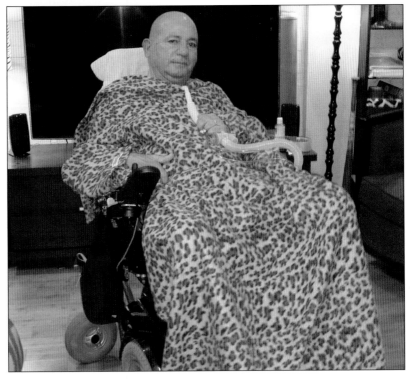

Here is Carlo with Kelsey in Montauk, New York, working
on *The Killer Within: In the Company of Monsters* in 2009.

Here Carlo is celebrating Easter al fresco in South Beach, Miami.
The beat must go on. Clockwise from right: Karen Scala, Laura Carlo,
Philip Carlo, Edward Scala, and Tatum Garofalo.

13. IPLEX—To Be or Not to Be

The following day, a miracle of sorts occurs. The IPLEX actually arrives. The pharmacist calls us and tells us he has it. Laura goes in the car and gets it, comes back within minutes. It is in this big box and when the box is unwrapped there is a much smaller box and within it are all these frozen vials of liquid. In order for me to be injected with it, it has to melt first. The rest of the doses must be kept frozen. The first day Laura gives me two injections, one on the left and one on the right side of my stomach, a total of 36 milligrams. I am hoping that within a couple of hours I will be up and walking, but that doesn't happen—I know that is a unrealistic pipe dream.

From that day on, every day, Laura gives me the two shots, sometimes in the stomach, sometimes in my arms. After a month of this, unfortunately, there is little difference in my condition. This unto itself is reason enough for me to become . . . depressed—morose. But I have been doing this knowing that it may not be the miracle drug we were hoping it is, knowing the effect might be minimal. Steve Byer told me it may take as long as six months to see a notable change. After all, it took years for me to get to this condition, he said. It is sound reasoning but still this is a letdown. I'd be lying if I said it wasn't. This is one of the very real pitfalls of new drugs and new treatments. When you are terminally ill, there is, if not on a conscious level, hope that a cure is just around the corner. After all, who really wants to die, especially if life is treating you well? I've always been wary of this new drug. But deep inside me somewhere, I had high hopes. One way or another, I will absolutely not allow this to rain on my parade. I keep working. I keep interviewing people. I look forward to dinner at various restaurants in South Beach. I love eating al fresco. I want to get out of the house; I must get out of the house. I want to go outside and mingle and act like I am normal.

I think, to a large degree, the beginning of the end comes when people who are terminally ill do not want to socialize anymore, do not want to leave their houses. I think it is imperative to be aware of your appearance, to continue to clean yourself, to shave and wash yourself. These things help bolster a positive attitude . . . a positive frame of mind. Therefore, rather than trying to involve myself in the various different treatments and possibilities, I keep my distance from them and let Laura look into them and talk to people and research them as opposed to involving myself in what amounts to my own death. To a degree, Laura has become a buffer zone between me and my sickness and the possible treatments and remedies.

On one hand, it seems like we have been in Florida for a lifetime. On the other hand, it seems like we have just arrived. Regardless of how you cut it, the days move swiftly here and the weather is beginning to change. The balmy pleasant weather of the winter is being replaced by a searing heat that makes the beach somewhat uncomfortable even under an umbrella. It is also becoming more humid. I don't like the humidity. It makes my breathing more difficult. But truth be told, I miss New York. I miss our garden. I miss my family and as much as I don't want to leave Florida, I want to get home and continue working. Because of the garden, we are able to be outdoors all day every day.

Kelsey and I begin at 10:30 in the morning and don't finish until 5:00 P.M., working all day. Often what drives us in are mosquitoes. I am also looking forward to planting our garden again, the vegetables and flowers.

It's finally time to go. Somewhat reluctantly, Laura boxes up most of our things and ships them back to New York. What Kelsey has we send back for her. We have a van specially designed for wheelchairs pick us up and take us to the airport. Leaving South Beach is sad. I kind of feel like my summer vacation is over and I am going back to school. In that I never liked school, anything that is even remotely comparable to that scenario is . . . uncomfortable. But all these are fleeting thoughts in my own mind and I know we'll come back next year, provided I am *here* next year. I am very pleased that Kelsey became comfortable with South Beach. She socialized, made friends, went on some dates, and seemed happy enough. This is important to me because she is an extension of what I am, and if she were miserable, everything would fall by the wayside, but that hasn't been the case. Plus with all the sun and the ocean, she looks marvelous. We all look much better than we did when we arrived, with suntans and wonderful fresh sea air.

Kelsey and I discuss *The Killer Within*—this book. It is a harder story to write than I thought it would be. I should have known it would be more difficult. I think, or rather I know, that under normal circumstances, the book would be finished by now, had it not been about me and the emotional turmoil of this unspeakable disease, coupled with all the murders involved.

The airport is crowded. I don't like being in airports in a wheelchair because everyone is walking this way and that all at the same time, all in a hurry, and I am fearful that somebody will fall over me, perhaps even knock me over. There is no way I can fall backward or forward because of the safety wheels, but I could easily be knocked over either left or right and in that I have no use of my hands, I cannot stop the fall and inevitably, the first thing that would strike the ground is my head. That thought really upsets me, that because of some incidental accident, I could be seriously injured, sustain a concussion, lose an eye or even worse. With the lack of muscularity in my neck, I could easily snap a vertebra, even break my neck. Having said that, I have become overly conscious and wary of accidents, being knocked over, falling down, and I sort of growl at people when they come too close to me. I guess it is a combination of what I just said plus my Brooklyn state of mind. I have it in me to bite anyone who gets too close to me. For the most part, however, people are extremely polite and quickly move so I can pass. Again, security is a breeze when you're in a wheelchair. The JetBlue people are extremely helpful; they carry me on the plane and stow my wheelchair in the cabin below.

Thank goodness I don't have to use the bathroom. This is always a concern and, to be frank, something I dread. The flight to New York is smooth and uneventful. When we arrive at Kennedy, it is dark and the night is clear. It is good to be back home, and soon Kelsey and I are in the backyard, working away. Kelsey is not only my right and left hand regarding writing, but she has taken over my e-mail corre-spondence, which is sometimes voluminous. Plus, I'm selling my books all over the world now and foreign rights agents and publishers need and want things and Kelsey takes care of that, too. Regardless of the state of my health, the beat must go on.

14. Coast to Coast

On the first day we are home, I have a long-planned interview on a radio show I do every now and then called *Coast to Coast*, hosted by George Noory. I enjoy doing this show because it is four hours long and broadcast on thousands of radio stations around the world. They have a listenership of some 32 million people. True, talking with the breathing apparatus is difficult, but I will manage it and make it work—I hope. This evening, I am going to talk about the difference between a serial killer and a contract killer, a terrorist and a Mafia assassin. I have a really strong coffee at midnight and begin chatting with George Noory. I like George. He's bright and articulate and rarely interrupts. He knows I know things that few if any know and is glad to give me voice. All of my appearances on George's show have gone well.

In that the show is four hours, it is an unusual opportunity for an author to talk in great detail. Not only is George interested in what I have to say, but we take calls from around the world and they flood the switchboards. I explain that what motivates a serial killer, simply put, is sex.

"All serial killers," I say, "are sexual sadists—from Jack the Ripper, John Wayne Gacy, Ted Bundy, the Night Stalker Richard Ramirez. What drove them all was sex, their need to have an orgasm, simply put.

"A contract killer, on the other hand, has no bloodlust as such. Killing for such an individual is a job, a day's work. He has no emotional or personal attachment to the task. Mafia assassins are similar to contract killers, but they have a feeling of omnipotence. They feel that they are part of an underground culture, a netherworld in which there are no rules or regulations but their own. They not only do not abide by society's laws and dictates, but they disdain them. They create their own rules and laws and they live by them. It's a simple equation. 'Fuck with me and I'll kill you. You have what I want, I'm taking it, I'll kill you for it. You disrespect me, you're dead.'

"A terrorist is a horse of another color. They are motivated by their obsessive religious beliefs. They feel what they are doing is for and in the name of their God and they are pleasing their God and therefore they have no conscience, no remorse—are as cold as ice.

"The three things that they all have in common are: no conscience, no guilt, no second thoughts. To put it another way: no predators in nature have any qualms about killing and eating their prey. That's what they are. Predators, no less, no more."

Toward the end of the interview, George asks me what I will be doing next. I don't mention *The Killer Within*, but I do tell him that I want to write a book about a very unusual mafioso in the Bonanno crime family, a man dubbed by his colleagues The Butcher.

This is a case I've been interested in for some ten years. It involved Tommy Pitera, a capo in the Bonanno crime family, and the superhuman efforts of the DEA to bring him down. The story took place, coincidentally, in the same place where I grew up—Bensonhurst . . . *Mafiadom*, as I call it. Pitera was not only a major drug dealer but he was also a hit man extraordinaire. In addition to killing for the Bonanno crime family, he murdered for all the five families and regularly cut his victims into six pieces, then buried them in a Staten Island bird sanctuary, where he knew the land was federally protected, could not be disturbed, and the bodies would not be discovered, I explain to George. Even other mob guys feared Pitera, wanted little to do with him, looked the other way when they saw him coming, enter a restaurant. Pitera scared scary guys. The problem is how to get a handle on the story when everyone is still deathly afraid of Pitera— and no one will talk. I've been back to my old neighborhood several times and tried talking to people who know the street well. When I bring up that name, no one knows anything. I keep hearing over and over how dangerous he was, how bad he was, how ruthless he was. I learned that he even killed a woman named Phyllis Burdi, cut her up and buried her at the bird sanctuary. As a boy in Brooklyn, I knew Phyllis Burdi very well. In fact she was the first girl I ever . . . soul-kissed.

We both lived on Bay 31 Street until her family moved off the block. I never saw her again. Pitera was the alpha wolf all the other wolves ran from. A friend of mine named Sal Clemente told me that Pitera walked around with a "shroud of death" about him; that Pitera had burial grounds where he'd dispose of his victims; that Pitera had an undertaker's autopsy table that he used to bleed and dissect the bodies. I've also heard that he was a karate expert and he studied martial arts in Japan. This is particularly interesting—the fact that he had the wherewithal, the independence to leave Brooklyn and travel to such a faraway place. The more I heard about Pitera, what he did and how he did it, the more determined I became to write a book on the case.

As I said, I am scheduled to be on the show for four hours but Noory likes what we are doing so much that he asks me to do the last hour with him. Under the best of circumstances, this would be a difficult task, talking nonstop for so many hours. But as you may imagine, for me, it is extra arduous because much of my diaphragm muscle has weakened and my ability to talk has considerably lessened. I manage to do the five-hour interview by periodically putting the air hose in my mouth and just bluffing it along. This is one of those times when the reality of my disease interferes with my work. These days, an author talking in such a venue is essential to the selling of books. If you truly have something to say, *Coast to Coast* is the place to say it. Many people are out there listening. Yet here I am, hiding the air tube from George Noory and his millions of listeners and making the best of it. I think for the most part nobody notices, I pull it off, but, still, the extra effort and the lack of normal breathing capacity makes it that much more taxing and tiresome. I am not complaining here. I'm just describing what ALS is really about, how it manages to insidiously slither, as though a venomous snake, into every aspect of your life. Because I have such a lack of lung capacity, when I sneeze, it sounds like a diminutive kitten's sneeze. I can't cough at all, which of course lends toward an excessive buildup of effluviums.

"So," George says, "when do you think we'll see this book?"

"As soon as I can put it together, George," I say.

"It's been a pleasure having you on the show, Phil."

"It's been my pleasure," I say.

Finally we sign off. It is five in the morning. I am exhausted. Laura is sound asleep. She tried to stay up during the whole show but it was impossible. I amaze even myself that I could talk for five hours. It makes me realize the extent of the information I have garnered over the years as a result of writing books about criminals and reading voraciously about them and, more important, having long, soulful conversations with the baddest of the bad.

Books . . . anything man ever knew about every subject is written in a book somewhere. Even the great novels written by the masters contain pearls of wisdom, eternal truths about human nature that have become somewhat lost by society's need to do everything in a hurry. When Camus and Victor Hugo, Maupassant and Flaubert wrote, when Shakespeare (the reigning king), Tolstoy, Dostoyevsky, Chekhov, and Gogol sat down with a blank piece of paper, there were no such things as sound bites, no computers, no obsession with saying things quickly. Ahhh, I shake my head and stop rummaging in the world of books that have become a part of me, that have taken up residence inside of me somewhere. *Bubble, bubble, toil and trouble,* I think.

A pale gray dawn descends on the backyard as if it were some kind of London fog. Birds begin to chirp. I can hear the faraway rumble of a garbage truck. It sounds like a giant dinosaur, insatiable and hungry.

I am soon lying in bed next to Laura; her sweet female warmth readily comes to me. In that I sleep better on my side, I turn to my right, close my eyes, and am soon drifting on a dark cloud away from this world.

When Laura wakes me, it is 2:00 P.M. As always, I am so tired because when you sleep with ALS, as I've said earlier, you don't expel carbon dioxide as you should and you are fatigued and plagued by aching bones and muscles. I feel as though I have been beaten up in a fight. Today Laura just about has to pull me out of bed. I have strong coffee, toast, and some fruit and sit down at the computer. There are hundreds of messages to me from listeners of *Coast to Coast* all around the world. Unknowingly, I am about to find the door that will open into a bloody netherworld created by a Mafia psychopath that few have known and come away from alive. Innocently, I begin reading the e-mails.

15. Enter the DEA

One of the many e-mails I receive that afternoon is from Dave Toracinta. He identifies himself as a DEA agent who worked the Pitera case.

"If you want to really know about Tommy Pitera, contact me. I was on the task force that arrested him," he writes.

This not only surprises me but kind of bowls me over. A while ago, I spoke to somebody in the publicity department of the DEA and they were not too cooperative and stopped returning my phone calls. Now I am hearing something completely different. I immediately write him back and within several hours, we are talking on the phone. Agent Toracinta is a cordial, outgoing man who has no qualms telling me about Tommy Pitera. Just the opposite. He immediately likens Pitera to a vampire. He says he was unusually pale and wore all black and enjoyed killing people in a way he'd never seen before. When I ask him where Pitera is, he tells me he's being held at Allenwood Penitentiary with seven life sentences hanging over his head.

"How many people do you think he murdered?" I ask.

"Over fifty. We got that from people around him who knew the truth."

"Amazing. Do you think he'll talk to me?"

"I have no idea, but I can tell you this: if you really want to know about the case, talk to Jamie Hunt."

"He is?"

"He ran the Pitera task force. He first uncovered what Pitera was doing. He was the street captain of our group."

"How long did you work the case?"

"Three and a half years or so," he says.

I ask him how I can get in touch with Jamie Hunt. He says he'll reach out to him for me. I thank him and we hang up. I know that much of his wanting to help me has to do with the fact that he heard me speak for five hours about crime, criminals, and—about law enforcement in a way that apparently impressed him. I'm sure that's why he eventually gets DEA Agent Jamie Hunt—who I soon find out is second-in-command of the DEA's New York office—to contact me, and a whole new world red with blood I know scant little about opens up before me.

The following day I get an e-mail from Special Agent Jim Hunt, giving me his phone number. I call Agent Hunt and he is somewhat guarded, though friendly enough. He agrees to meet me for lunch. We end up rendezvousing at Moran's, a restaurant near DEA headquarters on 19th Street and 10th Avenue. I tell both Laura and Kelsey to not ask questions, to let me talk with him—bond with him. There will be no note taking, no tape recording, nothing like that. Of course, I am an invalid and I have to bring Laura and Kelsey along. Even now, as I say that, "I am an invalid," as it rolls off my tongue, I feel uncomfortable. I have accepted my condition, my immobility, but when it comes out of my mouth, it is still difficult. It's like giving someone you care about dearly very bad news.

This is all new to me—interviewing somebody with the outward impediment of being in a wheelchair and having atrophy of my hands and the breathing apparatus and all the rest. On the one hand, I am uncomfortable; I feel as though I am imposing my condition on Agent Hunt. On the other hand, I know that none of this is my doing and anyone with a semblance of humanity would realize that and not be distracted or put off by my condition. Still, no matter what, I plan to write this book by hook or crook.

Moran's is one of those old-fashioned, Irish-oriented taverns with stained glass, shiny mahogany throughout, and a fantastic long, slate bar. I will soon learn that it is a cop hangout and that it was owned by a police officer who passed away. His daughter now runs the place.

DEA Agent Jim Hunt is an impressive specimen of a man, robust and obviously very fit, about five feet eleven inches, broad-shouldered,

thick-muscled with a narrow waist. He looks like a professional athlete who has just retired. Jim has dark red hair and a red mustache.
We take a table and order beers and burgers and start talking. In that
this is the first time we are meeting, it is imperative Agent Hunt gets
a feeling for who I am and what I am doing here. I give him a brief
rundown of the books I've written. He knows, of course, about *The
Night Stalker* and *The Ice Man* and, most certainly, about the
Anthony Casso book. He is, I quickly come to learn, an expert on
organized crime. In the world of La Cosa Nostra, Casso was a superstar, infamous among the infamous. I bring Jim Hunt a couple of
copies of my books, tell him I am interested in doing a comprehensive
story of the Tommy Pitera case.

"I don't want to write," I say, "a quickie book that just gets the
headlines. I want to do an in-depth study of the case, how you worked
it, who he really was, the effect the case had on you." He says he is
surprised a book hasn't been done already, that several writers had
talked to him about doing a book but none of those ever came to
fruition. He says, too, that he'd like to cooperate with me but first he
has to get permission from Washington.

"I don't think that'll be a problem, though," he says.

As we talk, I am taken aback by his encyclopedic memory. He
readily remembers names and dates, times and places and even what
the weather was like with unsettling, amazing clarity. I've never met
anyone in my life with Jim Hunt's memory. He makes me feel inade-
quate—downright stupid. I ask him about his prodigious memory and
he says, since he was a kid, it has been this way; his father, too, he
says, had an amazing memory. He explains that his father had a long,
stellar career in the DEA, that he arrested Mafia superstars Carmine
Galante, Vincent "The Chin" Gigante, and Vito Genovese. His name
was also James Hunt. His nickname was "James Hurt," for when bad
guys gave him a hard time, they inevitably were hurt. I also learned
that the Senior Hunt was a middleweight boxing champion in the U.S.
Army during World War II.

"So it's in your blood?" I say.

"Yeah, I guess you could say it really is in my blood," he tells me
and smiles.

"Fact is, my uncle, my brother, and both my grandfathers were in
law enforcement."

The more I speak to Jim, the more I am both appalled and fascinated by this case. Pitera had a penchant for not only cutting his victims into six pieces, but he always placed his victims in the bathtub, got naked, stepped into the tub with them, turned on the hot and cold water to just the right temperature so as to wash the blood down the drain, and proceeded to cut the corpse into six neat pieces, usually the head first. Hey, we all know people in the Mafia kill. That is no revelation. But what Pitera was doing was something completely different. The cutting up of the corpses that way was . . . medieval, truly barbaric. I will later find out that even mob guys were appalled by what Pitera did. To get naked with a corpse and then cut it up is ghoulish.

Years ago, I dealt with the Night Stalker and the Ice Man and Gaspipe but nothing I have heard comes close to Pitera's particular methodical barbarism. Mind you, it wasn't just one or two or three; we are talking about dozens of victims. When we finish lunch that first day I meet Jim Hunt, there is for sure a warm cordiality between us. He's only too happy to help Laura get my wheelchair out of the restaurant and help me get in the car. Several days later Jim calls me and tells me he's gotten the go-ahead from Washington to talk with me. I am elated by this. It makes the difference between doing this book and not doing this book, for without Jim Hunt there could be no book.

Every time I interview Jim, he never makes reference to or seems to notice that I am in a wheelchair with impeded speech, my hands immobile, that Laura has to hold the hamburger for me so I can eat it, and all the rest. There is a certain polite deference he shows that makes me warm all the more to him. It is obvious to me that he is a genuine tough man, but he is a tough man with a big heart.

As I learned more and more about the case, over a period of weeks and months, I realized the DEA did an excellent job bringing down Pitera. Everything was picture perfect. Through guile and cunning, they managed to wiretap cars and homes and get Pitera's main people to turn on him—no small task. In that there were multiple murder victims who had been cut up and buried at different bird sanctuaries, all the people who were on the Pitera task force truly felt that they brought down a real live monster—a nightmare come true.

They all are, rightfully so, proud of what they did and, ultimately, they decide to allow me to write a book about the case with their full input and cooperation. This is a milestone of sorts. The DEA very rarely gives journalists access to the inner workings of the agency. I feel privileged, and it is an honor that I am not about to misconstrue or misuse in any way. I will step up to bat and I will hit a home run, that is, do justice to the diligent, selfless work of the Pitera task force, of which Jim was in charge. When I ask Jim if he's married, he tells me, "My work is my wife."

Still I know, in a sense, I am walking on thin ice with this book—or rather rolling on thin ice, for Tommy Pitera is a very dangerous individual and writing about him extensively might prove to be a dangerous enterprise. Pitera still has people on the outside who are involved with the Bonanno crime family and I am certain he does not want me telling the truth . . . telling the world what really happened. I am concerned with only one thing really: writing a book that is a compelling page-turner about this remarkable story—this inside track of the war on drugs. As well as being a devoted killer, Pitera was a major dealer of both heroin and cocaine.

Oblivious to my disease, not letting ALS play into any of this, I interviewed people involved with the Pitera case—all the DEA agents on the task force, Pitera's associates while on the street, and family members of people Pitera killed. I tried very hard to talk with Pitera himself but he refused to speak to me. We exchanged numerous letters. In all his letters, he vehemently denied his guilt, blamed his crimes on everyone else but himself. I even interviewed other members and associates of the Bonanno crime family, who resided all over Bensonhurst and Gravesend, Brooklyn.

The Bonannos' relationship with narcotics was unique. The founder of the family, Joe Bonanno, made a fortune for himself and the family as a bootlegger in the 1920s and '30s. When Prohibition was lifted, Joe Bonanno saw the opportunity to continue making a fortune with another illegal substance—heroin. Bonanno, utilizing family contacts in Sicily, brilliantly set up a network of mafiosi to bring heroin from Afghanistan to Sicily, then to Marseilles, and ultimately to Canada and then the United States—to Brooklyn. This Joe Bonanno did in defiance of the full Mafia Commission. Unlike them, he did not see the pitfalls of the potential problems the selling of heroin could cause. Bonanno was so brazen and bold about his dope dealing that he and his family were ostracized from the other five families, the result of which was very nearly a full-scale war.

Joe Bonanno had been part of the great migration of Italians to America between the years 1888 and 1924, some 4.5 million of them. My grandparents, as I mentioned, were among that 4.5 million people. For the most part, the Italian immigrants landed in New York's Ellis Island. Many of them, however, went on to Louisiana and Northern California. Sicilians who were born fishermen quickly settled in San Francisco. The Sicilians used techniques they had mastered to fish the Mediterranean in the Pacific, and soon were taking in much larger catches than their American counterparts. A good example of this would be the DiMaggio family, who were fishermen that opened a fish restaurant in San Francisco's Wharf area. They also produced a son they named Joe DiMaggio, one of the most famous baseball players of all time. Northern California was ideal for growing grapes and Italian winemakers quickly planted seedlings and soon were producing fine Italian wines from American soil. A good example of this success would be the Gallo brothers.

However, with these honest, good, hardworking Italians came a dangerous, wily criminal element . . . La Cosa Nostra. Joe Bonanno, Tommy Pitera's inspiration and role model, was part of this early secret fraternity.

As an interesting, rather compelling aside: in the course of my research to write *The Ice Man* and *Gaspipe*, I learned that the Mafia was initially formed to fight the tyranny of brutal landowners and government in Italy. Also, perhaps more important, it was the Mafia that fought against foreign invaders that came to Sicily on a regular basis—the Normans, the English, Norsdmen (the Vikings), the Greeks, various Germanic peoples, the Moors, the Gauls, the Spanish, and the Bourbons, all of whom came to Sicily because it was a huge, sprawling island ideal for growing all kinds of crops. It was, in a very real sense, the breadbasket of all of Italy. Invaders also wanted Sicily because it was perfectly located to control the commerce that regularly came and went from Africa, Greece, and distant China. They, too, came for the women. On a regular basis, Sicilian women were stolen away and sold on slave blocks throughout Tunisia. Inside the Sicilians, a cold, vicious, deadly hatred brewed and ultimately the Sicilians refused . . . they refused to be abused and put upon and stomped into the ground; they refused having their food taken away; they refused having their women stolen away from their families.

It all came to a head on the so-called Night of the Vespers. It was March 30, 1282. On that date, the French were controlling Sicily. They were a ruthless, sadistic lot. They felt that they could do anything they wanted to the Sicilians and stole their food, their cattle, and their women—young girls were coveted, prized possession—and the French took to raping Sicilians girls and women. There were some twelve hundred French soldiers stationed near Palermo and they regularly raped Sicilian girls. A cry of "*Mia figlia! Mia figlia! Mia figlia!*" ("My daughter! My daughter! My daughter!") was often heard as these attacks took place. What some say these mothers were doing was calling for "Mafia, Mafia, Mafia!" not "My daughter, my daughter."

Fed-fucking-up, all the men of the island came together and made an agreement to fight back. To resist the French tyranny.

The plan was simple and extremely effective. At twelve o'clock midnight, when church bells sounded all across Sicily, every man and boy who could fight came forth to attack the French. They well knew they were going against highly trained soldiers but did not care. They evened the odds by using stealth and cunning, attributes the Sicilians were famous for worldwide. When the church bells sounded, the Sicilians attacked with a vengeance. The French had no idea what was afoot and were not only caught by surprise—but caught with their pants down.

Quickly, every French soldier was stabbed or beaten or shot to death. It didn't end there, though. What the Sicilians wanted to do was teach the whole world a lesson: they proceeded to cut off the genitalia of every French soldier and stuff the balls and the cocks in the dead Frenchmen's mouths.

When the searing Sicilian sun rose that day, the horror of what the Sicilians had done was there to see and know. Vultures and blackbirds and crows had picked out eyes of the Frenchmen. Sicilian feral dogs had opened up their stomachs, eaten their entrails.

This was, collectively, a horrible, unsettling sight. Word of what was done quickly spread far and wide . . . to Denmark and Sweden, south to Greece and beyond. The Sicilians' plan worked. No foreign power ever came to Sicily again until the Germans invaded during World War II and, again, with the help of the Mafia—specifically Lucky Luciano—the Germans, too, were sent packing.

In Sicily, in the years prior to the turn of the nineteenth century, the Mafia was known as the Honors Society. In America, they quickly learned the crooked ways of the government, Tammany Hall, and so on, and they not only learned about it but they became part of it and, ultimately, mastered it. Government manipulation; manipulation of the police; control of unions and construction and steel. Ruthless cunning was essentially the motor that ran La Cosa Nostra.

In America, when La Cosa Nostra came up against Jewish gangsters, they beat them, killed them, or, when advantageous, made them partners. They, too, went up against hard, tough Irish gangsters.

Diabolically and cleverly, they murdered them all. The famous Saint Valentine's Day Massacre was Italians killing Irishmen—specifically Bug Moran's gang.

They, the Mafia, created their own rules and regulations and strictly adhered to them. Like this, they multiplied and became the most successful criminal enterprise of all time.

Drugs, many would say, were the beginning of the end of the Mafia; they were certainly the end of Tommy Pitera—the focus of my new book.

Initially the mob viewed drugs as they viewed alcohol and bootlegging. They were just another illegal substance. No big deal. The difference was that the penalty for selling drugs was far stiffer. Long prison terms ultimately caused mafiosi to turn, to become informants ... "rats." These tough men whose entire lives revolved around crime suddenly found themselves with thirty-year-to-life sentences. Rather than take their time with their chins up and chests out, some of these individuals told all, which culminated in a chorus of singing canaries. When the federal government used RICO (Racketeer Influenced and Corrupt Organization Act) statutes against the Mafia, just merely talking about selling drugs—let alone actually selling narcotics—caused mob guys to be sent away on an unprecedented scale.

Of all the mob families that sold drugs, the Bonanno family was the most daring, connected, open—indeed, fearless. They so blatantly defied the Mafia crime commission that they were thrown off the board, became persona non grata.

Surely, no contemporary criminal enterprise had devoted, efficient killers like the Mafia. There was Albert Anastasia, Frank Nitti, Al

Capone, Anthony Bruno Indelicato, Joe Gallo, and Anthony Casso. But, for sure, the worst of the worst was Tommy "Karate" Pitera. Like all the others, Pitera killed as though he had a license, the blessing of the pope himself. But he took murder to new heights by summarily dismembering his victims and cutting off their heads.

I have come to learn, and I share this with you—what makes Mafia killers so ruthless is that they have no conscience, no scruples, no morals. They believe they are part of an age-old society in which murder is allowed, encouraged. Particularly in light of the fact that I am weighed down and distracted by ALS, the Pitera story, relatively speaking, will be a difficult book to write, I know. If there were a Mafia tree for the infamous, Pitera would surely be hanging high in it. I have come to think of the Pitera tale as a classic war between good and evil.

As soon as I know I have a green light from the DEA, I again try to communicate with Tommy Pitera at Allenwood Federal Penitentiary, to no avail. After much thought, I decide to put *The Killer Within* on the back burner for now. After all, I have been given a rare opportunity, which I have to move swiftly on. The door was just opened for me and I am going to take full advantage of it. The imperative of writing *The Killer Within* is: Will I still be around to write the book if I put it off, if I put another project in front of it? What I end up doing is I write a proposal based on the Pitera case and my agent and dear friend Matt Bialer quickly sells it to HarperCollins. I resolve to write Pitera's story as soon as possible and get right back to *The Killer Within*. All this greatly motivates me. It is precisely what I was talking about earlier— keeping busy, not letting the fact that I have ALS dissuade me or make me look away from my work. This is engaging. This is interesting. I'm in the race. I have the bell. *"And they're off!"*

Back to basics, I reach out and interview, always with Kelsey's assistance, as many people as I can find who knew Pitera on the street, who were involved with the Bonannos, and via these interviews I manage to get a very good take on just who Tommy Pitera was and how he got that way. I also interview one Frank Gangi, Pitera's right-hand man. Gangi testified at Pitera's trial. Gangi hammered the longest nails into Pitera's coffin. He is a wealth of information.

Special Agent Jim Hunt turns out to be a pleasure to work with. He is the best interviewee I ever had. All together, we interviewed him about thirty times. Whenever I interview Jim, Kelsey is always there taking notes, for at this juncture my hands have become truly useless. Many times we meet in Moran's and Jim also begins coming up to my home and we sit in the backyard and work. He is endlessly patient and gladly details the whole case to me, all its different aspects.

By the time we begin actually writing the Pitera book, my friend Mike and I plant tomatoes and zucchini, peppers and cucumbers in the backyard. Though I once really enjoyed gardening, getting my hands dirty, these days I'm not even remotely capable of gardening. I give my pal Mike instructions and he does what I now cannot do. I guess you could say I am gardening vicariously through Mike. The secret to having a good garden in an urban setting is cow manure. We manage to buy twenty bags of it out on Long Island and mix it in with the soil, put our vegetables in, and happily watch them grow. As the vegetables grow, so does the Pitera book.

My parents, Dante and Nina, are pleased that I am back from Florida. They are absolutely distraught over my diagnosis, watching me slowly deteriorate. Both of them want to help with all their heart and soul, but there is scant little they can actually do. When my mother is over, she tries to feed me and massage my hands, but what she can do is minimal. My father, at eighty-three, helps me exercise and stretch my legs and contributes whatever he can to my care. In truth, it is only Laura who deals with me on a daily basis, every hour of every day—feeds me, clothes me, brushes my teeth. I see the hurt and pain in my mother's face, but it is something that I cannot take to heart for it will only compound my dilemma. Now I act as though the way I am is—well, for want of a better way to put it—normal, that I was born this way, that I have never been another way. I have photos of me on Mykonos when I was naked and very suntanned and I marvel at the condition I was in then contrasted to what I'm like now. In any event, what I am about now is looking ahead, not looking back. Time goes by swiftly. I work with Kelsey on the Pitera book during the day; at night I watch movies, then sleep the dead sleep. I am still dozing off while working with Kelsey, slipping into that strange ALS limbo between consciousness and unconsciousness. As positive as my whole approach toward ALS is, I am noting that my breathing is getting more difficult. Laura and I go to see a pulmonologist named Dr. John Bach and he is very upset by the fact that I am holding the breathing tube in my mouth as I sleep. Like this, he says, I am not getting a restful sleep that includes the essential REM state of sleep. Like I've said, I have not been dreaming at all, which is clearly an indication of just how poor my sleep has become. Dr. Bach, a tall, gangly, affable man with a keen sense of humor, gives us an apparatus that straps around my head and will force air up both my nostrils rather than down my mouth. I tried to use this piece of equipment before but it was extremely cumbersome and I didn't like it. Now, however, I am determined to use it and see if, in fact, my sleep is more restful. The moment I view this as a challenge, as is my way, I become determined to give it a try. Initially, it takes some getting used to, but I clearly note that I do sleep better. I even dream for the first time in a long time. I see myself running on a beach in Conco, a beautiful Mexican island I had been to some twenty years earlier. As I run, I look left and note the distinct triangular fin of a shark parallel to me.

Knowing the new apparatus works, I take to using it every night and feel much more rested during the day. Unfortunately, I look like I'm a scuba diver when I have it on, but I avoid looking in the mirror and after a time I forget I'm even using it. My eyes don't close on me in the middle of sentences and I don't disappear while people are talking to me.

By the time fall rolls around and the vegetables are ripe for picking, we are just about finished with the first draft of the Pitera book, *The Butcher: Anatomy of a Mafia Psychopath*. We managed to get this done through sheer, old-fashioned hard work, by Kelsey and me working 10:00 A.M. to 5:00 P.M., five days a week. Sometimes, we have lunch; often we don't. We always, however, have strong coffee. A bad habit both she and I picked up. Thanks to our friend Jim Hunt we receive the actual DEA video taken the day Pitera's victims' bodies were found and exhumed by the police. Looking at this video, his unspeakable carnage, the many dismembered bodies, was unsettling, to say the least. We were able to experience in graphic color the decomposition of the bodies; most all of them were ensconced in cheap luggage or black plastic bags, cut into in six pieces . . . the head, two arms, two legs, a torso. Seeing this video truly brought home the severity and depth of just how terrible Tommy Pitera was.

Horrific.

I think of the Nietzsche quote, "He who fights with monsters should be careful lest he thereby become a monster. And if thou gaze long into an abyss, the abyss will also gaze into thee." If this isn't the abyss, what is?

By now, as fall begins to show itself, we have fresh tomatoes and cucumbers, zucchini and finger-sized hot peppers. The peppers are so hot you can only take a little bite of them. What I do with the peppers is put them in a bottle with olive oil and let the heat infuse the oil and then use it to cook shrimp and various other dishes—yummy. After about a month or so, the oil is hot—a homemade delicacy.

As the remnants of what we planted begin to die and leaves begin to fall from the trees surrounding the yard, it is time to head south. Clearly, the weather is changing. There is a sudden chill about the air. Some days I cannot go outside at all because of the cold. My right hand gets tight and clamps up and I cannot use the control for my wheelchair. We have already long planned our return to Florida and I have been looking forward to that day the way a kid looks forward to the last day of school. I am lucky I have been able to find and interview everybody I needed to in order to write the Pitera book. As Laura makes arrangements to have the car shipped to Florida, our bowls and pots and pans shipped down, she continues to inject me with IPLEX. It has been now several months that I have been taking the drug and there is . . . scant little difference. I am disappointed, but by the same token, I haven't necessarily gotten worse . . . I am bad enough already. Still, I'm willing to give it more time to see if there is notable change for the better. I'm open. I'm optimistic. I'm hopeful.

Meanwhile, I must call Laura if I have to go to the bathroom. I must call Laura if I have . . . an itch. Oh, how I have grown to hate itches, those little sons of bitches.

"Where?" Laura asks.

"My nose! My ears! My balls!"

We ship the car down to Miami and two days later, an ambulette comes to our door, picks us up, and takes us to Kennedy Airport to catch a flight back to Miami. It's a joyous day. I know for sure we will soon be surrounded by palm trees and blue skies, the spectacular sun, with the sea so nearby you can touch it. As we make our way to the airport, I see in my mind's eye the castles of cottony clouds, the weather suddenly changing, the wind building up, dark clouds appearing from nowhere. I hear the silky whisperings of the palm trees as warm winds tear through them.

For the most part, the people at JetBlue airlines are helpful and make sure I am comfortable, but, again, what I always worry about is what I will do if I have to go to the bathroom . . . eek! There is no way Laura could manage to get me into the lavatory. It is unsettling—embarrassing, the thought of that. The flight is uneventful, however, remarkably quick. I am used to flights to Europe, ten-hour flights to Greece. Two hours and fifteen minutes to Fort Lauderdale is like a walk in the park. As soon as we get out of the terminal, I smell the air and the palm trees. I quietly rejoice inside. If I could, I would get up and dance, I'm so happy to be back in this place that has embraced me with warmth and friendship and good cheer.

"Thank fucking goodness," I say to myself in my Brooklyn-ese.

We have a special van waiting for us out front. I direct my wheelchair into the van and soon we are back on Ocean Drive, comfortable in our oceanfront apartment. I wheel myself to the terrace and look out at the glorious beach that is my office. The moon is nearly full and I can see the ocean clearly in its silvery light, white, crescent waves gently moving toward the shoreline. Without realizing it, I have a smile on my face. I think I'm very lucky to be able to come here, avoiding the brutal New York cold, and write.

In South Beach, there are no grays, no sad, muted colors. Here there is a celebration of the most vibrant colors in nature, a circus of them.

This year Kelsey has an apartment just across the street from us. It, too, has a terrace and also faces the ocean.

In the morning, as is our custom, Kelsey comes to our apartment with espresso for Laura, her, and me and we get to work while Laura prepares for the office. As though we've been here all along, we get right down to it. If I may share this with you, I'm lucky for I never have "writer's block." For me, it's like a switch you can turn on or off. When it's time to work, I turn the switch on and it flows out of me in a steady stream of words, images, emotions, sights, and sounds, who and what and when and where. Most of this fluidity has to do with the extensive research I put into every book, and my ability to feel the pain, feel the anger, clearly see the sunrises, clearly see the sunsets. Sometimes when I write about a body, I can actually smell the body. Whether or not this is a curse is up for debate.

We soon leave the apartment and return to the office. We see all our old friends from last year, smiles and hugs and kisses. I'm pleased that the same people are still here, Carlos Mendes, the manager of the hotel, Vicki Bailey, Fernao Carvalho. However, our dear friend Sergio, the beach master, is gone. We soon learn that he was fired for arguing with customers. This does not surprise us, though we are saddened to lose him. He was a good friend and was always helpful.

We begin this much-coveted South Beach season with polishing the draft of *The Butcher*. What I'm doing now is removing the fat, getting rid of repetition, making it as succinct and to the point as possible. This is not actually writing; it is really rewriting. Not a thing I'm fond of, but something that must be done. There are some run-on sentences that have to be punctuated properly, metaphors that need to be straightened out, the color of blood described more succinctly. The day is clear. There are no clouds in the sky. The sun shines brilliantly. It's lovely to be back. I'm anxious to finish *The Butcher* and get it off the table, out of my mind. I want to go back to the compelling intimacy of *The Killer Within*, what you are reading now, dear reader. I believe *Killer* is an important story that should be told, for it encompasses the world of both murder and fatal disease: the criteria of suddenly being confronted with a terminal disease, lying down and dying, versus moving on with as positive an attitude as possible and living life to its fullest.

Finally, we do our last proof of *The Butcher*, dot the *i*'s and cross the *t*'s and hand it in to HarperCollins. My editor, Matt Harper, and my agent are pleased. Without missing a beat, one day, Kelsey and I go right back to *The Killer Within*, though this is harder than I thought. This is something I've never done, start a book and not finish it, but circumstances haven't given me the luxury of working straight through.

Now, no matter what, I will not stop until I finish *The Killer Within*. Kelsey and I continue to write under blue skies, on a white beach, next to a beautiful turquoise sea that rivals anything Gauguin put on canvas. As I lie there, writing the only way I can write now—with speech, sometimes crying, sometimes laughing, always deeply immersed—my eyes often move to the endless majesty of the ocean and sky coming together.

Both Kelsey and I have become deeply tanned. It's quite a phenomenon for me to be out in the sun, the outdoors, get a tan and be working, and while not being a lifeguard or a beach attendant. In a sense, we have the best of both worlds. I certainly don't appear as deathly ill as I really am. If it weren't for the breathing apparatus, as I said earlier, one would be hard pressed to know how dire my circumstances really are.

Here, with Kelsey's help, with Kelsey's diligence, I slowly manage to get this tale of murder and terminal illness on paper. Being out of New York and here in Florida is comfortable, user-friendly, and wherever you look there are tons of people at ease, on vacation, most everyone smiling and wearing skimpy bathing suits and bikinis. I'm beginning to think of South Beach as a kind of American Rio de Janeiro. It's got that hot, sexy, tropical feel to it—fucking in the air.

I'm happy.

I'm at peace.

My fate is my own.

Then, suddenly, I am thrown a curveball.

My friend Sol, the elderly gentleman with ALS who had the diaphragm pacer installed, died. When I first hear this, I am upset because I have gotten to know him and he was a nice, gentle soul and he was also afflicted with the same disease I have. Every time someone with ALS dies, a little part of me dies with them. I can't help it. I know it isn't healthy. I view us all as members of the same family and whenever you lose a family member, you lose a bit of yourself. Though I didn't know Sol well, I am deeply upset when he dies. I quietly mourn him.

It gets worse. I find out he did not die of natural causes. He had become so distraught about needing people to take care of him that he killed himself. He felt he had become an undue burden to his sons and their wives. Rather than feel this guilt, that he was putting those he loved out, my friend Sol took his life. I can readily understand his feelings. One of the most troubling aspects of this disease is that you become, for want of a better way to put it, helpless. You must count on others for all things. This is all fine and dandy for a child, but for an independent man used to taking care of himself, it is a very hard pill to swallow. You become, you feel like you become, a nuisance. I can tell you true it's a horrible feeling that unsettles you to the core of your being. *Poor Sol*, I think. *Rest in peace.*

Still, I am shocked and stunned and deeply hurt to learn that he took his life. He had been a stoic wall of strength for me. He had been the first person afflicted with ALS to tell me that life must go on, make the best of what you have, yet he killed himself. I become quiet, morose—introspective. After all, if Sol couldn't toe the line, how can I? I don't necessarily view suicide for terminally ill people as a bad thing. I can understand anyone with a fatal disease deciding to just end it. It seems an inherent right of those cursed that way. For me, I always think of suicide as a possible means to an end. To hell with this. I don't want this anymore. It's a matter of choice. I wouldn't do anything violent like shoot myself or hang myself or cut my wrists. That is a melodramatic overdo. What I would do is take a handful of pills, quietly lie down, and go to sleep.

But men who come from Bensonhurst don't kill themselves, I remind myself, and it would be a real stretch for me to do that. I have too much fight in me. When I speak to Dr. Onders, I first learn that Onders knew of Sol's plan.

"I understand perfectly why he did what he did," Onders explains.

Dr. Onders and I become closer and closer. He reads some of my books and we have lengthy discussions on the phone about writing. He is often writing papers in medical journals and I am able to give him insights into writing and encouragement. The operation that Onders created, inserting electrodes into the diaphragm muscle, seems more and more viable to me. When I look at the stats he sends on the test results of people who have had the operation, I become convinced it is the thing to do. Laura and I decide to fly from Miami to Ohio and get the procedure done. It is now the dead of the winter. Ohio is shockingly cold. I don't want to be here. The weather is dreadful, but I have no choice. The evening we arrive, we meet Dr. Onders and his wife, Tracy, and have dinner in a wonderful Brazilian restaurant just next to our hotel. Early the next morning, a cab takes us to the hospital, which is only a short distance away. Onders, I have come to believe, is a unique doctor. His specialty is hernia surgery but the acute curiosity of his mindset gives him a wealth of information about different aspects of disease and medicine. He has the insight and ability to think out of the box, is a bona fide genius, yet he has the caring temperament of a country doctor still making house calls in the dead of a winter night. I know I am in good hands with him, and without hesitation I have the operation.

After the procedure, when I come to, my chest burns and I demand more painkillers, which I immediately get, thanks to Onders. I float away on a pleasant cloud of morphine. I feel no pain; there is no ALS. Essentially, what Onders did was make an incision on the right side of my chest and plant four electrodes into the left and right sides of my diaphragm muscle, which are attached to a power pack the size of a garage door opener. We will not be able to energize the electrodes until the incisions have a chance to heal, about a week, he says. When I look down at my chest, I now have thin wires protruding out of the space just under my right nipple. I am the eleventh person to get the machine, the first one approved by the FDA.

"It will help you live longer," Onders assures me. Inevitably, he and I become good personal friends. I feel privileged to know him. The following day, Laura and I bundle into an ambulette cab, are taken back to the airport, and return to Miami, the embrace of its welcoming warmth. That night, I again dream I am running around Central Park: in and out of the shade, the smell of freshly cut grass strong, dappled light on and off me as I move under the shade of tall maple and elm trees.

I'm always running in my dreams . . . what the hell does that mean? I wonder.

16. Handicapped Sex

When we return to South Beach, I am still somewhat groggy from the drugs and the sudden dose of ice-cold weather. I tell Laura at about nine that evening that I have a pain in my chest just under the right nipple, from which the wires are protruding. It's an odd thing, having wires sticking out of your chest. They hurt so much that I need painkillers.

During the subsequent days of my convalescence, I am, however, able to work with Kelsey and *The Killer Within* moves forward. We find quiet corners around the pool and empty spaces on the beach, sit and write as though we are in some kind of football huddle.

People that we've come to know at the Savoy Hotel and on the beach ask why I write about "dark subjects." All through my career I've heard this . . . it has become a somewhat offensive mantra. I always say the same thing: it's because of the inherent drama. Everywhere you look there are tears and blood, broken hearts, broken bones, and broken bodies—trauma.

In theater, on the stage, there are two predominant aspects of human nature, Aristotle's smile and frown. I am drawn to the frown because I find that material compelling and three-dimensional—a mirror reflection of the human condition. I am able to write about the netherworld of human nature so vividly because I have studied it intimately, interviewed all the players, and, frankly, I feel a strong affinity to the drama inherent in human nature. No matter how you look at it, no matter how you cut it, it is always there—for writers to pick and choose from, mold into some of the greatest works of art seen by man. When I write, it's as though I'm watching a movie with surround sound. I see the blind eyes of blue-black guns, the malevolent eyes of killers, menacing hands, destroyed bodies . . . I hear the high-pitched, blood-curdling screams, as though they are the high notes of a Stradivarius in a master's hand. I see people in pain, stabbed and shot, dying. I see, too, pools of thick, viscous blood spreading across different sidewalks, dirty mean streets all over the world. Always where there are people there are pools of blood moving across the ground, snake-like. I've trained myself to visualize what actually occurs, smelling it, hearing it, knowing it better than I want to.

So vividly, too vividly, I see the knife wounds, I see the cut throats. I see the naked bodies laid out on unfeeling, aluminum Los Angeles morgue tables, cut open from their pubic hairline to just below the throat. I think of the Night Stalker case: the Stalker cut victims' throats so deeply that he actually severed their heads; I studied the crime scene photographs of his victims and they stay with me, stay with me, stay with me! I see these things the way people see paintings by the masters in the great museums all over the world. I draw from them.

This is what I think when people ask me why I write about the material I write about, but this is something I very rarely say. My object is to re-create for the reader with words exactly what happened, told candidly and impartially, though with taste and mindful that victims have loved ones. My object is to enable them to picture it themselves. That's my concern. It is a writer's obligation, an artist's mandate, to re-create what happened in the reader's mind. I think here of Hieronymus Bosch's work; I think of the drama inherent in Beethoven's Fifth and Ninth symphonies; I think of Steinbeck's *The Grapes of Wrath*; I think of Pearl S. Buck's *The Good Earth*; I think of Shakespeare's *King Lear*; I think of Truman Capote's *In Cold Blood*. I think of these different voices and I am *inspired*.

This weekend Laura and I have plans to go to Quattro, a fine Italian restaurant on Lincoln Road, for dinner. Dr. Onders is coincidentally in Miami for a medical convention and he joins us. We invite Laura's cousin, Tatum, for an evening of good food and conversation. After we dine, Karen and her husband, Eddie, join us for dessert. Laura has on a well-fitted cotton yellow dress and she looks marvelous. I fear that I neglect her as a woman because I'm so often wrapped up in what I'm doing—my sickness, my books, my work, my interviews. My, my, my. With me, everything is always on fire. But the truth of the matter is my books sell extremely well and generate real money. Not money for money's sake, but money for freedom, for us to be able to fly down to Miami, rent what we want, eat where we want, shop where the hell we want. Money so I have a clear head, so I can work unencumbered with the burdens of can-I-can't-I. To a degree becoming successful as a writer, monetary gain, is about luck, but I think to a much larger degree, it's about focus and dedication, not letting rejection dissuade you. I'm not talking about money now at all. I'm talking about writing a book that matters, about writing a book you can proud to have your name on.

If you're concerned with making money, I'd urge you not to write. The money only comes as a by-product of 10,000 percent effort over a period of time and some luck and unbending, unyielding, steely perseverance.

At Quattro, the food and wine are good. We have a very nice meal. Afterward, I have strawberry sabayon. All around us are attractive, suntanned people. Here, being outdoors, being back in the mix, helps me forget what an invalid I am. Dr. Onders has a good time. Rather than our driving home in the van, he offers to walk back to our apartment with me. Alone, he and I set off back to Ocean Drive, he walking next to me. It's about a three-mile walk but I very much enjoy Dr. Onders's company. At one point during a trip, the issue of suicide came up and he tells me with a serious face that if I ever decide to go that route, he will help facilitate it. Please, don't misunderstand this: he is not suggesting or encouraging suicide in any way. He is only saying if I ever decide to push that button, he will help raise my hand. This is a deep, profound statement and a soulful commitment from him. He understands the terrible ramifications of living with advanced ALS. He is just saying, "I feel your pain, my friend." I don't tell anyone this, not even Laura. I only say it now, here, to indicate what a wonderful man and brilliant doctor Ray Onders is. In fact, I have no plans to ever commit suicide. As I think I said earlier, guys from the place where I grew up do not kill themselves. Because being killed was an inherent part of that culture, you automatically developed a protective seventh sense.

Getting back to Laura: sex, when you're an invalid, when you're shackled with a terminal disease, is a hard thing to have, to do, to become a part of. I think most people, when they are disabled like this, tend to not think of sex, to not want it. Invariably, they believe that surely, they are not attractive; surely, nobody would want them, they understandably tend to think. My concerns have become breathing, brushing my teeth, eating, being able to relieve myself. For normal people, all these things are irrelevant, taken for granted, but when you lose the ability to do these simple things and are in my condition, they are monumental tasks. I pick up a utensil and watch my hands and arm quiver as though holding a hundred-pound weight. Still, I have a very active libido, which I have had to learn to marshal, taking into account my circumstances and the fact that I'm married to a very healthy, beautiful woman.

It's easy to get an erection when you have ALS, but what matters is what goes on in the big head, not the little head. The real sexual stimulations occur in the brain, not in the genitalia. Since I was a young boy, I have been very sexual. I don't know how or why it happened, but so it is. I chased my girl cousins; I coveted some of my teachers. I was forced to go to catechism class once a week, Wednesday afternoons at two, and the priest—I'll never forget—warned us not to masturbate, and if we did masturbate, he said, hair would grow prodigiously on the palms of our hands. For a while, when I woke up in the morning, I looked at my right hand first thing, but hair never grew and I knew the priest was a liar. I figured that out on my own. Masturbating, according to the church, was a sin. I figured I was going to hell, and I accepted it.

Early on, I had a sexual experience that was so bad it nearly caused me to lose my life, when I was seven or eight years old, young and wide-eyed and totally innocent.

17. Bad Bob—Innocence Lost

We are always talking about how great the weather is in South Beach. Sometimes it rains at night or late in the afternoon, but for the most part it is sunny and cloudless. We casually watch the news and the weather reports and it is raining all over Miami but rarely where we are. It is as though we are blessed by the god of good weather. This, the weather, plays into my life, my work, in a large way. After all, I came here to write a book. For me, going to the beach is a serious business for it allows me to get outside rather than stay cooped up indoors, where the only inspiration is four blank stucco walls. Sure, if I absolutely had to, I could write under any conditions, but it's a matter of preference—being comfortable. But for two days now, it has rained straight, and with the rain has come a chilled air. Both Kelsey and I are in jean jackets buttoned up tight. If I am careful, I am able to manipulate the wheelchair out onto the terrace. It isn't that big a terrace, but large enough for me to get out and turn the wheelchair around and have four chairs and a table. So we go out onto the terrace, Kelsey and the computer, me in the wheelchair, a turbulent sea stretching out endlessly before us, an angry gray sky above, lightning bolts way out at sea, tearing open the sky with practiced vengeance. What would happen, I wonder, if I got hit by a lightning bolt while sitting in this metal contraption? That would be a ready, quick end to it all.

BOOM—lights out.

If one had to go, I think that would be doable. Suicide, of course, enters my mind once in a while, but it is mostly within the context of a joke or some dark humor. As I stare at the foreboding sky and lightning, I think of death, I think of suicide, but they are fleeting thoughts that matter little. Still, I am able to draw a certain gloomy energy from the day, the lightning, cannon-like thunder, the darkness of it. It reminds me of the original movie *Frankenstein*, when the thunder and lightning come to be transposed into the monster and give him life. My eyes move from the sea to Kelsey.

"So . . . you ready, K?"

"I've been getting all this down," she says.

"Okay, let's continue . . ."

Bob was a tall, thin, hollow-chested man with salt-and-pepper hair that reeked of cheap aftershave. He had snake-like, beady blue eyes, razor-thin lips, a sallow, high-cheekboned face. He resided in the house where Judy had lived before she moved. Judy was my childhood girlfriend, the first girl I ever kissed. There was something off-key about Bob—the way he looked at me, an interest he had in me, that was . . . unnatural; that made me somewhat uncomfortable, and I tried to avoid him, but he kept coming over to me, sidling up to me like a snake does to its prey, and soon began talking to me about sex— a subject I knew very little about, but that didn't seem to matter to him. Not wanting to seem ill-informed, I readily told him about my experiences with Judy. She was gone by then and he promised me he wouldn't tell anyone, that it was *our secret*, which I would realize later is a classic tool, a jive-ass con child molesters use, to create secrets they can share with their victims . . . the first step to sexual abuse.

There was an alleyway that ran from my block to the backyards behind the buildings that lined Bay 31 Street, all three- and four-story structures. I liked playing in the yards, leaping from the garage roofs back there, eating the sweet grapes people grew on arbors. This was, for the most part, an Italian neighborhood. Here, many families grew grapes, tomatoes, and basil in their yards and the sweet smell of basil permeated the warm summer heat. Judy and I used to make out in the alley and in quiet corners we found in the yards, the smell of basil and ripening tomatoes about us. This particular block—Bay 31 Street —was teeming with kids. I had a lot of children my own age to play with. Sometimes my friends from the block and I had races from one end of the street to the other across garage rooftops. This was a dangerous, risky business—that's what made it fun—for some of the rooftops were three, four feet below the others and three or four feet apart. I always won. I was short and nimble, fast, with exceedingly strong legs. Now, as I write this, I again look at my legs and they look like two bones covered with scant little muscle.

In any event, one day as I was walking from the backyards to Bay 31, I ran into Bad Bob. He said he would give me a quarter if I let him play with my penis. This really caught me off guard. I had no idea a grown man would want to do such a thing with a boy, no less a prepubescent child, but it seemed like something he really wanted to do and I didn't want to hurt his feelings and the quarter sounded like a good idea. I said okay and in the next instant he was on his knees before me, performing fellatio on me. This stunned me. I knew nothing about oral sex but he sure the hell did and he sucked on me like he was a famished man and my small penis was some kind of precious sustenance. I was appalled by the blatantly carnal act there in the alley next to the garbage cans with flies buzzing about, but it was not painful at all, and I let him do his thing, thinking it was . . . really *weird*.

He seemed very nervous, kept listening to hear if someone was coming. Little did I know that if he was caught doing such a thing on this block in this Italian neighborhood, he would surely be beaten senseless, more than likely sent to the hospital, bones broken, perhaps even killed. I had no point of reference for such a thing; no one had ever told me about men like him. He, I realize now, apparently had an orgasm brought on by what he was doing and he suddenly stopped, his face red, covered in sweat—the pig. He stunk of Old Spice, a smell I dislike to this day. He gave me my quarter and made me promise not to tell anyone—that what he just did and what I had done with Judy were "our secret." I agreed, took my quarter, and went straight to Joe's Candy Store to buy a vanilla egg cream and a bag of candy.

Confused and unsettled by what happened, I went home. I wanted to ask my mother about it, but knew I couldn't. I had promised I wouldn't tell.

Sullen, from that day on I avoided the alley, avoided Bad Bob, but it was a small street, a small universe, and I inevitably ran into him and he was always syrupy-nice and all smiles, but I refused to go back into the alley with him.

"Forget it," I told him with as much threat as I could muster.

He started telling me about Manhattan, *the city*, a place I had never been. He made it sound like heaven on earth, said it was where all the important, the rich, successful people lived. I was very curious about the city. I had heard it talked about reverently many times, had seen it on television and in movies, but never had the chance to actually go there.

Soon, Bad Bob began asking me if I'd like to go to the city with him. He said he would borrow a car and take me. I said I had to ask my parents, get their permission for such a long-distance excursion.

"No, don't tell them," he said. "They'll never let you go. It'll be our secret. I'll take you. You'll love it. It's the best city in the whole wide world!" he assured me.

That, combined with my naturally adventurous, fearless nature, was enough for me to agree to go, and the very next day I met him around the block. He didn't want anyone to see me leave with him because he wasn't planning to bring me back, I later realized, but at this point, I knew nothing about such things. And off we went.

The city was, just like he had said, an amazing place. I had never seen such tall, majestic buildings, so many people and cars. Wide-eyed, I stared in wonder out the window as though I were a hillbilly seeing a city for the first time, fresh off a turnip truck. He showed me the Empire State Building. What a sight that was. It seemed like something created by some kind of supernatural power. This was the place I wanted to be; here was where all the action happened. Here was where I wanted to make my life.

"I told you you'd like it," he said, proud of himself. Back then, the thought of writing professionally, writing for a living, was as foreign to me as Mars.

Now, sitting on the terrace with Kelsey, watching the lightning bolts out at sea gathering around the horizon, tearing it up, feeling the strong sea wind, I think about how I would have never in a million years thought I'd become a writer. I was blind, oblivious to such a thing. But I think now, actually I'm certain, what happened that day would later become an element in my first published book, *Stolen Flower*, being about child sexual abuse. Though I *never* really consciously connected the two, it stands to reason that's the case.

Bad Bob parked the car, I still clearly remember now, on a wide, two-way street. I think it was West 57th. We entered a doorman building, went up to a high floor in a fancy elevator. I had never been in one before. It actually had music. Silently, we walked down a long hall with plush red carpeting. He rang the bell of a door at the end of the hall. A pretty woman with a lot of black hair opened the door. They kissed hello. He introduced me as his friend Philip.

"Hello, Philip," she said, smiling. "Would you like some soda?" I said I would. She soon handed me a glass of Coke with ice in it . . . how fancy. I wondered if she was going to suck on me like he had. I surely would not have minded that. Indeed, I was, somewhere in the back of my dirty mind, hoping she would. There were two other men there. They were not so friendly. I began to feel uncomfortable. I looked at the nice lady, her hair glistening. Surely, I was thinking, she wouldn't let these men do anything to hurt me. Bob soon invited me into a room in which was a large, canopied bed. He wanted to fellate me again and I was in no position to say no, I realized, and so I reluctantly acquiesced and the degenerate did it to me again. This time he wanted me to take off all my clothes. I refused. He said he wanted to "fuck" me. I wasn't sure what the hell that meant. I thought only men and women did that; I said no. This he didn't like. He became angry, his narrow lips tightening against his teeth. I thought about how I could fight him off if it came to that. I was barely up to his waist, but that wasn't about to stop me from resisting him. I remembered Jimmy Emma beating up Ralph the parkie. I stayed resolute.

"I want to leave," I said.

He seemed to sense that I would resist him, fight him tooth and nail, make a big fuss if he pushed me too far. If I could have, I'd have jumped out the window. He suddenly smiled and became nice again, but I was still uncomfortable. He was a venomous snake, a viper, and now I knew it. He could not be trusted. I said I had to use the toilet and went into the bathroom. When I came out, I heard Bob talking in strange, hushed tones to the other men, saying something about using a van instead of the car to take me to "the farm." I would never forget those words: *the farm.*

I wasn't about to let them take me to any farm, take me anywhere. I went back to the bathroom and found a pointy, red-handled pair of scissors in a drawer. I quickly put it in my pocket and returned to the living room. They became silent when I entered. I noticed now that there was a camera and lights near the front door. The woman was gone. Not good. One of the men asked me if I'd like to go for a ride to a "fun place" where they had all kinds of animals I could play with.

Knowing I could never resist three grown men, I said sure. "I'd like that. I love animals," I said, reversing the con.

"Okay," he said. "Good," seeming pleased. They all seemed pleased.

I'm sure if I had said no, they would have forcibly taken me, perhaps wrapped me up in something and just taken me. But because I acted like I wanted to go with them, they didn't have to force me.

"Afterward, can I go home?" I asked, all innocent, but what was playing in my mind was far from innocent.

"Sure," Bob said, and he and I and one of the men left. The other guy carried the camera and lights. No one was speaking. There was an eerie silence. We went down in the elevator, the music playing. The other guy looked like a rat, had a long, pointed face and dark, cold eyes. I imagined him with whiskers and a piece of cheese in his mouth. Now, back outside, Bob took my hand with more force than I'd have liked, a thing he had never done before, and we walked to a white van around the corner. I was looking for a chance to get away, looking for a cop, looking for help—desperate. My stomach turned. Sweat beaded on my brow. My heart raced. The horns of the cars were loud and intrusive. Though I was among thousands of people, taxis and cars and buses and trucks, I was alone—so alone.

"I don't want to go," I said, pulling away, trying to free myself. "I changed my mind," I said. Bad Bob would not let go of my hand, just smiled down at me. I began to panic inside. I pulled harder, with all my strength. I couldn't get free.

"You'll love it," he said, giving me a weak, annoyed smile. "I promise," he added.

One of the other guys opened the door. Desperate, I looked around. No one seemed to notice or care what was happening—everyone was blind. I took a deep breath and without a second thought, I pulled out the scissors and plunged the point into Bob's forearm with all my might. If I could have reached his face, I would have stuck it in his eye. He let out a wail, a moan, and let me go. I apparently had hit an artery for blood squirted up in the air, fountain-like. I ran off as fast as I could in my Keds sneakers. They did not chase me.

"My computer battery is dying," Kelsey says. As I have been writing this, dictating it to Kelsey, I have been looking out at the horizon, enjoying the freedom the horizon gives your mind to travel wherever the hell it pleases. I had been there, running down the street when I was a kid, not at all in Miami, when Kelsey's words brought me back. She knows better than to interrupt me with anything when I'm speaking rapidly, but the computer battery dying is good reason for me to stop.

"No problem," I tell her. Kelsey gets up and goes inside to get her plug. Now, larger, angrier waves are churning up the shoreline, and large numbers of rubber-suited surfers are taking advantage of the big waves. Kelsey returns and we resume.

Aimlessly, I walked strange streets crowded with strange people, all sizes, shapes, colors. I saw policemen, but was afraid to tell them what had happened—sure I would get into trouble for what I had done to Bad Bob, having no idea of the felonious gravity of what he had done to me, what he had wanted to do to me.

Now I was on a street called Broadway. There were many movie theaters, blinking lights, people hurrying to and fro. As I passed a subway station, I saw a sign that said Coney Island. What a relief that was! I was certain if I could get to Coney Island, I could surely make my way home. But what would await me back on Bay 31? I wondered. Would the police be there to arrest me? Take me to the big house? In my neighborhood, the big house was always a concern. There were men on my block, fathers and uncles of my friends, who had been sent to "the big house." It was a terrible, scary place. It was called Sing-Sing. You were lucky if you got out alive. Everyone was mean. The guards beat you for no reason. The food was terrible. We dreaded the big house.

Thinking these thoughts, worried, butterflies filling my stomach, I made my way down the subway steps, snuck past the turnstile, and asked a woman where the train to Coney Island was. She said she would show me and led me to a platform. It was crowded with people. The train soon came and I got on it. Luckily, it was the West End line, which went straight through my neighborhood.

Fascinated, I looked out the window, appalled though wiser. When we reached the Bay Parkway stop, I recognized my neighborhood and quickly got off the train. With great trepidation, I slowly walked down Bay 31 Street, sure there would be police cars in front of my house. There weren't. I made my way up the stairs to our small attic apartment. My mother was there in the kitchen making veal Milanese—my favorite dish. Boy, was it good to be home. I would never again, I vowed, go off to the city with someone I didn't know. I had learned a good lesson. It was that you couldn't trust everyone— just because someone was an adult and smiled didn't mean they were a nice person; indeed, perhaps, just the opposite. In years to come, this was a subject I would write about extensively—child sexual abuse. Learning about the depth and severity of how children are abused led me to understand the true building blocks of psychopaths.

Thinking any minute the police would ring the bell and the cops would be there, I put on *Popeye* cartoons—my favorite—and again watched Popeye save Olive Oyl from the villainous Bluto. Someone once told me Popeye came from Brooklyn. That made me like him all the more. I wondered where—if it was Flatbush, the place Judy Riley had disappeared to.

I thought about the city some more. Even though my first foray there had been a bad one, I was intent on living there someday, becoming part of the wonderful milieu I'd seen. Brooklyn was a backward tobacco road compared to the city. That's where the action was; that's where I wanted to be; that's where my destiny was, I knew.

Luckily for me, this experience with Bad Bob did not have a debilitating effect on me, my sexuality. Looking back on it now, thinking about it now, sitting here with Kelsey, telling her this, watching her reactions—which are minimal—I'm sure it has to do with the fact that I didn't allow myself to become a victim. I was willing and able to not only strike back, but strike back with very bad intentions. Like I said, if I could have, I would have stuck the scissors in his eye—killed him. More or less, from that day on, I carried a sharp knife. I didn't want to necessarily hurt anyone, but I was not about to ever become a victim. I knew, deep inside, that what Bob was about was a bad thing, that people like him were genuine outcasts of society from the beginning of time. As I said earlier, I wound up publishing a book about child sexual abuse and this experience, to a degree, might have leaned toward my taking pen in hand and writing the first book ever that portrayed what was really happening to abducted children. I wrote *Stolen Flower* in 1984 and '85. It was released in 1986, way before there

166 / P H I L I P   C A R L O

was the huge outcry about child sexual abuse that there is these days. In fact, I wound up doing many talk shows and too many news shows to count. I also lectured at symposiums on child sexual abuse around the world and lectured at Scotland Yard, the Manchester Police, INTERPOL, and the NYPD Police Academy. But I get ahead of myself. Forgive me.

I close my eyes; this is tiring. Without thinking, I try to cross my legs, but that proves to be an impossibility due to muscle atrophy. Last year I was able to cross my legs. This is a subtle though unsettling sign that the disease is progressing. Because I can do nothing about it, I ignore it. I open my eyes and again stare at the rough ocean, the stormy horizon where the sky and ocean meet, timeless lovers that are now, it seems, warring with each other. I hadn't planned on writing about the incident with Bad Bob, feeling it was . . . well, too personal. Is it anyone's business, really? Does it have anything to do with my getting sick? My interviewing killers? My swimming in the cesspool of human nature? My writing books about crime? Does it, in the end, have anything to do with my becoming a writer, I wonder? I decide that regardless of the answer, I'm going to tell it because it did matter, does matter, and it *might* have contributed to my becoming a writer.

As bad an experience as what happened with Bad Bob was, I had a wonderful, illuminating sexual experience a little while later. It involved the most beautiful teacher who ever graced the threshold of P.S. 128 . . .

18. Little Miss Goldilocks

As often happens in tropical climates, the weather can change dramatically very quickly. The winds suddenly die down, replaced by a clawing humidity. On my left, the thick, gray skies are opening up, revealing a friendly blue horizon as though a giant curtain is being pulled back. Now, on the stage that is the horizon comes a giant rainbow. Since *The Wizard of Oz*, I've been fascinated by rainbows and think of them as good omens. Though the waves are still strong, the water has become more subdued. Because it is wet, the beach is a tawny, leather-like color, contrasting sharply with its normal white. Walkers and runners and cyclists are back out.

As I watch joggers and cyclists on the beach, I collect my thoughts and begin; this incident I am sure played into my becoming a writer in a large way. I'll never forget her—my teacher, Miss Gold . . . certainly one of the most attractive women I was ever intimate with. For a while, she was the epicenter of my fantasies, but all that changed. It was 1962, eons before the more recent scandals of attractive female teachers becoming intimate with boy students.

I was in the seventh grade . . . thirteen years old. I was not a normal thirteen-year-old. I was precocious and outgoing and afraid of little. By that point, I had been in many street fights and won all of them. I had a natural confidence about me that exceeded my years. In retrospect, I wish I had been excelling at school rather than excelling at getting into fights and antisocial behavior.

Long, golden locks, large blue eyes, skin as flawless as the finest Chinese silk, Miss Gold was my substitute teacher. When she walked, or rather sashayed, down the halls of the school, every male head turned. Even the teachers, I noticed, blatantly stared after her. Our regular math teacher was frequently absent and Miss Gold filled in for her. I was completely and totally taken by her—seriously infatuated with her, smitten. When I arrived at math class—a subject I did not like—and she was there, I was all smiles, both inside and out. She was very nice, quick to compliment, and friendly, and she had this kind of ethereal, flirtatious gleam in her eyes that fascinated me; that made me think regular lustful, carnal thoughts about her—drew me to her. She wore short skirts, had shapely legs, and I often fantasized about how she'd look, naked and provocatively posed with her blue-eyed come-hither look. I even took to masturbating and thinking about her—having forbidden, illicit sex with her. I didn't want to think about any of those things, but much of it was hormonal and I had no choice in the matter.

Sometimes, when she sat at the front of the class, she sat with her legs slightly ajar, looking directly at me, I could have sworn . . . inviting me to look. I dropped my pencils so I would have to bend down and I could steal glances up her dress, see her silky thighs, imagine the secret, welcoming warmth between her legs—for me, at that age, the holy grail. She seemed to know what I was up to and had this slight, impish smile about her big, kissy lips.

I naturally told some of my friends about her; how she provocatively looked at me, about her sexy eyes. They all said I was nuts, said that I needed to see a shrink. But, still, I could have sworn she had hot thoughts about me, too.

I had a girlfriend named Debbie. She was very attractive, kind of looked like Natalie Wood, and her body was unusually developed. We kissed and she let me feel here and there, but it never got further than that. The more resistance I met from Debbie, the more I stared at Miss Gold. She was a grown woman and I knew she would not hold back her charms. At least I instinctively felt that way. It became . . . hotter—and heavier, in a sense, with Miss Gold. The stares were longer and bolder on both our parts. Her knees spread wider and still wider, I thought. I had no loyalty to Debbie as such. What was happening between Miss Gold and me, I was sure, was something special; the kind of naughty, illicit thing that happened in clandestine erotic books like *My Secret Life, The Story of O,* and *The Crimes of Love,* written by the much-misunderstood, infamous Marquis de Sade. I imagined having sex with her there in the classroom closet and bending her over the desk with her dress wrapped around her waist. At that young, inexperienced age, the idea of real sex was nirvana, a cherished mirage come true, the apex of human feelings and emotions.

I wanted her. I had to have her.

I took to winking at her and she winked back. *Oh my God, she's winking at me*, I thought, looked down, and I suddenly had an erection. How embarrassing. *What's wrong with me?* My goodness.

Here I stop. I look at Kelsey. The rainbow has grown bolder and larger. I begin to wonder whether or not I should tell this story. It doesn't seem . . . well, it doesn't seem germane to what this book is about—my having ALS and my writing about notorious criminals. I ultimately decide to tell about my experience with Margie Gold for it inadvertently opened the door to my becoming a writer.

Perhaps, back then, I already had ALS ticking away inside of me. Some of the experts say people are born with the disease, while others say it is acquired through toxins and poisons that permeate every major city around the globe. The truth is no one really knows exactly what causes ALS. There is, however, a type of ALS called "familial" ALS, which I do not have for no one in my family has ever had ALS. Now, while writing this, I remember how healthy my body was when I was a youth, how I ran seven miles a day for many years with no hint of disease, though these are things I do not allow myself to think about or dwell upon . . . So, getting back to Miss Gold . . .

I was saddened when the school year ended because that meant I wouldn't be seeing Miss Gold anymore, but out of sight, out of mind.

It was now the middle of the summer. I was sitting on a car fender eating a piece of pizza with my friends. We called ourselves the 24th Avenue Boys. School was the last thing on my mind that evening, but I could have sworn I saw Miss Gold, surely the sexiest teacher in the world, walking on the other side of Bay Parkway. I stared after her, certain it was her, but several times I had seen blondes I thought were her and had been wrong. Still this woman really looked like her—the sunrise and sunset of my fantasies. I crossed the street and began following her up 86th Street as though I were hypnotized, still chewing my pizza She looked in shop windows, wearing jeans and sandals and a white top. It was a lovely night. Many people were out shopping. The more I followed her, the more certain I became that it was

Miss Gold . . . the gait of her step, the tilt of her shoulders. The jeans accentuated her great butt, which undulated sensuously as she moved. I hurried to catch up to her, weaving around shoppers. She stopped to look in a clothes store window. I slowly approached her. It was Miss Gold—wow, there on 86th Street like a normal person. How could that be? *Could the sex goddess, Miss Gold, shop like a mortal being?* I wondered.

"Miss Gold?" I ventured, still not quite believing it was her. I had heard that everyone on earth had a twin. She turned toward me.

"Philip," she said, all smiles.

"Hi, Miss Gold. I thought it was you. What're you doing 'round here?" I asked, pleased but nervous.

"My parents live on Eighty-third Street. They're away and I'm watching their apartment," she said, all sweet, all smiles.

"Wow, it's so nice to see you," I said and it was. She had on a cotton halter top, no bra, and her boobs stuck out like the rubber bumpers on a fancy, brand-new Cadillac. Her hair had been cut shorter and you could see more of her beautiful face—those incredible eyes, the high arch of her forehead, the slopes of her triangular cheekbones. But her eyes were what really took me in, the sexual innuendo that issued from them.

"Do you miss school?" she asked.

"No," I said, and told her how I hated school; that for me it was like jail, how difficult it was for me to read, to sit still. She seemed genuinely interested. She told me I shouldn't have white sugar; that it affected some people in a bad way. Made them "fidgety," she said.

"I was going to take a walk down the bay. Would you like to come, Philip?" she offered.

"Yeah, sure—I'd like that," I said, and soon *the* Miss Gold and I were walking down Bay Parkway together, toward the bay, the same place I'd been many times over the years to watch the Coney Island fireworks display. As we talked, I kept calling her Miss Gold.

"Please, Philip," she said, "call me Margie; my name is Margie . . ."

"Okay," I said, loving the way she said my name, how it sweetly rolled off her full lips.

Though I had never been a good student, I had a precocious mind beyond my years, could readily understand abstract thoughts and theories, and saw beyond the surface of things, and as we walked, we began talking about life, society—about the intense feelings between men and women. She was open and candid and spoke to me as an equal, as though I were an adult. I liked her. It was hard not to. We reached the bay and walked on a promenade that ran along the water. It was a clear, warm summer night. A full moon hung low over Coney Island on the far side of the bay in a black sky. The moonlight shimmered on the water and made it easy to see. As we walked, we passed couples holding hands, kissing on park benches. We found an empty bench and sat down facing the water and the full moon laid a golden boulevard the color of her hair on the calm sea. We talked and talked. I kept looking at how the moonlight glistened in her hair, filled her eyes. We became silent. There was no sound but gentle waves lapping at the embankment.

"Would you like to kiss me, Philip?" she asked in a soft voice that seemed to be part of a misty dream, certainly not real. I thought I must be hearing things. She repeated it. I nearly fell off the bench.

"Yes, very much. I've wanted to kiss you from the moment I saw you," I said. "I know it's wrong, but that's all I've been thinking about since you first walked into the class . . ."

"I know," she said. "It was in your eyes. Very pretty eyes you have, Philip."

And with that, I leaned toward her, she came to me, and we kissed deeply. My toes curled. At first we kissed softly and gently, then . . . passionately. Her tongue, long and hot and probing, seemed to have a will and hunger of its own, exciting me in an atavistic way I'd never known before. I felt high; my head spun; the world spun; the earth had moved, I was sure.

Wow. Mamma mia.

She kissed and licked my neck with that long, hungry, silky tongue of hers. I was so excited, words could not adequately express it.

Then she really shocked me, said, "Would you like to come to my parents' house, Philip?"

I stared at her. Oh boy. I didn't believe she just said what she had just said. I didn't believe any of this. She repeated it.

"Very much," I said and she took me by my hand and off we went, me feeling as though I were suddenly on the yellow brick road to Oz. We began back toward Bay Parkway. I couldn't believe this was happening. Surely, I was dreaming. She kept holding my hand, seeming not to care that we were seen that way. This was curious. After all, I was only thirteen years old. I felt that I was walking from my childhood into some form of manhood, and my teacher, Margie Gold, had taken my hand and was leading the way. As we reached 86th Street, she said she thought it best if we stopped holding hands.

"Yes, of course," I agreed, quickly letting go of her hand, a hand I would soon get to know very well. We passed my friends. I ignored them but they saw me boldly walking along with "Margie"—the ones I had told I had the hots for her; the ones who had laughed at me when I said she had looked at me with passion in her eyes.

Who's laughing now, I thought as I moved alongside her, the woman of my dreams. I pinched myself. It hurt. *Wow; this is no dream*, I thought . . .

The phone in our apartment rings. Normally, I don't take phone calls when I'm working with Kelsey, writing, but it is Mickey Rourke and I answer the phone. It is always good to hear from him. We discuss the script. There are so many different ways to tell Richard Kuklinski's story that it is not so much a matter of where to begin but what will have the most dramatic impact and still remain true to what really happened, true to what the Ice Man told me. Mickey is up in New York but he says he may be down within the next couple of weeks. I hope he comes because I very much want to brainstorm with him over the script for *The Ice Man*.

The Golds lived in a six-story red-brick apartment building with a big, fancy lobby at 83rd Street. As we went up in the elevator, she kissed me so passionately there were goose bumps running up and down my spine. I was nervous, apprehensive. I didn't know what to expect—what to do. I didn't want to be out of line. I didn't want to disappoint her. I didn't know where this would end up going—but wherever it went, I wanted to be there all ready to sing *Hallelujah*.

When we entered the apartment, there was a large, square foyer, an umbrella stand, and a huge stuffed beige corduroy chair with a matching footrest. She took me in her arms and we kissed and, as we kissed, she adroitly unzipped my pants and pulled them down. I already had an erection and she quickly took it in her mouth. None of my girlfriends had ever done what she was doing to me now—holy mackerel—and my sex grew disproportionately. It was suddenly the size of a meatball hero. She stopped and quickly undressed herself and there she was, naked as a jay bird, all her charms there for me to see and know and do what I wanted with. My teacher.

Thank you, God, I thought.

She had a large, thick Venus the color of warmed butter. I'd never seen a full-grown woman in her prime naked like this and was amazed and excited. She undressed me and had me sit in the overstuffed chair and ate me everywhere.

Sometimes, as I'm dictating to Kelsey, I have my eyes open and I stare into infinity, most often out at the water or down toward First Street, palm trees tall and elegant and swaying. I don't need to close my eyes as such to be able to vividly see what I am *writing about*. However, today I find I am closing my eyes as I'm talking and as I open them, I look at Kelsey. I am somewhat self-conscious about describing this blatant sexuality to her because it is like nothing we've ever done. Though I have described to her murders in great, gory detail, which she has not been fazed by, I doubt if any of this is troubling her. I don't ask, she doesn't tell.

"Kelsey, are you all right with this?" I say, wanting to be sure.

"Cool . . . no problem."

Now . . . for the first time, I tasted a full-grown woman. I didn't really know what the hell to do with my tongue but she patiently and lovingly guided me. I was a willing student. If I had paid attention in school the way I did to her now, I would have surely graduated at the top of my class—an honor student.

She mounted me. I entered her. She ever so slowly moved up and down, fucking me, fucking me, and fucking me some more—telling me how she had wanted me, how she had fantasized about having me like this, in little more than a purr. I wanted to jump up and say, "I knew it," but I didn't want to seem cocky, even though my cock was in her.

My mind drifts. I stop talking to Kelsey. I begin remembering how strong and resilient my body was then. Back then, I could move myself machine gun–like. My God, what a different world—what a different place I am in now. I look at my useless hands as I think this and I remember how they touched and caressed Margie Gold. She was my teacher, the woman who stood at the head of the class for however many months as the responsible, respectable, well-educated adult, and there she was impaled on me and all I could think was—*This isn't true. I have to be dreaming.*

We both came at the same time. This was the first orgasm I had while inside a woman. It was tremendously exciting—I never forgot it. Like I said earlier, I hadn't planned on writing any of this but it was a turning point of sorts in my life and became more relevant as time went on.

Later, when I walked home, I felt different, taller, more sure in my step. I wanted to tell everybody in the world that I fucked my teacher, that I fucked Miss Gold! But I kept my mouth shut. I didn't say anything to anybody, a trait that would, in years to come, cause me to become intimate with a lot of neighborhood girls . . . the fact that I kept my mouth shut was like a golden key opening chastity belts all over the place.

Over the next several weeks, Margie and I were intimate nearly every night. After we finished, lying naked in her parents' home, we talked about life, drugs, sex, music . . . people. Many times over, she made me promise not to tell anyone what we were doing. She, far better than I, understood the severity of it, that she would get arrested, and all the rest. She explained that she would surely lose her job, would never be able to work in any school. I swore I would never tell—and to this day I never have . . . except this one time. But Lord knows, I wanted to share it with all my friends!

Then she shocked me again—she started telling me she loved me. This surprised and kind of bewildered me. Not that I really knew what love between a man and a woman was. I knew I didn't love her. I felt I could not trust her. I was sure that if she did such things with me, she was capable of doing *anything*, and so I reasoned she could not be trusted. Trust, to me, even then, was very important. I was born and raised in a place—a culture—where when people wanted to kill you they invited you to dinner, acted as though they were your friends, boldly lied right to your face, smiled.

Trust, for me, was essential.

Miss Gold—this teacher, this woman—did, however, do me a huge favor inadvertently that would, down the road, alter my life: she talked in great detail, with great passion, about books, how vitally, intrinsically important they were, how everything man knew about the world was in a book somewhere. I explained to her how I didn't like to read, that I kept losing my place; how the sentences transposed themselves up and down as though they had will and purpose of their own.

"Philip, you are dyslexic," she said—the first time I had heard that word. It was scary. Did it mean I was retarded? When I asked her what, in fact, that meant, she explained that my brain didn't see the words in the correct sequence. She said that many accomplished people were dyslexic, great writers and artists.

"Really . . . like who?" I asked, so very curious. This was a revelation. A golden door I knew nothing about was slowly opening. I repeated, "Like who?"

Bemused, "Winston Churchill," she said, "Walt Disney, Thomas Edison, Pablo Picasso, Lewis Carroll, Alexander Graham Bell, Henry Ford, John F. Kennedy, Babe Ruth, and Thomas Jefferson."

"Wow," I said, surprised and delighted by the company I was suddenly in. "How do you know all this?" I asked.

She said, "I wrote a paper in college on dyslexia."

"I see," I said.

With that, she took a book from the bookshelves in the Gold home and showed me how to read by using my fingers to keep my place, to keep my eyes where they belonged. I explained to her that I'd always tried to read using my fingers, that I felt stupid because I couldn't read, but teachers told me not to, even slapped my hand with rulers.

"They were wrong—idiots . . . forget them! Do what I'm telling you now and you'll see how helpful it is. This has nothing to do with being stupid," and with that, she gave me a book to read, *The Iliad* by Homer.

Later that evening, back home, I read the way she suggested and it really did help. Reading was still slow and awkward, but I could more readily follow the words as they were on the page. For the first time, I enjoyed what I was reading, and like this, by way of a teacher who had seduced me, I learned to appreciate the power and magic of the written word, a milestone in my short life, and a lesson that would show me much and take me far.

As the summer of 1962 passed, Margie gave me more books and I hungrily consumed them. As well as teaching me about literature, she also taught me about sex—the secrets and intimacies of a woman's body, where what was and why it was there and what to do with it. Armed with this valuable information, I was ready to do serious battle. Everywhere I looked, all over the neighborhood were beautiful girls and now I knew things about them that few if any boys my age were privy to. Margie Gold had truly become my teacher in a larger sense of the word. Though some would say that she had abused me, raped me, I always felt certain that my prayers had been answered. I felt indebted to her, not a victim.

My tempestuous, very unexpected affair with Margie Gold came to a sudden end when she went on a long, planned trip somewhere and left me alone with the reality of the life before me.

Though I never felt I'd been sexually abused by Margie Gold, I don't think it was happenstance that my first published book, *Stolen Flower*, was about the sprawling underground world of child sexual abuse. Armed with what I learned from Margie Gold, my mind filled with the erotic lessons she taught me, my body strong, my muscles hard and well developed, I moved toward my destiny, still having no idea what awaited me—the good, the bad, the successes and failures . . . the horror of the grim reaper a distant nightmare lurking in the shadows of the future.

19. Long Story Short

When I was eighteen years old, I left my parents' home and moved to the city. Still having no idea what direction my life would take, I felt free and was happy to be away from the restrictions and rules and regulations of my parents' house and to be living in New York. For me, New York was the center of the universe, the center of the world. Here it all happened. The best in the arts, business, sports, and fashion came here from all around the world to make a go of it. I still had a Brooklyn accent, a sharp Brooklyn edge to me, but I was away from Brooklyn, living in the city and moving closer to what I thought would be a meaningful life.

Unfortunately, what I did with my freedom, what I did with no one looking over my shoulder, was get myself in trouble. These were the wild and woolly times of the early seventies. Long hair, cultural freedom, new dress, new attitude, new music. The actual birth of a counterculture. I watched it happen. I was part of it. Truth was, I was smack in the middle of it. I let my hair grow long; I did what I wanted when I wanted. My parents no longer had sway over me.

Inevitably . . . I became involved with drugs. Cocaine was very popular, all the rage. Through a girl I met, I got hooked up with a large drug dealer and he fronted me all the coke I wanted. I was selling grams of coke at different hot, "in" clubs. I was not as cautious as I should have been and was arrested and my whole world turned upside down. I wound up beating a case of drug possession—after a long, bloody, expensive battle—and afterward, I got a job in real estate and went on the straight and narrow. My head was squarely on my shoulders now. I still smoked grass and did a little toot on weekends, but it was no longer an integral part of my life. I wound up opening my own real estate office on Central Park West and 83rd Street, an upscale residential area. I was twenty-two years old. I did well, but was never really satisfied. Making money was great but there was more to life, I started thinking, realized early on, than making money. I had always loved to read and I began to think about writing as a profession—writing about what I knew: crime, the streets, the Mafia, murder. I ended up closing my office and devoting myself to writing compelling books. Clearly, I had graduated from the school of hard knocks, and what I had learned I planned to weave into books, use to develop into realistic characters.

But where . . . where to begin? I started by doing what I had never done before: reading all the greatest writers who had ever lived. It wasn't hard to find them. All you had to do was ask, knock on the door, and they were in your hands. I read the greatest Japanese, French, Russian, and Italian writers, and, of course, the greatest American writers—Faulkner, Capote, Hemingway, F. Scott Fitzgerald. I was especially influenced and inspired by Hemingway, not because of his macho lifestyle or his public persona, but because of his unique way of marshaling words, of telling a story with simple declarative sentences, complicated tales that on the outside appeared basic and rudimentary but explore the human condition. *The Old Man and the Sea* had a profound effect on me and the story "The Short Happy Life of Francis Macomber" was, to me, magical. As I read it, I found I was suddenly in Africa. I could smell it. I could hear the roar of lions.

Early on, I came to realize that most of the best writers from all different walks of life, from all different cultures, had killed themselves with alcohol and drugs. This unsettled me. They were particularly bright, astute professors of human nature way above average in intelligence. *Why*, I wondered, *is this so?* Another of my favorite writers was Guy de Maupassant, a masterful storyteller who, like Hemingway and most great writers, drank himself into oblivion and was gone before he was thirty-six years old.

The more I read, the more I pined to live in Europe, to visit all the cities and countries I was reading about, all the places where these stories eloquently played out. France and Italy and Spain, the Mediterranean and the Alps, Cortina d'Ampezzo all beckoned me. I was intent upon learning the different cultures, peoples, places . . . how to ski. I planned to ski, when I could, from one end of the Dolomites to the other. I had money, my health, and the inherent street savvy that came with growing up in Brooklyn. I was free.

Then an incident occurred that caused me to be hospitalized and caused a radical change in my life. I got into a silly argument with a tall, broad-shouldered man while roller-skating at a club called the Roxy. He said something to a girlfriend of mine. He and I got into an argument, began fighting. I hit him with a hard left hook in the mouth and got a deep gash on my left hand. The bouncer broke up the fight and I had to go to Roosevelt Hospital. There a doctor stitched the wound closed and, foolishly, put a hard cast over the wound. Inevitably, because of the hard cast, the wound became infected and ultimately I developed gangrene. I went to see my doctor friend Richard Ash. He sent me to see an orthopedist at Bellevue Hospital. He, Dr. Richard Pearl, was appalled that any physician would cover a fight wound with a hard cast. My hand looked terrible. It was purple and black and swollen to the size of a grapefruit. He immediately admitted me to the hospital, put me on the ninth floor, and began an intense antibiotic treatment. While I was there, a woman in a ward several doors down was brutally murdered in her sleep, stabbed numerous times. I saw police and detectives walk by my room. When I asked them what happened, they told me and I was stunned. The killer might very well have walked into my room. Reporters showed up. That night, I didn't sleep much at all. There was a killer loose in Bellevue Hospital and I was not about to become a victim. I placed empty plastic containers around my bed so if the killer came, I would hear him. I managed to steal a pointed scissor from one of the nurse's carts and I kept it in my right hand. Thankfully, I didn't lose my left hand, as I could have. It healed quickly. When I got home, I thought that my experience would make a good book. For months, I struggled writing this book. I called it *Revenge Is Mine*. Its premise was a patient in a psychiatric ward manages to slip out every now and then and murder and rape women—female patients. Proud of myself, sure I had a great book, I tried to get it published. This proved to be very difficult, in fact, impossible. I received rejection letter after rejection letter. They piled up. But this did not dissuade me. I remained resolute. I knew I had something to say and I was going to say it in a book, no matter what.

By now, I was becoming tired of New York, living here. I wanted a change of scenery. I wanted to go to Europe, I very easily sublet my apartment. I packed a large steamer trunk, my parents took me out to the airport, and off I went. I first went straight to my roots—Italia. I landed in Rome and took a cab to a hotel on Via Nazionale. As I made my way around, I marveled at the incredible beauty of Rome. I sat at a small café in an out-of-the-way piazza, ordered an espresso. Sitting there, I closed my eyes and gave thanks for being able to be in this place with my mind and body and soul intact. Even now as I write this, I see it and know it and remember it vividly.

The smell of different foods wafting through the piazza made me hungry.

I found my way to an appealing trattoria in the Piazza Navona and, as is the custom, the food they served was laid out on long tables. I picked out an antipasto, prosciutto, and pine nut tortellini with pesto sauce and chicken oreganota. Even now, as I write this, I'm finding it hard to believe I was able to eat so much food back then and never be heavy. Be that as it may, I had a grand meal with an ice-cold bottle of white wine that first night in Rome. Having finished my bottle of wine and an espresso with an Italian aperitif made from licorice, I was feeling so happy to be alive, so happy to be in this world that I thought I knew so well, but had never known at all. As far as I was concerned, this trip was not at all about *la dolce vita*; it was about freedom and having the peace of mind, the wherewithal, to write a book—a book that mattered. That was my target. As I was sitting in the Piazza Navona in Rome, the place that begot the Roman legions, no check was given to me when I finished my meal. Here, you could sit and linger as long as you wished. I saw her walking by out of the corner of my eye, an exotic-looking brunette with bedroom eyes, sexy. I waved and she was soon sitting with me. Her name was Gabriella. I had no idea she was a prostitute. By the time I found out—after a second bottle of wine with her—it didn't much matter. She told me she had been a prostitute since she was a teen, that she used to work in a brothel in Naples.

"Really?" I said.

"Si."

"What was it like?" I asked.

"Terrible," she said.

"Why do you still do it?" I asked.

"Back then, I don't do for me, now only mine."

"You mean, you keep the money?"

"Si. I have bambino," she said.

"Oh," I said. My intention was not to have sex with her, but to use her as a source of information—a conduit. It was obvious that she knew the secrets I was interested in.

I explained, speaking slowly without syntax, that I wanted to write a book about child sexual abuse. She said that if I wanted to learn about such a thing, I should go to Amsterdam. We drank coffee and talked until the restaurant closed. We went to another outdoor restaurant and sat and continued to talk. She turned out to be a wealth of information about how children were being sexually abused all throughout Europe, especially in Amsterdam and the Scandinavian countries. She also told me about brothels for prepubescent children in Naples and Milan, in Munich and Hamburg. She told me about agencies that outright sold children to brothels in Sweden and Norway. She had no reason to lie. In fact, she cried several times and her tears spoke volumes about her sincerity, its truth. By the time we parted, it was getting light out. I walked her back to her apartment, which was near the Piazza San Marco.

As I made my way back to my hotel, I felt it—Rome was a haunted place. It was filled with the ghosts of those who were tortured and killed in the Coliseum and Circus Maximus. Rather than being a celebration of life, Rome seemed more a celebration of death. Still, it was magnificently beautiful. It had a magic quality to it. *I love you, Rome*, I thought as I walked back to the hotel, comfortable in this new place. At home. *Some day*, I thought, *I'll write a book here. I'll get an apartment and sit at different cafés and write without distraction every day.*

When I arrived at my hotel, I slept deeply and well, having no idea about the destructive force that was not a part of the outside world— the criminals I work with—but was incubating inside of me. Oblivious to that reality, I planned and plotted, researched and asked questions, intent upon writing a book.

20. The Villa Borghese

That first afternoon I spent in Rome, I discovered the Villa Borghese, a sprawling park smack in the middle of Rome. I walked about the park, imagining Roman legions camping out here, preparing for war, practicing the killing of human beings over and over again. The Villa Borghese was lush and green. It had wide-open fields, a thick forest, and hundreds of marble busts of famous Italians. There were also many statues of lions, representing the war-like mindset of the Romans and immortalizing the animals that ate human beings while still alive in the nearby Coliseum. I don't quite know why, but I coveted this place and felt like I had been here before, in another life. I felt this uncanny intimacy with it. I still do.

When I left the Villa Borghese, I made my way to the Coliseum and marveled at its huge size and splendor. Here I closed my eyes and imagined, quite vividly, the gladiators battling to death, lions and tigers eating people alive, as the crowd cheered and clapped and howled, as the Roman aristocracy stared on in wonderment. When I left the Coliseum, I was rather . . . depressed. People behaving so cruelly on a regular basis, as a way of life, is a difficult thing to wrap one's mind around. I had studied this place. I knew well the unspeakable acts that occurred here. One of the most hideous and unsettling atrocities committed in the Coliseum was this: a naked woman in the center of the arena was bound and tied into a position in such a way that most exposed her genitalia. A rag wet with the scent of a female cow in heat was then rubbed all over her exposed vagina. A male bull was then released into the arena, immediately drawn to the scent and aroused. What would ensue, as hard as this is to believe, is the bull would get a huge erection and he would instinctively mount the woman and insert his sex, killing her with its enormity, this as the Romans laughed and clapped and cheered. Who the hell were these people, I wondered, and how did they get that way?

A dedicated war-like culture, for the Romans, sex and violence, violence and sex went hand in hand. I could write a book about this alone. Perhaps someday I will.

After nearly three weeks of being in Rome, I wanted to have a change of scenery. A friend from New York, Cindy Ramsey, was working as a model out of Munich. Cindy and I had made plans for me to go visit her. I now phoned her up, got her answering machine, left a message.

That night, after still another remarkable three-course dinner in a small Roman restaurant where there were no tourists, I took a long walk and then wound up going to bed early. I woke up while it was still dark and went jogging in the Villa Borghese, a wonderful, exhilarating experience. As I jogged along, still not believing I was there, I heard the unmistakable bellowing roar of a lion over and over again. In all honesty, it was a frightening sound. I didn't know if I was imagining it, if the park was haunted by the spirit of a lion . . . it was outright supernatural. I changed my direction and ran toward the roar, rather than away from it. All my life I'd run toward the roar and was not about to change that now. Inevitably, my mind went back to lions eating humans in the Coliseum on a regular basis. With each step, I became more and more wary, frightened by the roars. As a shy, pale dawn crested the western horizon, I saw it—the source of bewilderment. I had no idea there was a zoo in the park, and as I drew nearer to it, I located the source of the roars. It was a giant male with a huge black mane demanding to be fed. I watched in wonderment. Zookeepers came and threw him chunks of meat bigger than Kelsey, which disappeared with shocking alacrity. Wow.

The mystery solved, I began to run again and soon found myself at a high point above Rome. From here, I could see the ancient splendor of the city spread out before me, just as the fiery, gold sun rose ever so slowly. The early-morning sun cast the whole of the city in a golden-crimson red. The majesty of the sight took my breath away.

I continued to run in the Villa Borghese early in the morning for the next few day getting stronger and stronger, farther and farther away from my life in New York. I even quit smoking cigarettes. I bought a writing pad and began writing short stories, while sitting in small cafés in out-of-the-way piazzas about Rome. I had books with me and I read for hours every day, thinking about my own book—it gestating inside me somewhere—remembering what an ex-girlfriend, Patricia, once told me—how her twin sister had killed herself because of demons that plagued her from her childhood. Their mother had prostituted the both of them, and Patricia's sister could not deal with the memories. There was an inherent dramatic arc about children being sexually abused. I knew if I could capture it honestly and present it in a simple, realistic setting, it would open people's eyes and be a hell of a compelling read. I thought, too, about Bad Bob the pedophile, the creep who abused me and tried to steal me away.

Mind you, this was in 1982, many years before the hue and cry of child sexual abuse sounded around the world. Even the Catholic Church, as it turned out, was a perverse hotbed of pedophilia. But back then, the sexual abuse of children was a never-discussed subject. I was sure that if I could capture the truth about that world, those happenings, and make it compelling and interesting, not me standing on some kind of soapbox, it would be a very good book. But how, I wondered?

In that I knew no one in Rome and my time was truly my own, I walked around the ancient city and learned its idiosyncrasies and appreciated it more and more. Thinking these thoughts, I jogged in the Villa Borghese for several hours early each morning. To keep my upper body strong, I took to running with five-pound dumbbells in each hand. After jogging, I would have breakfast, then go for long walks in different parts of the city, looking, watching, learning, writing short stories. Thus I learned Rome's many secrets. Like this, I made Rome my own. I was not a tourist staying at a hotel. I had become a part of Rome. What I enjoyed the most about Rome was sitting at small offbeat cafés I found around the city where you could order an espresso and sit to your heart's content, reading, thinking, watching people, writing a postcard or a book.

I had heard over and over again that short stories were good exercise, that if you could learn how to master a beginning, a middle, and an end within the context of a few pages, you had the basic rudiments of writing a book. I was learning how to cut away the fat, to write only about what matters. I wrote stories about running in the Villa Borghese, cocaine, robberies, women I saw walking down the block. It was an interesting enterprise done in a conducive setting, but what I was most interested in was the marathon race, not sprints. What I wanted was to write a book. Sitting here in different piazzas scattered about the city, it was easy to imagine Roman legions walking up and down these cobblestone streets, some in regimented marching form; others as civilians on their days off looking for a good meal, a good woman, a good time.

I had always been fascinated by ancient Rome, its war-like culture, its politics, its unique sexuality, how it had gone from the very summit of human accomplishment to an abysmal failure. The Romans did not just conquer other peoples and nations, but what they did that was so unique was welcome the conquered into the fold. Rome made the vanquished part and parcel of what Rome was—their success. The one thing that was uniquely Roman was the Coliseum, its brutality. For me, being in Rome was like a high. I planned to spend more time in the Coliseum and visit Circus Maximus, but I wasn't ready to rub shoulders with tourists quite yet, though I had books about these places and had read about them voraciously and looked forward to knowing them personally, to touching and feeling them and imagining what happened there.

My mind kept going back to what Gabriella had told me about brothels with children in Naples and other places.

I thought that if I did go to these places, with my guile and street cunning, I could find out things most journalists would be hard pressed to learn. I did not yet know about Tiberius and his sadistic obsession with children. A whole netherworld of information was slowly making its way toward me, or rather I toward it.

In any event, my friend Cindy finally called me back from Munich and invited me to come visit. I had heard Munich was an exceptionally beautiful city in Bavaria and I knew it was the home of the Nazi movement. I was curious to see the place and to understand it the way I understood Manhattan and now Rome. As it turned out, Munich was a well-built, quaint city with wide thoroughfares. Smack in the middle of the city was a huge park, the English Garden, which very much reminded me of Central Park and the Villa Borghese. By the time I arrived in Munich, Cindy had left to go to a shoot in Nuremberg.

I grew fond of a main thoroughfare called Leopoldstrasse. On it, there were many fine restaurants hailing from all over Europe—French and Spanish, Portuguese and Italian. I stayed at the Holiday Inn on Leopoldstrasse, and they had a large, extremely well equipped spa with an Olympic-sized pool and a sauna. Interestingly, the sauna was coed. That is, men and women took saunas together, all quite naked. It was just something the Germans did as a matter of course. There was nothing sexual about it. At first, I was a little surprised, pleasantly so, for some German women were attractive, but I grew to admire their open mentality toward nudity and sex. The Germans were far less judgmental than the Mediterranean, Catholic countries—Italy and Spain—I came to know. It seemed wherever the pope and the Catholic Church held sway, normal human sexuality was repressed. I mention this because it dovetails into what I had swimming in the back of my head somewhere . . . a book about child sexual abuse. On Leopoldstrasse, I found a bookstore with a large stock of English texts. They had a mystery section and I discovered, quite fortuitously, Raymond Chandler, Dashiell Hammett, and James Cain. Somehow I had never read these authors before and I was drawn to the hard-boiled characters they so realistically created and their amazingly simple prose. Suddenly, there was a spark in me that wasn't there before—the voice I would use to tell my story, when I figured out exactly what story to tell. Through the concierge at the hotel, I found a typist whom I hired to type up the short stories I had been writing in Rome and in Munich. I thought I should keep a record of them, even though I had written them only for myself. What they were, what I wanted to remind myself of, were these days when I was free as a bird in Europe, and of what my early writing was like. It seemed every time I sat down to write a short story I got better and better still, more comfortable with a blank page—my characters more vivid, the background more realistic. Of course I had no idea that, in years to come, I'd be walking into prisons and death rows all across America and sitting down with a colorful variety of killers, seeking the truth about what really made them tick.

As the weather grew colder and colder still that year—it was 1984—I resolved to learn how to ski and to ski in every good resort throughout Europe, all the while reading Chandler and Hammett and

Cain. I had a book bag filled with books that I was intent upon reading. I didn't watch television because it was all in German. I read constantly.

In Munich, I heard more rumors about rampant child sexual
abuse in Holland, in Amsterdam, but I wasn't quite ready to deal with
what I knew I would confront, write about. Winter was just around
the corner. Snow was falling in the Alps. I took a train from Munich
to Cortina d'Ampezzo, checked into Hotel della Posta in the middle
of town. The next day I took a few skiing lessons, and because I had
been a die-hard roller skater, I was soon on the steep slopes of Cortina,
speeding down difficult trails. Life was good. I was very pleased to be
away from New York. I felt like some kind of super human being who
was not skiing but rather flying in this most beautiful of places. On
my left there were pine forests, on my right, endless mountains covered in cake frosting—the mighty Dolomites. I had no idea the grim
reaper was on skis just behind me following me, following me. No
matter what mountain I skied down, no matter how fast I went, he
was there lurking, stalking me. Now as I sit here writing this, telling
Kelsey this, on the terrace facing the ocean, I'm so very glad I had
those days, that wonderful celebration of life, skiing in Cortina and
across Europe. No matter how sick I get, nothing can ever take that
away from me. It was like an investment that I am now getting divi-
dends on.

When I left Cortina, I skied Switzerland, Spain, Germany, Austria,
and France. At night, I ate fantastic meals in rustic French, Spanish,
Swiss, Austrian, and Italian restaurants and cafés. I drank wine with
every meal, always with a book, always reading.

Weeks turned into months and soon spring came knocking and I
was ready to write my book. But it wasn't just a matter of sitting
down and writing. It was a matter of research.

Toward that end, I finally was ready. I got on a plane to Amsterdam and I checked into the Victoria Hotel on Damrak, a main avenue
that cuts through the middle of Amsterdam, opposite the central station. As I left the hotel, intent upon learning the secrets of this place,
I stopped at a coffee shop for an espresso. To my delight, they not
only sold espresso but also sold all kinds of hash and cannabis over
the counter. I bought a few grams of some excellent Afghani hashish,
which I would check out later.

I left the coffee shop and began walking, thinking about my life—where I'd been and where I was going. My birthday was just around the corner. I was going to be thirty-three years old. Where had all the time gone . . . a thing I wasn't about to dwell on, though.

Amsterdam is a town made for walking. I had rubber-soled Reebok shoes on and I walked and walked and walked and little by little, piece by piece, a portrait of what was really happening here formed inside of my head. From a practical point of view, it wasn't that difficult. What I was intent upon writing about was everywhere you looked.

I made my way up and down streets in the red-light district where women were in windows selling themselves, selling any part you could want. You want the mouth, you got it. You want the pussy, you got it. You want the ass, you got that, too. None of this surprised or delighted me.

This, the obvious, the prostitution, had no real relevance to why I was here. I was here to learn about child sexual abuse and that, too, was just as prevalent as women in windows selling themselves. I didn't especially like prostitutes; in my mind, they represented the baser commercial aspects of human sexuality, but to each their own; whatever consenting adults did was their business, not mine.

But then came the revelation, shocking and disconcerting. There it was, plain as the nose on your face. As I made my way past a picturesque church, just next to it was a shop selling hard-core pornography, books and videos, and right in the window—to this day, I still can't believe it—there were open magazines featuring prepubescent children having sex with both adults and other children. I had a hard time believing my eyes, especially because there were two gray-uniformed Dutch policemen talking to each other, casually smoking cigarettes right next to the shop . . . some five feet away. I went inside and looked at the magazines. There were stacks of them. The more I looked, the more shocked I became, but most important, the more I learned.

Most unsettling of all was the fact that in the back of the magazines there were personal classified ads offering children for sale to adults for sex. Here are some of them taken verbatim from a magazine called *Lolita*:

GERMAN male, father, travels extensively, wishes to view sexually explicit films of young girls. Willing to pay for club memberships, etc. 624X

HANDSOME FATHER in late 30s with beautiful young daughters interested in meeting others interested in sex education. Discreet. 602T

WOULD like to correspond in English with parents of girls ages 5–10. Am interested in establishing long-term sexual liaison. 578T

HANDSOME Spanish man, 45 years of age, willing to pay $3000 to parents of pre-teen children who will pose and have at my estate in Spain. 487W

UNMARRIED woman in late 40s is looking for a partner who also loves having sex with young children. Wants a lasting relationship. Please send photo. 518L

AMERICAN male, early 30s, with young daughter willing to have sex with like-minded men. If interested in meeting us, write 614T.

PRETTY MOTHER with a 6-year-old daughter wishing to find unmarried man looking for a mate who loves young girls and their sexuality. Travel and relocation a possibility. Write 592L.

FRENCH male, 45, willing to pay top dollar to spend a week with your pre-teen daughter. Please include photo. 511X

AMERICAN gentleman with extensive film library of pre-teen girls would like to hear from anyone interested in viewing my rare collection. 638T

SUBMISSIVE pre-teen and her uncle seek meetings with older men. Please reply with detailed letter and photo to Box 670X.

40-YEAR-OLD Swedish man wishes contact with parents of daughter age 4–10. Will pay $3500. 401W

GOOD-LOOKING Canadian man in early 30s would like to have sex with Oriental pre-teen children. 600 X

Inevitably, I wondered what happened to these children. I wondered about their mindsets, their lives when they grew up. These thoughts, this curiosity would wind up leading me to the jails and prisons across the country where the outcasts of society dwell, where the baddest of the bad hang their hats. *Is it nurture or nature*, I wondered, *that makes sociopaths, psychopaths—remorseless killers?*

Disgusted, my head filled with these questions, I went back to my hotel, changed into running shorts and shoes, took a couple of hits of the hashish—it was very good—and headed for a long run. That first night I was in Amsterdam, I ran for nearly two hours straight, going up and down both scenic, well-lit canals and somber, dimly lit canals. While running, I studied this city, this modern Sodom, got to know it in a most unique way.

For the next two days, I went into every porno shop in Amsterdam's red-light district, and they all had these materials, no one giving a flying fuck about the content—not the store owners, not the police, not the least of which the people who were buying them. I could feel myself getting angry. I could feel myself wanting to set these places on fire, wanting to curse the people who sold these materials, wanting to say to the cops, "Are you fucking blind?" But I was not there to judge or moralize or point fingers or to be a cop. I was there to learn, and learn I did. I stayed in Amsterdam some three weeks and when I was ready to leave, I had more than I needed, for I had actually met the cretins, both men and women, who made these magazines and films, who were responsible for them, produced them, sold them—coveted them. I had also met the people who actually sold children, which is a book unto itself. Shockingly, these people, these miscreants, looked like everybody else. Some were in their early twenties; some were in their late fifties, early sixties, slick and well dressed, gray-haired and frumpy. One thing that they all had in common was an unapologetic lust for children. They spoke with gusto and without inhibition about having sex with children, proud of themselves. I had presented myself to them as a rich Texan, a man who wanted to buy a child, a man obsessed with children. I spoke with a ridiculous accent but I managed to fool everyone whom I dealt with. There was a bar on Prinsengracht, several blocks away from my hotel, that was the home base for people who were brokering children to pedophiles. The man who had initially told me about it warned me it could be "dangerous."

"You must be very careful," he had said. "They are paranoid. They are concerned with police. There was a father here some weeks ago looking for his daughter and he stabbed one of them to death. So you be careful."

I had mixed feelings about going to this place. I already had more than I needed. After all, this was not going to be a full factual account; it was going to be a novel based on the truths. But my curiosity got the better of me, and I walked over there, somewhat wary, carrying an eight-inch razor-sharp knife with me. Again, here is an incident where what I learned growing up in Bensonhurst came in handy. If need be, I knew I would have used a knife on one of these people in a heartbeat. I don't say this proudly or think of it as necessarily a good thing, or, for that matter, a bad thing. It just was. If I had to hurt somebody, I would do it in such a way where I had the upper hand, where I was not defending myself—I was striking first. I had no intention of getting into any kind of trouble in this place. My object was to get in, get this story, and get out. That's all I wanted. That's all I was concerned with. I didn't want to confront anyone, but if it came to that, I'd go for the throat—the jugular . . .

The bar was on the ground floor of a narrow two-story structure and had a tinted window facing the street. The second story was obviously empty. The bar was called Candlelight. I walked in and ordered a beer and I copped some hash and smoked it. I wanted to *blend*. After a while I offhandedly told the bartender what I was interested in. He pointed to a man in a corner. I sashayed over, introduced myself, and told him I wanted to buy a child. He reminded me of Jerry Garcia; he had short, stubby hands and sausage-like fingers. In front of him was a mound of tobacco that he was mixing heated hash with. The poignant, sweet smell of hash pleasantly hung in the air. It was the only pleasant thing about this place.

He asked specific questions about the kind of child I wanted—sex, age, coloring, and so on. His attitude was such that I felt like I was buying a car, that he was selling automobiles, not children.

"No problem," he said. "Sit down."

I sat. He offered me a Marlboro. I declined. I asked if he had any photographs.

"*Ja, ja,* sure. Where do you come from?" he asked.

"Texas," I said.

"Ah. I hear it's very big."

"Very big," I said.

"If you make an agreement with me, it will have to be guilders," he said.

"No problem," I said.

And with that he drew out a photo album and showed me pictures of naked girls. I picked out a blond. He said five thousand. We went back and forth. I agreed to pay him four thousand guilders. I was supposed to come back the following night and the girl would be there.

192 / PHILIP CARLO

When I left, I slowly walked all around the red-light district along the color-reflecting canals. The shops with girls in the windows were all closed now and the never-sleeping lights from these places played on the calm water. A shy dawn slowly began to light the Dutch sky. I walked back to my hotel. On the way back, I stopped and had a breakfast of ham and eggs. I was not yet sure whether I should actually go through with this. I began to think I was overextending myself. After all, I was alone and had no backup. I thought hard about going to the police but I was sure the police knew all about this already, were perhaps an intricate part of it—certainly weren't doing anything about it. I knew for a fact that the police were aware of it because children were boldly being sold in magazines, which were sold in public places. Here, with the Dutch authorities, it was a laissez-faire, do-as-you-wish attitude. With these thoughts playing in my head, I returned to my hotel, lay down, and fell asleep.

Later that day, I went to the bank and withdrew the money. I returned to Candlelight the following evening as instructed, ready to buy the girl and turn her over to the authorities. That was the right thing to do, I had decided. He wasn't there. I waited for two hours. He never showed up. I went back several times and no one knew anything about where he had gone. Every time I returned to this place, I got angrier.

Ultimately, one night, near three in the morning, the place somehow caught on fire. Screaming fire engines came to a stop in front of it. The following day, I was in a cab, heading out to Schiphol Airport, leaving Amsterdam behind me, but taking with me everything I saw and had learned.

I was a man possessed now. I had a story to tell. I knew something the world didn't know, or didn't seem to care at all about. When I arrived at Schiphol Airport, my intention was to return to Rome and begin my book, but I missed that flight and took the next flight out, which happened to be to Paris. With the French cabdriver's help, I found a lovely hotel called the Madeleine Princesse on the Rue de Cambon.

The following day I found a quiet café just off the Champs-Élysées. I had a blank pad with me and a merry-go-round of images circling inside my head. It didn't take me long to realize, however, that the story was not quite ready to come out of me. I could readily liken this whole process, the writing of a book, to gestation. There was the planting of the seed and the growing of the fetus. This book had not yet taken form inside of me. At this point, it was merely a seed. As I was dictating this to Kelsey, I had been back in Paris, the great-grand City of Light, the place where all the best artists of our time had gathered and put down on canvas and paper their thoughts and images and changed the way mankind looked at the world. Paris, unlike Rome, was filled with life and light. Paris was a celebration of life. As Papa put it—*Paris is a moveable feast.*

Now I am back at South Beach on the terrace. I look left. The sky is filled with large cottony clouds the color of gunpowder.

"I think it best if I end here and pick up tomorrow," I tell Kelsey. "I'm tired. The story will be moving to Spain."

21. Ibiza

Though I grew fond of Paris—its food, the wine, the Champs-Élysées, the Louvre, the Luxembourg Gardens, the beauty everywhere you looked—it was cold and I didn't want to be in a cold climate anymore. I had heard about a Spanish island called Ibiza—how user-friendly it was, how pretty on the eyes it was; that there was a writer's colony there, that many writers went there to pen books, enjoy its quiet solitude, its inherent scenic beauty, and, of course, the Spanish culture. Bullfighting, paella. I decided to leave Paris and move my act to Ibiza. I wanted to be where the sun was hot and welcoming and would embrace me, not be indifferent.

By the time I left Paris and arrived in Ibiza, it was the end of April and I was a year older. In that it was still the off-season there, most of the hotels were still closed. However, I found one open in San Antonio, a small, out-of-the-way town with a little piazza facing a calm, scenic harbor lined with palm trees and small cafés. The weather was much warmer here than it was in Paris. People smiled and were friendly and gracious. There is a radical difference between Mediterranean countries and peoples and those of Germany and northern Europe. I am Mediterranean—comfortable in Spain, France, and, of course, Italy. I felt at home. Instinctively, I knew this would be an ideal place to write, create. Everywhere you looked there were soft, rolling hills and mountains, the sea, lush palm trees. The country was dotted with white structures called *fincas*.

The first day on the beach, I was able to jog in shorts without a shirt. I ran ten miles, turning over in my head what I had seen and learned and come to know in Amsterdam.

When I got back to my hotel, I was in a hurry to get to work. I had a light breakfast, went to the small plaza, and found a little café with outdoor tables. The chairs all faced the harbor. It was amazingly scenic, tranquil . . . the perfect place for what I had in mind. I knew precisely what to do, how to structure the book, how to develop the characters and plot. It was clear in my mind's eye. My recent reading of Chandler and Hammett and Cain, plus voraciously reading what Hemingway had to say about writing, had armed me and prepared me well.

My intention was to write the first draft in under six weeks. Hemingway said if it takes longer than six weeks to write a first draft, you're dawdling; you're wasting time. I was intent upon writing all day, every day, seven days a week, no respites, no stops, no holidays.

Like this, at ease and comfortable, I began: on the first page, I wrote what I thought was an excellent title for the book, *Stolen Flower*, and, by using an ex-cop private detective, proceeded to tell the story of an eight-year-old girl abducted by pedophiles to be sold into white slavery. I told the story of not only her abduction but of the mindset of the people who did it, the culture and belief system that they were a part of, and I put down exactly what a parent feels when losing a child that way. This was heart-wrenching, hurtful material and I actually cried several times while writing. It was difficult not to. In other words, I constructed the story so it ran the full gamut of emotions, from A to Z, for both the victims and the predators. Each day, I went back to that same little café in that small, quiet, very lovely piazza with its palm trees and mosaic tiles and I wrote prodigiously; no matter what, I made sure I wrote ten pages a day. Some days it poured out of me. Some days I wrestled with it, I fought with it. It was like a big, toothy alligator. But no matter what, I got my ten pages done, and in six weeks I had finished the first draft. I believed in my heart of hearts I had something special here, original, something that had never been seen before. I had done what I had set out to do, I thought. I had no idea that I was opening Pandora's box, sounding a clarion that would be heard round the world.

There was no one there, though. No one there to share this with. No one to tell about it. It's interesting because I had become so used to the concept of being alone and writing that I accepted it as normal reality. I had no girlfriend, no wife, no friends. No one to turn to and say, "I finished my book today. Hey! I finished my book!"

But none of that mattered. For me, it was not about bouncing what I had done off anyone else. What I was doing was being a professional writer, lucky to be able to write in such a scenic place.

I grew to love Ibiza and, by extension, Spain. Every day after I worked, I went and had a glorious four-course meal and wonderful Spanish wine. When I walked into one of my regular restaurants, the waiters and the owners always smiled and welcomed me and hugged me because I loved to eat and they knew it. Not only did I love to eat but I ate with gusto. It was my gusto that made them all happy to serve me. And now, as I sit here in South Beach, a machine forcing air in and out of my lungs, my hands uselessly resting in my lap, I look back and I smile. It's an interesting smile because it has no outward manifestation. It's all inside—deep inside, a place the ALS can't touch. I never thought in my life I'd ever share this with anyone, but here I am blah blah blah, blah blah blah. I think my love for the written word has enabled me to fight the disease, contain it. Of course, that also has to do with me being comfortable with myself, in my own skin, and perhaps I found that innate comfort in Ibiza, Spain.

But the book was irrelevant unless I got it published. Unless somebody else picked it up, said, "Bravo," and wanted to publish it, it would remain my secret. What all writers since the beginning of time want more than anything is to be read.

So, back in Spain, I moved from San Antonio to Ibiza City. It was much livelier and there was an amazingly hip crowd that congregated in Ibiza City. There was an outdoor café called Mar y Sol where people met to make plans for the evening. The first day I sat down there, it was late in the afternoon and everywhere around me people were smoking hashish-laced cigarettes. Here, hashish was legal. This was great. I was home. I ordered a cappuccino and smoked a joint, crossed my legs, sat back, and watched the world go by. The sun here was very strong and by now I was extremely suntanned. I fit in. My first day in Ibiza City I met, of all people—considering what I had just written a book about—Roman Polanski. He was at a table just next to me and we started talking. I knew some people he knew. He was very nice, affable, but he had also run away from charges of child molestation. I knew the truth about what really had happened via a girlfriend of mine back in New York who had been in the house the night the alleged molestation took place. Having said that, suffice it to say here, it didn't involve a man. It involved an underage girl and a white German shepherd. I started hanging out with Polanski and his friends, going to dinner with them, going to clubs with them, and getting to know many people.

I began having too much fun. My objective was to do a rewrite of the first draft of *Stolen Flower*, but Ibiza was becoming distracting. I wondered about where I could go where I knew nobody, but was still beautiful to the eye. I decided to go to Mykonos, Greece. I had been there ten years earlier. I bought my ticket, said farewell to the many friends I'd made, and was soon gone. I would not return to Ibiza for several years, and when I did, I would have one of the greatest actors who ever lived by my side.

Now, back in South Beach, it suddenly starts raining cats and dogs. The wind blows so hard we are forced to stop working on the terrace. All this reaching deep inside myself is tiring, emotionally draining. Laura has showered and is getting dressed. We are going to grab a bite to eat. The rain suddenly stops outside but the wind continues unabated. When we leave the apartment, we cross the street and eat at a restaurant called Barolo. It is a small, intimate place. We know the owner, Malcolm, well. I say little. I am tired and somewhat worn out, but I know I'll be able to pick up strong tomorrow. The wind off the ocean blows hard, palm trees bend, and large, wet leaves crack like bullwhips. Here, in the tropics, rain comes and goes with the bat of an eye. Enjoying the tumultuous beauty of the wind and the storm brewing about us, we have our lunch. It has been a good day.

The following day is a Saturday. The rain clouds that harassed and chased us are gone. Again, the sky is a clear blue, the winds mild, the sea calm and friendly. Kelsey comes to work at eleven o'clock, carrying a strong espresso for me. After downing my coffee, the three of us go to the office. By now, we always call ahead to give everyone a chance to get ready to help me get on the beach, and ten minutes after we leave our apartment, I am sitting on the comfortable lounge with Kelsey next to me all ready to continue. Today the sun is very strong. It always seems to be so after a storm. The beach attendant asks if I want an umbrella and I say yes and he dutifully posts one in the sand. Kelsey turns on her Mac. Laura begins reading a magazine. It's hard for Laura. I have repeatedly told her not to interrupt me when I'm writing, not to talk to us. I take writing very seriously. I don't think she, or for that matter any lay person, can understand the basic tenets of what really motivates people to write books and how wrapped up they become in the writing. Books get written for one reason and one reason only, a burning desire to say something, fused with discipline. Whenever you look at someone who has a large body of work, you can safely say that person did without a lot of love. Love, children, wives, girlfriends, lovers are all distractions when you're trying to write a book. There really is a reason people go off in solitude, travel around the world to write books. I am blessed, for I am on a comfortable lounge on a beautiful beach in a safe haven. If it weren't for this sickness, the breathing apparatus, this ridiculous tube sticking out of my mouth, I'd be in Nirvana, I'm thinking, but not saying.

"Are you all right?" I ask Laura, feeling guilty for neglecting her, for what I'm doing . . . for what we are doing, Kelsey and I.

"I'm fine," she says.

"Do you want to go in the water?" I say.

"No," she says. I can't fathom why she doesn't like to go swimming in the beautiful sea right on our doorstep. If I were healthy, I'd be in the water half the day. To each his (or her) own, I guess. I stop looking at the water and start looking at Kelsey. She's ready, I can see it in her eyes, but she doesn't want to push me. Many times she has asked me if I'm ready and I tell her, "I'm thinking!"

But now, I say, "I'm ready."

I'm sure Kelsey's innate awareness of what I do comes about because she is a writer. She has the inherent sensibility of storytelling, cohesively stringing sentences together. Kelsey loves writing and she loves books, and whether or not it's conscious or unconscious, her affinity for books is helping me get from A to B to C.

Two tall, hot-looking women in their late twenties lie on towels just near us. Both of them are topless. I look for a moment or two but I've become so used to seeing attractive topless women on the beach that it's irrelevant. It doesn't distract me.

I am ready to start a new chapter. I call it "Pandora's Box."

22. Pandora's Box

Whenever I sit down with Kelsey, I remember that right before we went to Italy, we were on this beach. I begin the process of clearing my head and writing with her. Just as I am about to start, my cell phone rings. It is my friend, Steve Byer. Steve has discovered a team of doctors in Monterrey, Mexico, who, unhampered by George Bush's restriction on stem cell research, have perfected a way to inject stem cells into the brain and help people with motor neuron diseases . . . people with ALS. Steve wants to make me part of a group going down to Mexico soon. I resist this. I feel uncomfortable about Mexican doctors drilling holes in my head and sticking needles into my brain. I trust Steve, but his enthusiasm seems to be running ahead of logical thinking. I tell him for the fifth or sixth time that I want to see the results of the first group having the procedure. He writes my request up as a big waste of time, but I don't. When I consult Dr. Ray Onders, he feels it is a very taxing trip with little guarantee of success. Steve is stubborn, and the more he insists, the more I back off. I put him on the phone with Laura. He wants to argue the pros and cons, and I don't argue. I'm too sick to argue and debate with anybody about anything. This disease is helped along by strife; chaos is its best friend. Again, I look around at the beautiful setting and I am pleased, pleased that we can be here, pleased that I can enjoy the outdoor splendor and continue to work, while being so sick. As bad as it is for me, I know with ALS it could be far worse. As Laura talks to Steve, I turn my attention back to Kelsey, this book. I say, "Where . . . where to begin?"

"You were starting a new chapter called 'Pandora's Box.'"

"Right. I've got it."

I had no idea I was opening Pandora's box with *Stolen Flower.*

Initially, it was difficult to get *Stolen Flower* published. Editors told my agent that nobody wanted to read about child sexual abuse. However, E. P. Dutton ultimately bought the book. For the first time, I made money, good, substantial money, by writing—a milestone. A wonderful high. Finally, I came to believe that my wanting to write was not a futile effort. Because the book brutally addressed the truth about what motivated pedophiles and what they did, the news media came knocking on my door, and I ended up getting an inordinate amount of press and ultimately appeared on many television shows. I had no kind of training in public speaking, but I knew what I was talking about and was passionate and angry and I would never allow anybody to shut me up, and soon I was appearing on all the important news programs, and I did a full hour on the *Phil Donahue Show*. Back then, the *Donahue* show was watched all around the world by many millions of people. In a sense, you could say it was a precursor to the *Oprah Winfrey Show*. Doing the *Donahue* show was a turning point because I not only held my own but I brought a hard-core, undeniable truth to the forefront—how rampant child sexual abuse was around the world. I told about *Lolita* magazine; I talked about classified ads offering children for sale. The audience was shocked and horrified but the truth was out.

To a degree, because of *Stolen Flower*, because of what I was saying on all these different news shows, a debate began about how society, the police, the school system, parents were all miserably failing our children. Ultimately, *Stolen Flower* had a domino effect. I did one show and the producer of another show would see me and invite me on that show. It got so that I was so distracted by doing these news shows that I wasn't writing. Though I was passionate about what I had written in *Stolen Flower*, it was never my intention to become a spokesperson for sexually abused children. My job, what I was good at, the fire I had burning inside me, was about writing—researching the darker sides of human nature, finding out all the dirty secrets and weaving them into compelling stories.

I was invited to speak at symposiums on child sexual abuse in Switzerland and England. I also lectured at the New York Police Academy and various law enforcement entities around the world, telling INTERPOL, Scotland Yard, the Manchester Police what I had learned. There was also another interesting turn of events. Again, long story short, through a mutual friend of mine, Sandy Beale, I gave Joe Pesci a copy of *Stolen Flower*. Everyone who read the book told me it would make a great movie. Joe read it, saw the tremendous film potential of the story, and, without my knowing it, he gave his copy to Robert De Niro. This occurred on a Friday. Monday Joe called and said he wanted to have lunch with me to talk about the book being taken to the big screen. No matter how you cut it, *Stolen Flower* being made into a major motion picture would be a monumental event. My book would be read by thirty, forty thousand people, scant little compared to the millions of people who would see it if it became a film. I had come to know Joe Pesci through a very popular late-night hangout/restaurant on New York's Upper West Side called Café Central.

They served dinner until two o'clock in the morning. In those days, a lifetime before I was stalked by the grim reaper, I went roller-skating every night and because you could not enjoy the sport on a full stomach, I was forced to have late-night meals. My skates slung over my shoulder, I began going to Café Central for dinner. As it turned out, Café Central could readily be likened to a popular Left Bank café during the expatriate years in Paris. There was an amazing abundance of burgeoning talent hanging out at the place, well worth my mentioning them here. Bruce Willis was the bartender; Bobby De Niro, Joe Pesci, John Ford Noonan, John Savage, Danny Aiello, Paul Sorvino, Peter Weller, Peter Riegert, John Heard, John Goodman, Bruce McGill, Chris Walken, Harvey Keitel, Bill Hurt, Paul Herman, Sean Penn, Eric Roberts and his very young sister, Julia Roberts, Debra Winger, Cher, Ellen Barkin, Elizabeth and Lorraine Bracco were all regulars. It was an inspiring place to be. There were electric sparks in the air. All anyone ever talked about here, passionately, was writing and acting. It was about this time that I committed myself to the enterprise of writing. I read all day and wrote short stories at night. Because of Café Central, I became less reclusive and, inadvertently, plugged into an underground, artistic subculture that drove me and motivated me. Café Central was New York at its best. Whereas before, I was thinking about how to commit crime, now I was thinking about how to effectively write about crime. Here, too, during this time, I became aware of how important it is to do research, ask questions; how important it is to know a subject backward and forward before even thinking about picking up a pen.

Back to Joe Pesci . . . we met for lunch that Monday and Pesci was very cagey. He said that "a very good friend" of his had read the book and really liked it. I knew it was either Al Pacino or Robert De Niro. Pesci kept talking about how important this person was, how the whole industry revered him.

"Who is it?" I asked.

"Well, we'll get to that, but the point is, we want to option it."

"Okay, great. Who is this person?"

"Well, like I said, it's a little early. What we're going to do is have our lawyer call you and make a deal and you'll be happy. Mark my words, you'll be happy."

I was pleased that this person really liked my book, but I was a little miffed by the fact that Pesci was being so secretive, mysterious. It wasn't necessary. In any event, Joe and I finished lunch and I went home. Joe's girlfriend, Sandy, happened to be an ex-girlfriend of mine, a very good friend. I called her and soon found out that the mystery person was Robert De Niro. With this, I wanted to jump up and do a jig, but I remained calm and cool and steady. I knew I had to keep my wits about me. Sure enough, their attorney called me later that afternoon. His name was Jay Julien. He had a reputation as being a very wily, hard guy. He represented a stable of A-list actors including Christopher Walken, De Niro, Peter Falk, John Cassavetes, Ben Gazzara, to name a few. He asked me what I wanted. I told him the figure I had in mind. It was a lot but I felt no amount of money was worth what I had done. Mind you, I didn't write *Stolen Flower* as a commercial enterprise as such. I wrote it because I saw what was being lied about, denied, swept under the rug, all of which needed to be dragged out into sunlight, kicking and screaming. By the same token, I had invested blood, sweat, and tears in this, and I wanted to be compensated appropriately. There were other books I wanted to write, other stories that needed to be told, and none of that would happen unless I could underwrite myself, my travel, in order to interview people in the know all over the place. He thought the number I named was . . . funny, for he laughed. I asked what was so funny.

He said, "This book is not a bestseller, has not even been reviewed yet, and you're asking for this kind of money?"

I said, "I'm offended by the fact that you think this is funny. Listen to me, Jay: I put my life on the line to write this book," I said. "I lived on the road for a year."

I was mad. I hung up on him. This is exactly why people shouldn't represent themselves. I had a book agent, Max Becker, but he was in semi-retirement and I didn't think he was up to dealing with the likes of Jay Julien, a bona fide barracuda. My getting emotionally involved, my getting angry, was a mistake. In order to negotiate wisely, you have to stand back and be impartial. Still, I was passionate about this book, what I had done, and I would have gotten angry at anybody who didn't respect my work. In any event, within minutes Joe Pesci called me up and asked me what was wrong.

"Your lawyer insulted me," I said.

"He didn't mean to insult you! He didn't mean to insult you!" Joe said.

"Well, he did," I said.

"Calm down."

"Okay, I'm calm," I said.

"Let's you and me meet again," Joe said. We made plans to meet the following day.

That evening, I went to dinner at Columbus Restaurant, which was on 69th and Columbus Avenue, the new hot spot; by now Café Central had closed. It was here I had had a book party for *Stolen Flower*. It was also here that I had met Mike Tyson before he became heavyweight champion of the world. Mike's shoulders were as wide as the door and he was young and innocent and wide-eyed—a very nice guy. It was obvious that he would eventually become a legend. Tonight, I was meeting a dear friend, Paul Herman. Paul Herman was one of the owners. He was also an accomplished actor. He, too, had worked at Café Central. His job was to bring in celebrities and he did that very well. He was a nice-looking, affable man with blue eyes and a pleasant way about him.

A week earlier, I had run into Tommy Mottola here, who would later marry Mariah Carey and become the president of Sony Records. The night he had been with Daryl Hall, the tall, blond half of Hall and Oates. I was friendly with both Tommy and Daryl and so they had invited me to their table. I had run into Daryl while I was living in Europe, specifically in Munich. Hall and Oates were doing a concert there. I had gone to see the concert and afterward went out with the band for dinner. I told Daryl about *Stolen Flower*. "Sounds interesting," he had said.

Back in New York, the evening I had run into Daryl and Tommy at Columbus, Daryl had asked what had happened with "the book you were writing." I explained that I had finished it, it had been published, and I would send him a copy, which I did the following day, via Tommy's office.

When, a week later, I walked into the restaurant to meet Paul, Daryl was there. When he saw me, he rushed over to me and said that he had read *Stolen Flower*, that it was a great book and that he thought it would make a wonderful film. He was very effusive in his praise. This was something I was not used to. All I had ever received were rejections for my literary efforts. I liked praise a lot better. This had nothing to do with ego; it had to do with vindication; it had to do with the fact that others saw the world the way I saw the world, understood and felt not only what I had to say, but, more important, what I was laying down about the world of child sexual abuse. I sat down with Daryl and Tommy and to my surprise, Tommy Mottola said he wanted to make it into a movie.

"You know it's funny," I said. "I just recently heard from Joe Pesci." And I explained to Tommy what had happened with Joe and Jay Julien. Tommy had the very sharp business sense to know immediately that it was De Niro who was behind this and he said he had wanted to do something with Bob for a really long time. The very next day, he had a contract drawn up by super agent Mike Ovitz, the founder of CAA, and I got everything I asked for and more. Of course, Pesci got back to me, and I told him, "Joe, I'm sorry but I optioned it to someone else." He was not pleased.

As soon as we signed the contracts, Mottola called De Niro, told him he had the rights to my book, and they quickly made an agreement that Tommy would produce it with Bob and Joe and Bob would star in it and direct it, his directorial debut. When I heard this, I was flattered—vindicated. The world would know about what was really happening to children, how severely they were being used and abused. This not only made me feel good in that immediate moment, but gave me a confidence, a confidence I would end up using throughout my career, indeed, throughout my sickness, that would enable me to march into prisons, knowing exactly what I was looking for, knowing exactly what I needed to breathe life and electric energy into stories. *Stolen Flower* became like a booster rocket for my sensibility as a writer.

The following day, I had the pleasure of meeting Robert De Niro. At this point in his career, he had won two Academy Awards, one for *Raging Bull*, one for *Taxi Driver*, and here I was sitting next to him and he was asking me questions, curious, concerned, interested. I was humble . . . flattered. He wanted to know how I wrote *Stolen Flower*, why I wrote *Stolen Flower*. He also wanted to know how much of it was true. I answered him as candidly as I would my own doctor. He told me he wanted to go to Europe and see every locale the story played out in.

"Fine, no problem," I said.

Several days later, De Niro and I were in the first-class section of a jumbo 747, speeding toward Rome. Over a three-week period, we visited all the cities where *Stolen Flower* took place: Rome, Naples, Hamburg and Munich, Ibiza and, of course, Amsterdam. We were together day and night. He had a lot of questions. He was unusually perceptive. I started asking him questions so I could give him what he needed on a larger scale, more insightfully. It was always about the truth—he was obsessed with the truth, learning it and portraying it. It was funny, because my own sensibilities told me that it was what really mattered in good writing—the truth. We became friends. It was a privilege getting to know him. To this day, I hold him in high esteem. When he and I went to Ibiza, we stayed in Ibiza City but we did go to San Antonio, the place where I wrote *Stolen Flower*. The plaza, as usual, was sleepy and quiet. De Niro and I sat at the table where I usually had sat some two and a half years earlier, writing *Stolen Flower*. One of the waiters I knew well came over and greeted me with a hug and a kiss. I introduced him to De Niro. Bob had a full beard and his hair was in a ponytail. He had just finished a movie called *The Mission*, an eighteenth-century drama. Though he was hard to recognize, the waiter's eyes widened when he realized Señor Robert De Niro was sitting at his café. I explained to Bob how I had come to this café every day for some six weeks and wrote the book. For me, at this point, it was no big deal, but he was interested. I think, in retrospect, as I write this now, I realize that De Niro's curiosity is exactly what makes him such a great actor. Our cappuccinos were served. Quietly, we sipped the coffee and enjoyed the solitude of this lovely Spanish plaza. Just beyond the plaza was the San Antonio harbor. The water was calm and small fishing boats gently moved to and fro with the current. Seagulls with large wingspans swooped and dove. Bob had a copy of *Stolen Flower* in his hand. He turned to me and said, "You know what it is . . . you know what it is about your writing that got me?"

"No," I said, "what?"

He said, "You write from here," pointing to his heart.

"Why thank you, Bob. I appreciate that," I said. Those words, coming from him, meant an awful lot to me.

We sat there for a while, and I told him more and more about what I had seen and learned while researching *Stolen Flower*. It was I who had burnt down the Candlelight bar in Amsterdam, which I had never admitted to anyone, though I told him what I had done. He didn't say anything one way or another. A pleasant breeze blew off the harbor. The large leaves of the Spanish palm trees that lined the plaza moved as though they were fanning us. As we headed back to Ibiza City, I wondered about my next book. *What the hell can I write to top this*, I thought, knowing that sooner or later it would come to me— perhaps in the form of a newspaper article, a magazine piece, even something I'd see on television. I would be patient. I would wait. I would read between the lines. Often the truth about a story is not what's said or shown; the truth is hidden, often between the lines. This I knew to be a fact.

When I began writing this book, I wasn't going to mention De Niro or my trip throughout Europe with him, but as I have worked on the story I realized that it is important and should be told. For me, this has been like sharing a secret. It is almost as though I have been talking to myself and Kelsey has been typing. Though I want to stick to what the story is about—killers and my having a fatal disease— what I learned in Amsterdam and my trip with De Niro played a large part in my ultimately dedicating myself to writing.

"Water! Ice-cold water!" shouts the black man who passes the Savoy beach every day carrying a dripping wet bag filled with bottles of water and ice.

I buy three bottles of cold water from our friend, who is always smiling, has no teeth, no home, no life, yet is always smiling. Go figure.

I look up and Laura's sister, Karen, and her cousins Ari and Tatum have joined us. I have an appointment with Virginia for a massage on the beach. I have been very lucky to find such a good masseuse. She knows human bodies very well and Virginia can see, I think better than anyone else, the devastating effect ALS has had on my muscles. Virginia soon shows up and begins working on my legs. Careful muscle manipulation and a happy ending are very important to people with ALS—just kidding. Now, whether I like it or not, because of Laura's cousins and Virginia, my work for the day is finished. We order piña coladas and mojitos. I never drink alcohol while I'm working. Just to my right the sun has begun its descent. I ask the beach attendant to take away my umbrella. The late afternoon sun is not as hot and a cool breeze is coming off the ocean. As I look around me, at all these beautiful women I am surrounded by, drinking my piña colada, I am thinking I'm a lucky guy. My eyes slowly close and I soon doze off, as Virginia works on my legs, as Laura is chatting away with her cousins, as the world slowly goes by without me.

23. The Big Itch

Something that drives me absolutely nuts is having an itch on the top of my head, my face, my ears and not being able to reach and scratch it. That is a fucking curse.

"Laura! Can you *please* come scratch my head!"

Can you imagine?

The ultimate insult I've suffered from this stupid disease is the loss of my hands—more relevantly, the lack of ability to pick up a pen and write. Of course, brushing my teeth and eating are necessary vitals, but the conduit between my brain and my hands is no more. The hands that I used to write with are no more. Because the loss of them has been so gradual, a little bit each day, I didn't realize how the disease was slowly stealing away my hands—insidiously.

Also, insects. When I'm sitting and a bug lands on me, I can't swat it. I can't even shoo it and it really upsets me. The other day there was this giant fly boldly walking up and down my arm and I could do nothing. By the time Laura got it, it had abused me and probably crapped all over my damn arm. I think I'm going to start carrying around one of those bamboo scratchers they sell in Chinatown, I tell Laura, but then I realize I wouldn't be able to hold it.

Another thing that upsets me to no end is having to go to the bathroom. As I have mentioned, ALS has weakened the muscles that control the bladder and also has weakened the sphincter muscles and there I am, on the beach, working hard in the office, and I gotta take a leak but I can't. However, it's very necessary to always be ingenious when you have this fuckin' disease and what we do is bring urinals down to the beach and Laura hides them between my legs and covers them with a towel and, if we're careful, we're not discovered. But I feel like a child, like I need diapers or something, and it chips away at me as a person, as a man. I won't go any further here about bodily functions.

It's time to leave the beach. We talk about having a snack and we are soon making our way over to the News Café. I know I've said it, but I really enjoy being in South Beach. Here it is, the middle of the winter, yet the temperature is near eighty degrees and all I am wearing are shorts and a strap T-shirt. As I look around, I can't help but again marvel at the striking deco buildings painted in fabulous pastel colors. I am at home here. I especially like the News Café. It's got such a variety of people and we can sit there undisturbed and eat and drink and watch the scantily clad world of South Beach move all around us. I think more than anywhere in the United States, Miami, South Beach, has the largest collection of peoples from different places, mostly Europeans and Canadians, few Asians. As we make our way up Ocean Drive to the News Café, quiet and introspective, Kelsey is walking next to my wheelchair. Laura, her sister and their two cousins are a few steps behind us, chatting away. I must admit, I enjoy being around attractive women and Kelsey, Laura, Karen, Tatum, and Ariel are eye candy.

"By the way," Kelsey says, "what happened with *Stolen Flower* and De Niro, if you don't mind my asking?"

"I don't mind. I tell you everything, silly. It's a rather long story, but to make it short, after De Niro and I got back from Europe, he asked me to write a script, which I did. Both he and Pesci proceeded to rewrite it and Bob wasn't happy with that either. The project ended up on the back burner; Bob got involved in other things and . . . unfortunately, it's still languishing on the back burner," I say, not pleased.

"Bummer."

"Tell me about it. I think that what first drew him to the subject— how truly taboo it was—ultimately pushed him away. He wound up making *A Bronx Tale* his directorial debut. I think he was ultimately more comfortable with the Mafia genre. But who knows? Maybe someday, he will make it. It ain't over 'til the fat lady stops singing."

We move on in silence for another block. Kelsey's questions have got me thinking about *Stolen Flower*. As we wait for traffic to clear so we can cross the street, I say, "Still, I think it's a crying shame *Stolen Flower* did not make it to the big screen because it would have been the first time society would have been exposed to the scale on which children are being sexually abused around the world."

I'm always wary when crossing the street. If a speeding car comes, I do not have the ability to move swiftly, and I'm apprehensive, though Kelsey always stays close to me and makes sure no cars are coming. As we now cross the street, we pass a circle of fresh blood near the curb. I wonder where the blood came from. I start thinking of Richard Ramirez, the Night Stalker—the voluminous amount of blood he caused to stain homes all over L.A. County. I also remember photographs of Ramirez as a young boy, at ages five, seven, and nine. He was an unusually attractive, wide-eyed child, as innocent as the day is long. For the hundredth time, I again wonder how an innocent child can turn into a monster. To try to find an answer to that question, I remember well how I began writing letters to the infamous who lived in prisons across the country, looking for the links between how an abused child becomes an abuser. One of the killers I wrote to was Ramirez. He responded to my letter and I wound up writing a book about his case, which took me three years, far longer than I thought it would. Though it was a very difficult and painful book to write, detailing the gruesome murders of the elderly, the brutal raping of multiple women, it became an important book, for it shed an incandescent light on the murky world of serial murder. While we move closer to the café, I look right and can see between the dunes that line the beach. I am just about able to see my old, dear friend—the Atlantic Ocean. Seeing the ocean, seeing the Atlantic, takes my mind away from murder.

When we reach the News Café, we get a large, round table, place our orders, and have a pleasant late lunch, though I'm really not that hungry. All I have is guacamole and chips. The café is crowded. All around us there are many different languages being spoken at the same time. I am kind of quiet, drained from writing all day. While the girls talk, I enjoy people watching, particularly female people watching. When we finish, I pay the check and Laura and I say good-bye to the girls and make our way home. Gray clouds suddenly rush in from the sea. The air abruptly becomes cooler. Strong winds rustle the palm trees. Near Fifth Street, we pass a *New York Times* kiosk. Laura buys me a copy and places it on my lap. The wind is so strong now, I have to hold the paper down with my hand. At this point, my hands are in such a sorry state that I can no longer, as I said, hold up the *Times* and read it, but as we move along, I note a story on the front page about the rampant sexual abuse of children in the Catholic Church—specifically Boston—that captures my attention. I read the first few lines, look away from the article, and now somehow all the vibrant colors of South Beach become flat and muted.

I shake my head in disgust, thinking about *Predators and Prayers*, the book I wrote about sexual abuse within the Catholic Church, which delved into the terrible specter of men dressed as priests sexually abusing children while threatening them with God, Hell, damnation. Of all the criminal behavior I have studied, read about, researched thoroughly, and written about, nothing is more heinous than pedophiles dressed as priests sexually abusing prepubescent children. Because of my writing *Stolen Flower*, I wound up learning the truth about how pedophiles were infiltrating the Catholic Church. In 1993, a play I wrote called *Swear on God You Won't Tell* was staged on Manhattan's Theater Row on West 42nd Street. This play was a result of all my interactions with child advocates and people involved in fighting child sexual abuse. I learned that it had never been about good-priest-gone-bad, as many think. What it was really about was dedicated pedophiles becoming priests because they knew they'd have access to trusting children; knew, too, that children, in their hands, would be very pliant. They also knew the church would protect them either by legal counsel or by moving them from one parish to another—hiding them. I think of the case of John Geoghan, a priest who had, shockingly, been moved to thirty-two different parishes. Every time he was accused of abuse at one parish, he was moved to another, never stripped of his collar, never arrested. I only hope that all the priests who are abusers are put in general populations of prisons and the inmates mete out justice. Geoghan was eventually arrested and convicted of molestation and placed in Illinois State Prison. A fellow prisoner got Geoghan alone in a cell, stuffed a rolled-up pair of socks in his mouth, and proceeded to beat him to death. I remember when I first heard about this, I wrote the prisoner a letter. I am not going to divulge what I wrote here for no doubt it will make many people angry. Suffice it to say, I felt justice had been served.

When I was ready to write about the rampant pedophilia in the Church, I moved back to Rome, wanting to be near the Vatican while I penned the story. I took an apartment two blocks from the Vatican. Every day I worked on *Predators and Prayers* and jogged in the Villa Borghese, having no idea that my strong, sturdy muscles would one day slowly leave me. I couldn't help but become incensed when I saw priests, bishops, and cardinals marching about Rome as though they were something special, disciples of God, when I knew many of them were sexual deviants cloaked as religious men. On the one hand, I again very much enjoyed Rome, the food, the pace of life, and the like. But the grave injustice of what the Vatican was allowing to happen appalled me to the point of distraction. I tried to see the Pope but that didn't pan out.

Initially, my agent, Matt Bialer, was not able to find a home for *Predators*. Eventually, however, we did find one, with Leisure Publishing. Publishers—who often have their heads in the ground like ostriches—did not get that I was an honest, compelling voice telling the truth about things people apparently did not want to hear, but impartial reviewers got what I was doing and the book received some exceedingly perceptive critiques. For example:

> There are some books that grab your attention from the first word. Such is the case with this outstanding work, Predators & Prayers. . . . As details are revealed you want to laugh, you want to cry and your emotions spiral within you.
>
> I really can't say enough good things about this work. Philip Carlo brings out a hidden truth of sexual abuse that plagues the very institution that should be a haven of safety, the Catholic church. Yet, understand this, he makes it plain that it is not the belief in God, nor the soundness of such a belief that is to fault, but the concept that predators always find openings to feed upon their prey. He opens our eyes to a problem that is sweeping our country, infiltrating many sacred institutions and touching those who cannot defend themselves.
>
> This read is one of pain, revenge, love, hate, forgiveness and frank honesty that you will never forget. This is a must read that you will not be able to put down. Highly, highly recommended.
>
> — Shirley Johnson, Senior Reviewer, *Midwest Book Review*

I subsequently did talk shows and news shows and over 150 radio shows and on each one, I told the uncensored, brutal truth about what I had learned; how the Catholic Church became an underground cadre of pedophiles. Often, so-called good Catholics would call up the station I was on and berate me and this only made me angrier because I was telling it like it was. For some unfathomable reason, one could readily count on one hand the number of priests who had been prosecuted. Police and prosecutors regularly and consistently—sinfully—gave the Church a pass, looked the other way.

The name of this work is *The Killer Within*. Writing about degenerate priests here now might seem a deviation from that premise—my having ALS. However, what these pedophiles dressed as priests were doing was creating a long list of serious psychological problems for those they abused—their victims. Drug abuse, alcoholism, marital problems, sexual deviance, antisocial behavior, suicide, and irrational violence all stemmed from what had been done to the many thousands of individuals who had been victimized by priests not only in America but around the world. Ireland, Germany, and Norway are all hotbeds of child sexual abuse done by priests. Just recently, a bishop in Norway, Georg Mueller, resigned after admitting he had sexually abused children, that he was a pedophile. In response to the worldwide uproar of child sexual abuse within the Church, Pope Benedict said, "Now, under attack from the world which talks to us of our sins, we can see that being able to do penance is a grace and we see how necessary it is to do penance and thus recognize what is wrong in our lives."

What temerity, what unmitigated gall—what f . . . bullshit. His child-abusing brethren should be arrested, prosecuted, and sent to jail like any rapist, yet he's talking about penance as if it's some magical cure-all, justice served. Absolutely criminal. The Pope more recently referred to pedophile priests as "stray priests." Please, give me a break. These are not stray priests. Nobody becomes a pedophile after having a clerical collar put on his neck. They are surely pedophiles way before that. Referring to these pedophiles as "stray priests" is a con job, subterfuge. As Abraham Lincoln said, "You can fool some of the people all of the time, and all of the people some of the time, but you cannot fool all of the people all of the time."

In a very real sense, these molesters dressed as priests are true wolves in sheep's clothing and they eat up and spit out the hearts and minds and souls of the innocents they molest. Now that I think of it, slowly moving down Ocean Drive with Laura, the wind blowing, warm raindrops beginning to wet my face, I am proud to have written *Predators* for I feel it is what people in the arts should do—expose the unspeakable injustices man perpetrates on man. Picasso's *Guernica* comes to mind; Hemingway's *Farewell to Arms*; Steinbeck's *Grapes of Wrath*. Though many filmmakers over the years have done exactly what I'm saying, not enough of them have gone out on a limb and exposed the iniquities rampant around the world. Yes, films and books should be entertaining, amusing, a way to escape the mundane, but that does not mean they cannot be expository and informative at the same time.

Now, as we approach our building, I fleetingly wonder: Is the reason I got sick because I attacked the Church? Could I have, in some way, crossed the line, offended God? Ultimately, I decide that this is impossible because all I did was tell the truth and if any God would try to stifle someone trying to expose the abuse of children, it would surely be the devil, not Jesus Christ or, for that matter, Allah or Buddha or whomever. It couldn't be. I remember a quote from the Bible regarding child molesters: "It were better for him that a millstone were hanged about his neck, and he cast into the sea, than that he should offend one of these little ones," said Jesus Christ in the book of Matthew, chapter 18, verse 6. I couldn't agree more, amused by the things that pop into my head, often for no rhyme or reason.

I have an itch in a private spot and I cannot get to it—scratch it. *My goodness*, I think, *this ALS is a fucking curse.* I do not like thinking these dark thoughts in this beautiful place of light, palm trees, the ocean, gay art-deco colors, but I am not about to turn away from the reality of these things because they're distasteful. I slow for Laura to catch up to me. The question of nurture versus nature. That is, are people born bad or is it learned behavior? After interviewing all the criminals and serial killers I've worked with, I've come to the conclusion that it is surely a combination of the two. It's like minestrone soup, a matter of many different ingredients in a pot stewing on the stove on low heat and it bubbles and simmers and bubbles and simmers and in the end you have an individual with no conscience, no scruples, and no morals. If you repeatedly abuse any creature in nature during its formative years, as soon as that creature has teeth, it will bite. Take a puppy and tie it to a tree and whip it every day; when that puppy grows up, you better run. It's like that with human beings. Abuse a child over and over, hurt it over and over, and when that child becomes an adult, it's going to do what was done to it, for sure. There are, of course, exceptions to this rule, but for the most part the abused tend to become abusers. It's a simple equation.

We arrive at the building. Laura opens the door for me. I carefully guide my wheelchair inside just as a torrential rain falls and thunder and lightning rip apart the South Beach skies. Laura checks our mailbox and there is a film from Netflix—Mel Gibson's *Apocalypto*.

"Great," I say. "I've been wanting to see that."

Silently, we go upstairs in the elevator. Inside our apartment, Laura puts on the film for me. I'm excited. I so very much enjoy watching good films.

"Would you like some popcorn?" Laura offers.

"For sure."

The film starts. As I watch *Apocalypto*, Laura feeds me Newman's Own popcorn. I have the best of all worlds: a good movie, thunder and lightning outside, and popcorn.

24. IPLEX—Not

Soon after breakfast, Laura injects me with another dose of IPLEX directly into my stomach. I've been taking the drug now for some eight months. I'm noticing that my speech is getting somewhat stronger. Sometimes, actually most of the time, it had been weak, but lately it seems more . . . robust. I wonder if it's the IPLEX. I ask Laura her thoughts; she thinks it is the drug. She's optimistic; I'm skeptical. I can't afford to be let down. Yet hope, I know, is an essential part of getting through every day; hope is the foundation of why and how I can work without distraction, every day.

Kelsey shows up carrying my double espresso to get my creative juices going. Soon the three of us head down to the office, me in my wheelchair, Laura and Kelsey in bikinis. It's a gorgeous day, no clouds, no wind, though perhaps a little too hot. If it went to one hundred degrees, I wouldn't care—if I were only able to go in the water. All through my childhood, my mother took my sister and me to Coney Island's Sea Gate. I was in the water all day, every day, throughout the summer. I grew to love the ocean. Now all I can do is sit and stare at my old, dear friend. We begin working. After an hour or so, we have more iced coffee. Kelsey goes for a swim. I miss Sergio coming over and telling me the latest gossip on the beach. Kelsey returns refreshed. We resume working. For some reason, while we are in the office, on the beach, time goes by unusually fast.

Sultry, tropical days turn into weeks, which turn into months. Without fanfare, spring arrives. We know the weather in New York is changing, beckoning us back home. We've so very much enjoyed being here in South Beach, the outdoor cafés, the perfect weather, the gorgeous beaches, but we have responsibilities in New York, and as long as the weather is warm in New York, I have no problem living there. Indeed, I very much enjoy the Upper West Side. With my motorized wheelchair I get around well and we are close to Zabar's and Citarella and all kinds of outdoor restaurants. In that summer is just around the corner, the weather here in Miami is getting prohibitively hot, and with the higher temperatures comes unpleasant humidity.

When I first met Laura, she was driving an Audi SUV. The step up into the car was high off the ground, but back then, by using my hands, I was able to lift myself into the car okay. As time went by, however, that became harder and harder, to the point where Laura actually had to help lift me into the car. Here again was one of those small, subtle changes that on the surface doesn't seem to mean much, but was indicating that my muscles were weakening further still. It got to the point where it was so hard for Laura to get me in and out of the car that we weren't using it much at all. On several occasions, however, we had places to go and had to use the Audi and it became . . . dangerous for me. As an example, one incident sticks in my mind. My friend Tony Danza came down to visit me. Tony and I have known each other a long time and we are tight. He is a good, loving friend. As a young man, he was a professional boxer, was discovered in the ring, and ended up starring in two very popular television series—*Taxi* and *Who's the Boss?* When I was healthy, Tony and I regularly skated in Central Park and we also ran a lot together, jogged around the Central Park Reservoir. Tony was a very athletic, strong man. When he arrived in South Beach, he hung out at the office with us, and it was nice having his company. He was attentive, caring; he didn't know what to do for me.

So, one night we were going to dinner with his daughter, Katie, and his wife, Tracy, who had also come down for Katie's graduation from the University of Miami. To help me get in the car, he came to our apartment and Tony, Laura, and I left together. When we got to the car, he and Laura struggled to get me in and I ended up toppling over. I was sure Tony wouldn't have any difficulty putting me in the SUV because of his unusual strength, but strength has nothing to do with knowing how to manipulate someone with ALS, dead weight that can readily fall in any direction. What complicated the situation further was the fact that I had a breathing tube in my mouth. So Tony took my left side and Laura my right side and as they tried to maneuver me into the car, I fell over, flat on my face, unable to stop the fall. My breathing tube was torn from my mouth. When I'm prone, breathing is very hard for me; fact is, I can barely breathe. I started panicking, my heart racing. This only made the circumstances worse. Because Tony had not been dealing with me, did not know I couldn't breathe when I was lying down, this made the situation even worse still, for I kept indicating that I needed it with my hand—not able to talk—and he didn't know what I wanted. Laura ran around to the driver's side of the car and finally stuck the tube in my mouth. I caught my breath. The two of them righted me up and off we went. Tony sat in the backseat.

"I'm so sorry," he said.

"Don't be silly," I said.

The dinner was at Phillipe, one of the many chic, fancy places in South Beach. We had a nice meal and I enjoyed spending time with Katie and Tracy. Tracy is a beautiful blond woman, gracious and warm. I think the world of her. When we were leaving, Tony attempted to pick me up by himself and place me in the car. He had one arm under my legs and the other around my back. As he tried to maneuver me into the car, I literally slipped out of his grip and my head swiftly dropped toward the sidewalk. Somehow, Tony managed to break the fall by putting his knee against my back, and there I was upside down with him struggling to hold me. Mind you, this is in front of a big crowd of people who are waiting for their cars to be brought up or waiting to get into the club. A stranger rushed over to help and grabbed my arm. The two of them started trying to get me into the SUV, but the stranger let go of my arm and I went down again and again was upside down. From that position I looked at the crowd of people gawking at me and this was really absurd. All through this, the breathing hose kept falling out of my mouth. Finally, with Laura's help, they righted me up and got me in the van, all crooked and disheveled. I was upset, shook up.

"This sucks," I told Laura.

She had had a drink, which she normally does not do, and it didn't seem to bother her that I twice almost broke my head, or it didn't seem to bother her as much as I wanted it to bother her.

"That's it!" I told her. "I am not getting in the van anymore! We have to get rid of it! No more!" We talked about trading the SUV in and getting a special van for wheelchair-bound people. This was anathema to me because it was the kind of milestone that marked not only a decline but a life change so radical that you become a rare species: a permanently handicapped individual.

Still, this aside, we are hoping some kind of cure comes down the tube, a way to again strengthen my muscles so I can readily get in and out of the SUV. Laura continuously searches for new drugs or procedures, unfortunately, to no avail. On another front, we are anticipating the perfection of stem cell applications to help people with motor neuron diseases.

Thankfully, thank God, Hallelujah, Barack Obama has been elected president and we, the collective group of people who would directly benefit from stem cell research, those with motor neuron diseases, are more than hopeful. Kelsey, Laura, and I had watched the election returns with great interest and enthusiasm, and when Obama won, we saw the horizon of a new day—a day of reason and scientific common sense. When I saw Obama at the victory celebrations, I applauded. As I applauded, I looked at my hands. I really couldn't clap because the fingers were curled. Still, I applauded as best I could, feeling that a new day was upon us. I felt so moved that I dictated a letter to Kelsey shortly thereafter, which I am putting here for you to read.

Dear Mr. President,

My name is Philip Carlo. I am a New York Times *bestselling author. I felt absolutely compelled to write you and congratulate you on your momentous victory against all odds. When I saw you speak at the Democratic Convention in 2004, I sat there with my mouth open, immensely impressed by your depth of feelings, how truthful and insightful and how honest your powerful words were. I had never seen anyone in the political arena speak in my lifetime with such strength and insight into politics. Forgive my presumption in sending you the enclosed books, which I wrote. I'm giving them to you because I wanted to let you know that I am one of the millions who would benefit from stem cell research, which I know you advocate. Bravo to you. I was diagnosed with Lou Gehrig's Disease some four years ago. At this point, I can't walk, use my hands and have to breathe with a machine. As you might know, ALS is a fatal disease and my days are numbered. I have spoken to the foremost neurologists in the world and they, as a collective whole, tell me that the answer and cure for ALS would be stem cell research. My professional career has been spent researching and writing about the dark side of human nature, the most heinous criminals in modern times. I have been visiting death rows and prisons across the country interviewing killers, looking for the reasons why, the links that bind them together, ways to avoid them in the future. In a sense, my career has been about shining light in dark places. Unfortunately, one of the most dreaded killers of modern times, ALS, is now stalking me. I can no longer write because I've lost the use of my hands. I'm managing to speak and that's how I'm constructing this letter to you—by dictating to my assistant, Kelsey, who, by the way, thinks you're hot.*

Mr. President, I wish you luck with the many difficult, complicated problems you'll be facing. I feel confident that you will consistently make the right choices, using the right people, strategies, and setting a tone that will welcome us back into the world community with the respect that we once had. Again, congratulations on your victory and Godspeed to you.

Very Sincerely,
Philip Carlo

Time to go back to New York. There is no way I can handle the twenty-four-hour car ride back home. It would definitely be a strain on me, as well as monotonous and boring. We therefore make arrangements to fly back north out of Fort Lauderdale. The flight from Fort Lauderdale to New York is only two and a half hours—a much easier task than the twenty-four-hour car ride. Here, as I enter the terminal, is one of those junctures when the hard-core truth of being a handicapped person rudely smacks you in the face. Again, most everybody is on their two feet, walking a hundred ways at once with little regard for the ease with which they can take a step. I'm a little person whose eye level meets everyone's crotch. People walk fast and don't look where they're going and almost end up in my lap. That's the downside. The upside is the fact that I'm able to blow right through security, and all the security guards bend over backward to be nice to me and I'm never made to feel like there's something wrong with me. Once we're through security, off we go. I'm able to take my fancy wheelchair right to the threshold of the plane. There, male flight attendants transfer me to a box-like apparatus, which they strap me into, pick me up, take me to my seat, pick me up again and place me in my seat. It's all done very quickly and efficiently and I'm genuinely grateful for their kind handling of me, their polite ways. We take off on time. As we fly back to New York, Kelsey and I continue to work on this book. We soon land. Laura has arranged for a wheelchair accessible van to meet us at Kennedy. It is raining and cold and I get wet waiting for the van and being transferred. I hope I don't seem like some kind of namby-pamby, but getting wet could lead to a cold, a respiratory problem, and because I have no ability to cough, to clean my lungs as such, it's a potential problem that could lead to pneumonia—death. With ALS, most people who pass on do so from respiratory complications that strain the heart; also, interestingly, another killer is falls on the head. Laura and I know several people with ALS who have died that way, by falling. It's funny because when you fall, it's nothing like what you experience when you're a healthy person. You just quickly, as fast as the blink of an eye, go down, and because of the lack of strength in your hands and arms, you cannot grab on to something and stop yourself. Several times I've fallen and I dread it. I am inordinately frightened of falling. It's like the phobia I've had all my life about sharks, irrationally fearful of them to the point where I wouldn't go in water above my thigh. If I feel like I'm tipping over when Laura's transferring me, for instance, I get disproportionately panicky, which, of course, always makes things worse.

At the airport, we get in the van and start out. The driver is very accommodating. We drop Kelsey off at her apartment in Brooklyn and go on to Manhattan. The rain stops. New York, despite its capacity for sprawling brutality, is a very beautiful city. For me, it has an unspoken majesty, like someone born to royalty. As we make our way up West Street, which runs parallel to the Hudson River, I marvel at the width and enormity of the river, how the different colored lights on the Jersey side play on the water. We pass Jersey City, the place where Richard Kuklinski, the Ice Man, was born and raised. The making of the movie based upon *The Ice Man* has moved forward. The producer, Marty Beckerman, turned out to be a pleasure to work with, always there, always able; very much unlike a Hollywood producer. We will be shooting in the exact locales where the story truly happened. Mickey Rourke is still slated to play the Ice Man.

We are soon home. We've been gone six months but it seems like only six days on the one hand and then on the other hand, it seems like we were gone six years. We are tired. Laura washes me up and helps me get in bed. We have one of those Tempur-Pedic mattresses that hugs you when you lie down. I love it. I roll on my right side. I have the breathing tube sticking out of my mouth. Laura shuts the light. It seems we never left.

Outside, the rain returns . . . a gentle pitter-patter lulls me to a far-away place. Soon, I'm in a deep sleep, unmoving, as though I were paralyzed. When I wake up, I don't feel rested at all. My muscles and joints ache. I'm still tired, yet I've got to get up and start the day. *Why, I wonder, do I have to get up? Fuck it. Where am I going? I'm staying in bed. I don't feel good. I have aches and pains.* Laura's been up an hour already. She walks into the bedroom. She wants me to get up. I don't want to get up.

"Kelsey's here," she tells me.

"Okay," I say. Kelsey is often the only reason I'll get out of bed because she is here to work, and that's really the only thing I'm interested in these days. I start thinking of words and sentences and themes and before I know it, I'm up. I want to get *The Killer Within* finished. I'm planning another book about Juan Carlos Ramirez-Abadia, the Colombian drug kingpin whom I mentioned earlier. We are on the threshold of beginning this new book. What I plan to do is enter into the black heart and soul of one of the most feared, cunning drug lords in history. The first thing I did toward writing this book was hire a second assistant who spoke five languages fluently to work with Kelsey and me. I wanted all the newspaper articles ever written about Juan Carlos Ramirez-Abadia in Spanish, Portuguese, and English. I also had her locate all the photographs of him and his homes and where he came from. Thus, the process, the in-depth research needed for the new book, has begun. Still, the actual writing of this book is down the road. I know it would be a good idea to go to South America, Colombia and Brazil, to interview police officials who investigated and arrested Ramirez-Abadia, discovered millions of dollars in his homes. According to the DEA, this dude made $1.8 million during his career. Throughout my career, I've always made it a point to actually sit down with the people involved and pick their brains. But now this is an improbable stretch, considering my condition. However, there is more than one way to skin a cat and we are managing to interview the main players via telephone and webcam. With the help of GoogleEarth, both Kelsey and I are able to get a bird's-eye view—literally—of all the places where the action plays out, the actual streets, the actual homes.

Meanwhile, we are gearing up for the book party for *The Butcher*. There is going to be a lot of press, DEA agents and FBI agents there. The entire Pitera task force is coming. There will be a lot of media. It bums me out that I have to be in a wheelchair with a breathing tube sticking out of my mouth on such an occasion. After all, I wrote the book yet here I am, not able to stand up or shake anyone's hand. But I'll make the best of the situation and hope people understand. Still, I hate the idea of being at my own party with a hose sticking out of my mouth, having to look up at people when I should be eye-level with them. No matter what, I am excited because it is a cause to celebrate. I'll make the best of it.

25. Home Sweet Home

Locanda Verde is located at 377 Greenwich Street in lower Manhattan. Right now it is one of the hottest restaurants in town. We have chosen to have the book party for *The Butcher* there because Bob De Niro is one of the owners and the people there are very accommodating. Last year, we had the book party for *Gaspipe* there and it went well. The chef, Andrew Carmellini, is one of New York's finest and it takes weeks to get a reservation. Because of my relationship with Bob, the party room has been made available to us at a discount price, otherwise I could never have afforded it. I think, too, that Bob and his partners are cutting me a good deal because of the fact that I have Lou Gehrig's Disease and have persevered, kept writing. Most important is the fact that people are reaching out to me with warmth and genuine care. Ultimately, I think that works somewhere deep in one's psyche and has a . . . curative, positive effect. Also, the book party is a reconfirmation of my going on, my being willing to go out in public in a wheelchair with a breathing apparatus. I looked in the mirror yesterday. I'm still very tan, not gray and sickly-looking. Of course, a lot of this has to do with the fact that we recently came back from Florida. I have left it up to Laura, her sister, Karen, and Kelsey to make plans for the party: what's going to be served, the drinks, and so on. These days I keep my focus on my work. I'm adamant about not being interrupted or getting involved in the mundane. My idea of a perfect day is to write all day with Kelsey and watch two or three movies during the evening, fitting dinner in somewhere, when I'm hungry and feel like it. In that I can't cook any longer, one of my greatest pleasures in life, food, has become far less important.

The weather has gotten warm and working in the backyard is a pleasure. It is a far cry from South Beach, but in its own right it is quite beautiful, safe, and large enough so I don't feel claustrophobic at all. We have laid tiles in the yard and put up a new fence and my good friend Mike and I put down twenty bags of cow manure mixed with topsoil and planted flowers and a half-dozen tomato plants, which will give us ripe, delicious tomatoes. We also planted peppers and zucchini. I actually had nothing to do with the planting other than directing Mike. The actual gardening is out of the question for me, in that I have little use of my hands, though I've acclimated to this lack of being able to garden and I've grown accustomed to telling my pal Mike what to do.

Laura is not really interested in gardening. I try to get her involved but she's . . . indifferent. I understand her lack of interest and don't press her to participate. However, there is a heated bone of contention between Laura and me and it's about, of all things, transportation.

26. The White Van

Going to family functions, on shopping expeditions, just going out to dinner downtown are difficult, arduous tasks when you're wheelchair-bound. In that my chair is motorized and top of the line, it is 350 pounds and rather large and doesn't fit into any kind of conventional SUV. Handicapped vans are expensive, but it is much better to buy, invest in, a van that can actually accommodate my wheelchair, say Laura and my sister. Fact is, my family strongly advocates my buying one and Laura wants one also. They all feel it would be easier for me to get out and go visit them, go shopping, blah blah blah.

Getting a van has become a source of friction between myself and pretty much everyone around me. Even my mother's brother Lenny has gotten involved. At my sister's insistence, she convinces my uncle Lenny that I have to have a van. I've always been close with my uncle Lenny. Everyone in my family has always been close. Without my blessing, my uncle and my sister begin going around and checking out vans and, naturally enough, they find a little-used van owned by a woman whose invalid husband had used it and recently passed on. I want nothing to do with this van. I don't want to spend the money; I don't want to buy a van when the man who formerly owned it died. It could have a negative effect on my psyche, I tell everyone. It is also my admitting that I will never walk again; that I am accepting the severity of my illness rather than fighting it. I realize all this is nonsense when I think about it, that I am thinking with my emotions and not my head.

Ultimately, Laura says she wants it, that we can go shopping again because I'll be able to take my wheelchair into stores like Costco and Target and Whole Foods and Home Depot. I haven't been in a Home

Depot in some three years and I always got great joy from looking at all the stuff for homes. I finally acquiesce, and we buy the van, sight unseen, on my uncle's recommendation after he has a mechanic look at it. So, lo and behold, as I write this, the van is parked outside, just in front of the building, and it really has been easier to get around and I think it is a wise investment. Having it doesn't bother me at all. Fact is, I feel kind of cool. Over the last month, we have gone to Costco and these other large stores and it's just good for my head— to be able to get out, go shopping, pick out things makes me feel as though I'm in the mix, not ostracized, not locked in the house. I think the beginning of the end for people with terminal diseases comes when they take on a mindset in which they are on an island by themselves.

For me, things are looking up . . . we have a new white van, the book party, new projects on the horizon.

27. The Worst Possible Critic

Tommy Pitera is the last person in the world you'd want mad at you. I've always known this. The fact that he went to trial and never testified against anybody and never opened his mouth about what he knew—and he knew a lot—does not bode well for me. Essentially what that means is that he still has connections and friends, confidants, on the outside who respect him and will do his bidding. Though he went to jail so many years ago—nearly twenty—I thought that most people he knew who could be a threat to me were long gone and forgotten, but I may have been wrong. I just heard that he somehow got a copy of *The Butcher*, read it, and was pissed off. I feel that my friend Jim Hunt at the DEA, who cooperated extensively with me and enabled me to write *The Butcher*, will protect me. Jim and I have become friends and I portrayed the DEA agents involved in this case as the righteous heroes they really are. Fact is, I dedicated the book to the task force that pursued and brought down Pitera and I named the many agents who were killed in the line of duty. Some of them were not just murdered—they were unspeakably tortured. Through an attorney who is close to Pitera and my wife's uncle, I found out that Pitera's sister had gotten early copies of *The Butcher* from my UK publisher, Mainstream, and like that, he was able to get the book in federal prison and read it. Little by little, I put together what amounts to a moat around myself, a moat filled with white sharks with sharp teeth.

One of the sharks I speak of is a good friend of mine of thirty years, Chuck Zito. Chuck is a very rare guy. He had been the president of the New York chapter of the Hell's Angels. He is a martial arts expert and he is 220 pounds of muscle and fighting acumen. Over the years, I've seen him get into fights, twice with three men at the same time, and he knocked all three of them out. I first met him at Studio 54. I later wrote an article for *Seconds* magazine about that meeting, about Chuck Zito:

> *The first time I met Chuck Zito, the president of the New York chapter of Hell's Angels, I was at the bar in Studio 54 with my girlfriend, Patti. The year was 1979. The bar was crowded, the music hot. I noticed an argument off to my right, looked and saw this one guy, Chuck, arguing with three guys. As fast as the blink of an eye, a fight between Chuck and the three men broke out, and within fifteen seconds, Chuck knocked all three guys out cold and went back to talking with two blonde women. I was born and raised in Bensonhurst, Brooklyn, and I've seen a lot of street fights in my day, but I never saw anyone with the controlled, precise aggression possessed by Chuck. Watching him fight was like watching some kind of natural disaster—a hurricane or a cyclone—in action.*
>
> *Soon after the three came to, the police were called. I knew Studio 54 well and its serpentine basement leading to its back doors. When I saw the cops coming towards Chuck, I hurried over to him and told him to follow me—that I'd lead him out a back door. Without asking me a question, he followed me to the basement, then across to the other side of the club. As we made our way there, we passed a small group of people standing in a loose circle passing around thumb-sized vials of cocaine, talking animatedly. Truman Capote, Andy Warhol and Halston were part of the group. Truman was wearing a baggy white caftan and a big straw hat. Chuck apparently knew Andy, for Warhol greeted him like a friend. Chuck said he had to go and we made our way to the rear entrance of the club and I opened the 53rd Street exit for him. He said, "Thanks," and took off into the New York night. I made my way back to the bar and Patti and I watched two of the three guys—with obviously broken jaws—get taken away by paramedics . . .*
>
> *The next time I saw Chuck, two weeks later, was at Café Central on West 74th and Amsterdam Avenue. Café Central was truly an in-spot then. Bruce Willis, still a struggling actor, was the bartender. Some of the café's regulars were Danny Aiello, Bobby De Niro, Joe Pesci, Peter Weller, Peter Riegert, Tony Danza, Paul Herman and on and on. Chuck*

saw me, came over and again said thanks. We sat and had a drink—he a Coke, me a beer; he told me he didn't drink alcohol at all. I asked him what happened at Studio 54. He said those three guys said something rude to the women he'd been talking to. "They were," he told me, "just friends of mine, but those jerks didn't know if one of them was my girl or wife or whatever. You've got to draw the line somewhere." I told him how two of the three "jerks" had to be taken away by paramedics.

"Good," he said. "Maybe next time they'll have some respect."

"No doubt they will," I told him.

And that's how I became friends with Chuck Zito. Over the years, our friendship grew and I now consider him one of my closest, dearest buddies. If I ever had to be in a foxhole with anyone, I'd want it to be him. He is, without a doubt, the most stand-up guy I've ever met, the best person in the world to watch your back. He is a loyal, sincere man automatically willing to make your battles his, your enemies his enemies. Though I hasten to say, if you've ever done anything to make Chuck mad at you, leave town right away and don't come back . . .

Some two years ago, Chuck retired his patch and quit the Hell's Angels. They're still very tight and if there is a problem, he can readily call upon them. People do not realize how really bonded the Hell's Angels are and just how many of them there are. There are chapters all over the United States and Europe as well as several in Japan. Of all these thousands of badass men who reject society's mandates and protocols, Chuck Zito is thought of as a superstar. One, because he's so physically tough, and, two, because he was blindly dedicated to the club. Some years ago, he got arrested in an FBI sweep and was accused of selling an ounce of amphetamines. This was a bald-faced lie, something he never did. Chuck doesn't drink, doesn't smoke, and he's never used drugs in his life. But suffice it to say, he ended up getting railroaded and he did five years in federal prison. This further bolstered his reputation as a stand-up guy within the club because he never told the truth about who really had the drugs. The Angels all knew it, and they rallied behind him. If I ever have a problem, Chuck is probably the first person I would call. He and I are close. The Mafia even respect the Angels. They know that the Angels are absolutely stand-up; they know that no Hell's Angel has ever testified against another Angel. The Mafia cannot say that about themselves.

It was Chuck, in fact, who first introduced me to Mickey Rourke. They are tight. I found out later that Mickey had offhandedly mentioned to Chuck that he had read my book, and seen the HBO specials on the Ice Man, and that he really wanted to play Richard Kuklinski. Chuck said he knew the writer, called me up, and put Mickey on the phone. I now call Chuck and tell him about my concerns regarding Pitera.

"Don't be concerned," he says. "I'll make sure word is passed along."

This is reassuring, but still, I know for sure there are a lot of people in this world not playing with a full deck, who will not listen to reason. Pitera is one of those people. He could very well know a maverick psychopath and, from jail, ask him to come look me up. With Chuck's intervention, however, I feel . . . insulated.

28. Locanda Verde

Locanda Verde is a stone's throw from the Hudson River in a neighborhood of Manhattan called Tribeca. This was once an industrial area known as Washington Market. Here, all manner of fruits and vegetables were sold both wholesale and retail to the citizenry of New York. Because of the proximity to the river, beginning in the 1850's and tapering off in the 1920s, numerous factories were built and flourished here. It became a hubbub of commercial activity. Few people actually lived here then. Tribeca still has an Old World charm about it. Over the last twenty years or so, drawn by the many lofts with oversized windows, a long list of artists, actors and painters, sculptors and designers comfortably settled here, foremost of whom is Robert De Niro. Tribeca became a hip place to live. De Niro opened several restaurants in the area—The Tribeca Grill, Nobu, and, most recently, Locanda Verde, where we're having the party this evening. He also began Tribeca Films, which encouraged the film community to open offices here and, naturally enough, restaurants and a host of other businesses followed suit. De Niro also initiated the now popular Tribeca Film Festival. I myself have never liked this neighborhood; it still has a gray, soulless, factory-like feel to me. There are few trees. I very much enjoy being near the green splendor of Central Park. Down here in Tribeca there are no parks. On the night of the book party for *The Butcher*, my friend Mike drives the white van downtown. Both Laura and Karen have new dresses on and each of them looks great. As we try to find a parking spot, I am rudely jostled about because most of the streets here are still cobblestone.

De Niro wanted Locanda Verde to have the look of an old-fashioned Italian villa and he has managed to achieve that. On the night of the party, I arrive at seven o'clock and the place is already crowded. With my friend Mike's help, following Kelsey and Laura, I slowly roll through the crowd and into the back room. Already the bar has been set up and my sister-in-law, Karen, is there giving everybody orders—something she's adept at. Karen has a brilliant sense of space as a decorator and I know with her here, it will work. The problem with Karen is that everything has to be her way or the highway. You can't have an opinion but, still, she knows what she's doing, and we all stay out of her way. It's funny how when I arrive there are only a couple of people in this big room with a wooden floor and only a few tables; I feel like I am in some kind of dance hall in which everybody will be dancing but me.

Again, it starts bugging me that because I am in a wheelchair, my eyes level with everyone's bellybuttons. I raise my wheelchair so I will be higher up but I am still quite low, like some kind of belligerent, book-writing midget. I say belligerent because I was born belligerent and since I've gotten sick I've only become more belligerent. Sitting here watching everything being prepared, the posters being put up, and so on, I imagine myself as a dwarf smoking a big cigar, a kind of perverse ringmaster, boss of all the midgets. It's a wild thing to be sitting and looking at somebody's privates while they're looking down at you and asking, "What inspired you to write this book?"

Clearly, the party is all because of a book I wrote. Yet I feel like I've been brought here because I am somebody's child that nobody could find a babysitter for. I kind of feel like I don't belong. It's not the easiest thing in the world to overcome being this handicapped. But fuck it, I say to myself, I'll make the best of it, with this stupid breathing tube sticking out of my mouth and my hands listlessly resting in my lap. I have hired a publicist to help me with the marketing of *The Butcher*. His name is James Sliman and he is very thorough. He knows what he is doing. It is a pleasure having him as part of the team. I think that another reason I have warmed to James is the fact that he gets the significance of what I've been doing—writing prolifically while burdened with a terminal illness. I guess to a PR person, my condition is a bit of a gem. In any event, I get along with James and like the way he does most everything. James is working harmoniously with Karen. He is a tall, thin, well-dressed man. The publicist from

HarperCollins is also here. His name is Adam Rochkind, a young, nerdy-looking individual. Also present is my editor at HarperCollins, Matt Harper. Matt has been a real pleasure to work with, a good editor, sharp and insightful. We have eight big posters of the book cover all around the room and we put out two hundred books. Before I know it, the room fills up with my family and friends and a lot of media and it seems to be going very well. There is an open bar and delicious appetizers are being served. Mickey Rourke has promised he'll come and sure enough, he does. He arrives with my pal Chuck Zito and the photographers swarm all over them. He takes a seat at a table where I have been sitting and gladly poses for pictures and answers questions about *The Ice Man* and signs copies of *The Butcher* for people because I can't sign them myself. He is gracious and supportive.

The room becomes more and more crowded. People are surrounding our table. I am beginning to have a hard time breathing. This is a combination of anxiety and fatigue. After all, no matter what my mindset is, my muscles have diminished so greatly and I am so weak that anything out of the ordinary is unusually taxing. When the breathing tube falls from my mouth, it is difficult to pick it up and put it back in. I can't raise my hands above my pectoral muscles. This is something new but I am not about to let this or anything else put a damper on the evening, especially with my new best friend sitting on my right side doing everything he can and more to make the night a success. As I write this now, I can't help but think of the Ice Man— the real Ice Man, Richard Kuklinski. Because Mickey's instincts as an actor are razor-sharp, he knows Kuklinski is both an interesting and a repulsive character at the same time and any actor who portrays him well will hit a home run. Here we have a married man, Kuklinski, who has children, living a seemingly happy, suburban life, but is traveling around the world killing and torturing people at will. His specialty is making people disappear forever. Here is a man who also slept on the floor of his eight-year-old daughter Merrick's hospital room when she was suffering from a bladder infection; a man who brought other children on the ward toys and candy; a man who paid for medicine for the children of the poor on the ward. Mickey sees, and I agree, that this, *The Ice Man*, will be his *Raging Bull*. Surely, he will be nominated for an Oscar.

Jim Hunt also shows up with the members of the DEA Pitera task force. I have been writing about these individuals for some two years but have not met them all. It is really a pleasure to finally get to meet them and shake their hands. We gave Jim a box of books a week ago and he has given them out to his colleagues. They've all read it by now and start discussing it with me. They don't like what I've done, they love it. For me, this is the ultimate compliment. After all, the book is about what these men do in real life. One of them, Mike Agrifolio, says to me, "You know, the book made me cry," truly the cherry on the cake.

"What was it that made you cry?" I ask, curious, wanting to know what struck home so.

"You captured the camaraderie between us, the brotherhood," he says.

Well, that makes my heart soar. "I'm very pleased to hear that," I tell him, and I genuinely am. I have done my job.

Then, out of nowhere, one of Tommy Pitera's main men, Manny Maya, walks into the room. I don't recognize him at first, but then I do. There is, in fact, a picture of him in the book. I get tense. I look at Chuck Zito and any trepidation I have disappears. When Chuck sees Manny, he gets up from where he is sitting with Mickey, walks over to Maya and shakes his hand, and brings Maya over to me, smiling, and says, "This guy is a friend of Tommy's . . . he's in the book!"

"I know," I say. I shake hands with him. He is all smiles and friendly. He isn't here for any reason other than the fact that a good friend of his, Paul Vario Jr., was invited by Chuck and it soon becomes clear to Maya that I am tight with Chuck and, as such, have the muscle-bound umbrella of his protection. Of course, word of this will very quickly spread through Mafiadom and ultimately reach Pitera and, regardless of what he wants to do, he can do nothing without consequences. That type of violence, a murder contract issued from jail, is a two-way street. People in jail are just as vulnerable to retribution as those on the outside, perhaps more so. I should mention that Paul Vario Jr. is the son of the very infamous Paul Vario, a capo in the Lucchese crime family. Paul Vario helped mastermind the famous Lufthansa heist at Kennedy Airport.

The party is a success. It is written up in newspapers and magazines and generates substantial media attention, in both New York and Los Angeles. Media attention is not something that I'm fond of.

Truth is, I think it's a bunch of baloney, but these days it's an essential part of being a writer, selling books. The competition is incredible. When you're in New York, you're competing against the best writers in the world, and I'm not just looking to get published, I want a best-seller, a book that's bought and read all over the world. What all writers have wanted in all places since the beginning of time is to be read. Can you imagine the disappointment God would have felt if nobody had read the Ten Commandments? The more people who read your work, the better.

When I was just starting out, getting published and having a book that was a success was the most important thing in the world to me. Back then, I was healthy and had no physical impediments at all; I exercised daily no matter where I was, what city I was in, what the weather was like.

As I look around the room now, even though I'm wheelchair-bound, staring at people's bellies, I have truly accomplished what I set out to do, and regardless of how sick I become, nothing will ever be able to take that away from me.

29. South of the Border

The following day is beautiful. The sky is a rich, clear blue, the temperature in the mid-seventies. I am by myself sitting in the backyard. Kelsey has gone to lunch. Laura is on the phone with her sister. I am quite pleased. The party went well. Everyone was kind and warm and I think we hit a home run. I swing my wheelchair around and face the tomato plants. Some of the tomatoes are ready to be picked, others are still green. A squirrel has been stealing the ripe ones and I am at a loss. I don't want to hurt the squirrel, but by the same token, we've worked hard for these tomatoes. Mike has gone uptown to an exterminator on Amsterdam Avenue who has a cage in which we can, if we're lucky, catch the squirrel. If we catch the little thief, we plan to release him in Central Park.

I wheel myself closer to the ripest of the tomatoes. Without thinking, I try to reach out and grab it, wanting to take a bite out of it, but I cannot lift my hands more than an inch or so off my lap. Though I have completely lost the use of my limbs, what bothers me the most is the loss of my diaphragm muscle. Because of that, I must use the ventilator twenty-four hours a day, even when I sleep. We keep it in a small knapsack hung on the back of the wheelchair. A tube connected to a mouthpiece runs from the ventilator. In order for me to breathe, I must hold the mouthpiece between my lips, between my teeth. I don't say this with rancor for I have come to accept all the pitfalls of having ALS, but imagine that a tire on your car needs air. You pull into the gas station. You go to where the air machine is. You grab the air hose, but instead of putting it on the tire, you stick it in your mouth. Well, that's kind of what I look like—a guy with an air hose sticking out of his mouth. I can't go anywhere without this absurd air hose. However, I've gotten so used to it that I sometimes talk to people like the hose is not in my mouth—waiters, shopkeepers—and inevitably all I get is, "What?" and creased brows. I'm so nuts that I start getting offended because people don't understand blah blah blah blah. Sometimes, I do radio shows and I don't realize the air hose is in my mouth and I am mumbling away. Laura has to give me the high sign. Fact is, I'm doing a radio program tonight, *The Joey Reynolds Show* on WOR, for two solid hours. I know this is going to tire me. I know this is going to be, for want of a better way to put it, a pain in the ass. It doesn't even begin until one o'clock in the morning, but we will go down to the studio and I'll do it and make the best of it. I am a trooper.

The good news is that the disease has not weakened the muscles needed for speech. With air in my lungs, I can speak perfectly well. Perhaps that is attributable to the IPLEX. It's hard to say, though, because we have no idea what my speech would be like without the IPLEX. It's kind of a catch-22. Laura comes outside. She sees the dilemma about my face.

"What's wrong?" she says.

"I wanted that tomato but I couldn't grab it."

Without effort, she picks the tomato, saying, "I'll go inside and cut it. Want anything on it?"

"Salt and pepper and a little olive oil," I say, and she walks off with my tomato. I wait with anticipation because nothing is as good as homegrown tomatoes. Sitting there, I begin thinking of stem cell application. Steve Byer has repeatedly suggested I go to Monterrey, Mexico, and have the stem cell implantation done there. I am still wary about this for I haven't seen definitive proof that the procedure in Monterrey is helping people with ALS. I do know that the longer I wait, the worse my condition could very well become. Still, I am not going to allow them to drill holes in my head and jam stem cells into my brain unless I know it is safe, unless I know I will benefit from it. As I said earlier, I think that Steve's enthusiasm is running ahead of good logic—science. I'm open to new ideas, procedures, tests, and all the rest, but just because I'm shackled with this terrible disease, I'm not about to put my head on a chopping block. Laura has been speaking with the spouses of people we know with ALS who have had the

Monterrey procedure done and what she's been hearing, telling me, is the improvement has been marginal. We have talked extensively about going, looked into the itinerary. It entails flying out of Kennedy, stopping over in Mexico City, and then on to Monterrey. From there an ambulette would take me to a hotel. This would be a difficult, arduous trip. The following morning, the four-day process would begin, culminating with them drilling holes into my skull and injecting my own stem cells, with the hope that they will multiply and make strong the ailing motor neurons. That's the theory.

Regardless, I still firmly believe that one day—whether from a newly discovered drug or stem cell application—I'll be able to get up and walk, though I already know it will be a slow process. It has taken me some five years to get to this stage. I'm sure, though, that because I was an athlete prior to my getting sick, my muscles will rebound quickly if they are just given the chance.

The only thing I have left, regardless of any property and material things, is my talent—my ability to write. I'm deathly afraid that if they drill holes in me, in my brain, I'll lose the capacity to imagine, to get outside of myself . . . to make something from nothing. After all, now, I have scant little to help me with the trials and tribulations of life. This whole thing about being a cripple, being wheelchair-bound, you can get used to. But the thought of losing the ability to write, a discipline that took me thirty-five years to develop and perfect, is as disturbing as a deadly earthquake. What would I do every day? I can't cook. I can't ride a bike. I can't skate. I can't even read because I can't hold up a book or a fucking newspaper. If I couldn't write—I don't think I would want to go on. That could be a death toll. Thus, I'm so hesitant about having this procedure done. If I were to have an experimental stem cell application done on me, I would be much more comfortable if it were at Columbia University Medical Center or Mount Sinai Hospital. Mexico . . . I'm frightened. I cannot lose the one thing I have that this disease could never touch—the integrity of my brain.

Laura returns carrying the plate on which is my tomato. She gingerly forks a piece into my mouth. It is sweet and juicy, delicious. I eat it with a pepper-infused hard biscuit. Yummy.

"I spoke to Steve a little while ago," Laura says.

"Where was I?"

"I looked in the yard and you were napping."

"I was just thinking about him. What did he have to say?"

"Well, like he's been saying, he really thinks you should do this."
She feeds me another piece of tomato.

"Laura, let's say I do this and I can't write anymore. What do I
do? Who do I turn to? Who do I yell at? Who do I get mad at?"

Of course, she has no answer. She can't have an answer, and that's
part of the problem. I do not like gambling with cards or in Vegas or
in Atlantic City. I've gambled with my life many times, however. Becoming a writer and closing a successful business was a gamble. Going
off and living out of a steam trunk for two years all over Europe was
a gamble. There were many times when I was alone in somewhat dangerous places and I did these things without second thought or reservation. These were all gambles. But now it's really not about me at all.
I have to trust Mexican doctors that I know nothing about. Yes, Steve
and his wife, Barbara, have told us effusively how wonderful the doctors are, how polite, how attentive, how clean the hospital is, but still
I know scant little about these Mexican doctors. I turn away from
Laura and my attention is again drawn to the tomato plants. They
are now over seven feet high and are a testament, I'm thinking, to the
will of all things to grow and fill their destiny according to nature.
What happened to Ernest Hemingway pops into my mind. I forget
the tomato plants, my nemesis the squirrel. I imagine Hemingway putting the shotgun in his mouth and pulling the trigger. I wheel my chair
around and face Laura.

"Laura," I say, "you know, Ernest Hemingway was having some
mental issues and they wanted to give him ECT (shock therapy). He
didn't want it done but his wife, Mary Welch, agreed and against his
will, she signed papers allowing him to get shock therapy and from
that day on, he never wrote again. What they did was they burned
away his memory. He couldn't imagine or recall anything. If you can't
remember, you can't write."

"I didn't know that," she says in a small voice.

"As far as I'm concerned, his wife was responsible for stealing
away one of the most influential, important writers of all time. It's a
telling lesson—be careful if you put your head on a chopping block,
for a guillotine can come down."

"You're being dramatic," she says.

"That's what I do," I say. "I'm a dramatist, but I'm not allowing anyone to drill holes into my brain." She doesn't answer me. What can she say? Much of the burden of my illness has fallen on Laura's shoulders. I well understand how any possibility of improvement is an important thing to her, but I am not about to gamble with what little I have left for anyone.

A breeze blows and the strong smell of the tomato plants comes to me. My attention again turns to them and the tomato-stealing squirrel. *It's a dog-eat-dog world*, I think to myself, laughing quietly.

30. A New Lease on Life

The tomatoes and our other vegetables have come and gone. Abruptly, the days grow short and dark comes on quickly. Mike and I put out the trap for the squirrel but we never caught him. Everything we tried was foiled by his guile. Kelsey and I are now sitting in the backyard. Leaves, still green from the summer sun, though tinted with reds and browns, are slowly falling, leaving a somewhat bare canopy of branches hanging over the yard. I can see between the branches and there's a V-shaped formation of geese going south. I can hear them communicating with one another by faint, distant honks. I'm thinking that they have more sense than most people.

There has been some new news on the stem cell front. We have heard some positive results from the stem cell application procedure in Mexico and I am now seriously entertaining the idea of going. I wheel myself inside, find Laura, and tell her that I don't want to go to Mexico from New York; that it will be easier to go from Florida to Mexico as it is a shorter trip.

"If we decide to go," I add.

She thinks this a good plan, though I think she knows that what I'm trying to do is stall the trip. I still want more proof that it works. This is creating an unspoken tension between Laura and me—my vacillating.

Every day the weather gets a little colder. Every day more leaves fall from the trees and carpet the yard. Some days, it's so cold I don't go outside at all. One of the effects of the cold is that my hands stiffen into claws and it's hard for me to work the joystick on my wheelchair; the other day, I drove it into a garbage can.

It is time to return to South Beach. To hell with New York and its freezing weather and gray skies. I loathe gray skies. At the prospect of going back to South Beach, I am as excited as a boy on the last day of school. I've never liked winters in New York—all the clothes you have to wear, the barren trees, icy winds—and since I've gotten sick, I've become deathly afraid of getting a cold, which could readily turn into pneumonia—serious respiratory problems. As I watch Laura pack, I think of myself on the beach with the smell of the ocean and the warm sun soothing what muscles I have left, my aching joints. I can readily see palm trees basking in the sunlight; I see them being beaten and battered by strong winds and stormy weather, the large leaves whipping.

"To hell with winter," I say to Laura.

"No winter for us," she says.

The door opens and Kelsey walks in carrying a red suitcase larger than she is. The three of us are ready to go. Laura gives the apartment a quick once-over. There are a lot of things we have to take and we want to make sure we have what we need. The special vehicle for a wheelchair is somewhat late, but finally it arrives. Happily, anxiously, I steer my wheelchair out the door and onto the street, not looking back as I go. It is gray and raining. The cold rain feels like it's biting my face and my hands . . . like little needle pricks. *God*, I think, *I want out of here!*

I drive my wheelchair into the wheelchair-accessible vehicle. The wheelchair is buckled down by the driver. We have arranged to have our van shipped down to South Beach. It will be waiting for us when we get there.

Kelsey and Laura sit behind me. The driver puts the car in gear and we are soon approaching Kennedy Airport. Hallelujah. Because of the bad weather—the rain and gray skies—our leaving today seems all the more fortuitous. I feel no loss or sadness because we're leaving New York, my hometown. In fact, it's just the opposite. For the most part, I've emotionally separated myself from New York. Yet I know we will be coming back in the spring and I can't help but look forward to that. For me, New York is the kind of city you love to leave and you love to come back to. In the meantime, I can't wait to get back to the different places that we like so much in South Beach—the News Café, Fratelli La Bufala, Prime Italian, and all the rest.

Without difficulty, we check in at the JetBlue terminal, go through security, and board the plane with the help of friendly flight attendants. As I'm strapped into my seat, I think of my family. They are the only thing I will miss while I'm away. I hope I can convince my parents to come down to South Beach sometime during the winter. I close my eyes. The plane begins to taxi. Before I know it, I'm sleeping. When I wake up, we're arriving at Fort Lauderdale Airport. I had been dreaming that I was running on a beach in Puerto Vallarta, Mexico, one I ran on years ago. Surely, I think as the flight attendants pick me up and bring me back to my wheelchair, this is a good omen.

It's great to be back in Miami. The blue skies, the strong sun, the tropical feeling in the air . . . my cup runneth over. Even with all the difficulties I'm having, being here encourages me to forget them or, rather, to not think of them. In that Kelsey and I are just about finished with this book, we will soon begin entering the writing stage of *The Prince of Cocaine: The High Times and Bloody Crimes of a Colombian Drug Lord*. It's kind of ironic that we have ended up in Miami. It's a known fact that many Colombian drug lords chose to live here, bought real estate here, built high-rises all over South Miami, send their children to school here, have fortunes stashed in plastic waterproof boxes buried on their properties. One of the last things I did upon leaving New York was contact the DEA agent whom my friend Jim Hunt has put me in touch with regarding the trafficking of cocaine from Colombia into the United States—specifically, into Miami.

We are soon on the beach, back in the office, finishing this book. It's interesting because I'd like to end the book with my getting well, my being better . . . perhaps even writing these words on my own. But that is not in the cards just yet. Even if I were given a drug today that helped bring health and vitality back to my motor neurons, it would take months for my muscles to build up again. As I dictate this now to Kelsey, I'm looking down the beach and watching people walk, run, bike—seeing in my mind's eye myself walking along, my legs moving forward a slow step at a time, supporting me, not letting me down, not buckling under me. I think, though, if I'm going to fall, the beach is the best place to do it, so I resolve to take my first steps here on the beach, near the ocean, being reborn, as though I were some kind of amoebic creature leaving the sea to become a *Homo sapiens*. I want to be really reborn, not the kind of reborn that George

Bush became. Reborn, my ass. The donkey. Forgive me for saying it again but I think of Bush vetoing two bills that would have underwritten research into stem cell application that, very likely, could make the difference between life and death for millions of people, including myself. I wonder what kind of Christian would do that. I think I may have said this before. I certainly have thought it before. But it can't be said enough. I believe it was the most un-Christian thing I've seen in my lifetime, condemning so many people with motor neuron diseases, fatal illnesses, to the torturous slow death that comes with these maladies.

Mexico—we have to go, Laura says. Though I am still very reluctant about going, I have agreed to travel there and talk to the doctors and see what it is all about myself, perhaps even speak to some of the people who had the procedure done. I am still not keen on going to Mexico but if I have to go, the plane ride from here will be considerably shorter. I tell Laura I'll be ready to go in a few days; that I have to muster up the will to go. The following week, on Monday, she makes the reservations and packs what we'll need, which really isn't much. We're going from one warm climate to another. What weighs a lot is this ridiculous breathing apparatus and the batteries and chargers and wires we need for it. That's a good sixty, seventy pounds right there, but we manage to pack everything okay and, kind of nervous, quiet, and sullen, I drive my wheelchair into a special SUV, which takes us to the airport. As usual, the Fort Lauderdale terminal is crowded with people walking in every direction at once. Most often when I travel I have a feeling of joy and pleasant anticipation, but today I feel apprehension. I don't want to go. Even though this is an exploratory trip, I am wary . . . very wary. What concerns me more than anything is the end result—the fact that there will be needles going through my skull and inside my brain, and I can't help but worry that these Mexican doctors will make some kind of mistake, a blunder, and it will affect my ability to write—imagine. I remember my uncle Philip, my father's brother, my namesake. When he returned from World War II, he had serious mental issues. He had a form of shell shock and wasn't quite there. Doctors told my father's family that there was a new brain operation that could help him. All of the thirteen children and my grandmother were at Methodist Hospital in South Brooklyn where my uncle was operated on. He actually died on the operating table. That is playing, as if an old-fashioned, grainy, black-and-white film, inside my brain somewhere. Laura asks what is the matter, seeing the shadow of gloom about my face.

"I don't want to go," I say. "I don't want anyone putting needles in my brain. I'd rather wait until they develop something here, until Valerie and Project ALS and the people at Columbia University come up with something. I'm not going to Mexico. The one thing that I have that is special is my brain and my ability to write. I'm not going to subject it to what these people want to do. Forget it!" I nearly shout, surprising even myself.

"If that's how you feel, fine," she says.

"Let's go back," I say.

"Okay," she says.

I tell Kelsey what we are doing, she says fine, and the three of us are soon on our way back to South Beach. Each of us is quiet, a heavy burden on our shoulders. I am willing to take the chance to wait for something to be developed here, and I am not going to become distracted or dwell on this excessively. *Fuck Mexico*, I think to myself. *I ain't going*, I say in the Brooklyn-ese I sometimes use when I speak to myself.

As we speed back to South Beach, off on the right there is a large rainbow. It seems to stretch for five or six miles, the bright yellows and reds and blues and pinks.

"That's a good omen," I say softly, pointing with my bent finger.

No one else seems to hear me, but I hear me.

Straight ahead, the sun shines brightly, and the sky is a vivid pastel blue, free of clouds.

"Let's go to the News Café and get some piña coladas," I suggest.

"Let's!" Kelsey says.

"Good idea," Laura says.

When we get back to South Beach, we drop off our luggage and head over to the News Café. It is late in the afternoon now and the place is quieting down. As usual there is a flock of wild parrots in the palm trees above the outdoor seating area. They squawk and make noise, but they are a delight to see, with their long, elegant, sweeping tails and their emerald-green feathers and golden eyes. Laura goes into the café and comes back with a copy of the *New York Post*. She begins reading Page Six. A waiter I know well from New York named Michael, who used to work at Elaine's restaurant, comes over.

"What can I get you?"

"Three piña coladas," I say, a smile about my face, watching the bikini-clad women walk by, thinking it's not such a bad world after all.

The following day, it is beautiful outside, clear skies and bright sunshine. Kelsey and I are back on the beach—where this story began—writing. I do not have an umbrella yet and the sun feels marvelous on my browned skin. I'm gleefully soaking up the Vitamin C and Vitamin D. As I say these words, I watch Kelsey's fingers quickly and nimbly move over the keyboard. I once saw the great Nureyev dance. I also saw Mikhail Baryshnikov dance at Lincoln Center. Kelsey's fingers moving over the keyboard remind me of these great dancers, elegantly vaulting, jumping, twisting, turning . . . effortlessly, without thought. I feel confident that, someday, my legs will be muscular again, and I will be running on this very beach, the place we've dubbed "The Office." At this juncture, I don't know if it will be stem cell application or a drug, but I do know there are better days yet to come; that scientists all over the world are actively pursuing a way to stop the insidious march of ALS and its cohort, the grim reaper. Meanwhile, I'll keep writing. I will keep putting words on paper, and regardless of what happens to me, these words will live on. These words will never die.

The beach attendant comes over and asks if I want an umbrella.

"No, thank you," I say. "I want to feel the sun."

Salud,
Philip Carlo
South Beach, Miami

INVICTUS

William Ernest Henley (1849–1903)

Out of the night that covers me,
Black as the Pit from pole to pole,
I thank whatever gods may be
For my unconquerable soul.

In the fell clutch of circumstance
I have not winced nor cried aloud.
Under the bludgeonings of chance
My head is bloody, but unbowed.

Beyond this place of wrath and tears
Looms but the horror of the shade,
And yet the menace of the years
Finds, and shall find me, unafraid.

It matters not how strait the gate,
How charged with punishments the scroll,
I am the master of my fate;
I am the captain of my soul.

Afterword

My dear friend Gaby Monet passed away on October 31, 2009. Of all the people mentioned in this book, she was one of the nearest and dearest to my heart. I met her while researching *The Ice Man*. For some three years, we lunched every other week and shared our thoughts with each other. Gaby always insisted on picking up the check. She read everything I ever wrote and warmed in a big way to all of it. When I first told Gaby I had ALS, she made it her cause to try to assist me. She was so very supportive and helpful and loving. Gaby Monet was one of the best friends I ever had and I miss her deeply and profoundly. Though she is gone now, she will always be alive in my heart. Rest in peace, sweet friend.

Her obituary appeared in the *New York Times*:

> Gaby Monet Jacoby, October 31, 2009, passed away peacefully after a long illness, surrounded by family and friends that adored her. Gaby was the beloved wife of legendary comedy writer, Coleman Jacoby, for over fifty-four years and magnificent stepmother to Catherine and Antoinette Jacoby. Née Marilyn Lagoria, Gaby was born in Oakland, California, became a flamenco dancer as a young girl, and came to New York City at age 19. Gaby danced on Broadway in "By the Beautiful Sea" in 1954 and in "Mask and Gown" in 1956. She went on to become a choreographer of live industrial musical shows, as a partner in production company Concepts Unlimited Inc. Concepts produced the documentary film, "Norman Rockwell's World: An American Dream," winning the Academy Award for Best Short Subject Film in 1971. In addition, Gaby produced and wrote many other suc-

cessful documentary films for television, garnering several Emmy awards and critical acclaim. Gaby had two passions, her love of her family and her love of her work. After forming Jacoby-Monet Productions with Coleman, Gaby began a new chapter in her ever developing career, writing and producing for HBO documentaries, including the highly successful "Autopsy" series with medical examiner Michael Baden. Working closely for the last several years with friend and colleague, Sheila Nevins, President of HBO Documentary Films, Gaby additionally produced "The Iceman Interviews" and "The Iceman and the Psychiatrist." Gaby was known and loved for her kindness, generosity, humility and strong, quiet convictions. In 1963 Gaby marched on Washington with Dr. Martin Luther King Jr., and was pleased to live to see Barack Obama elected President. Despite her illness she continued working on the HBO documentary about the Barnes art collection, currently in production. Gaby is survived by her husband Coleman Jacoby, her stepdaughter Loria Parker and husband Gerry Janssen, brother, Jack Lagoria of San Francisco, niece Kitty Dorazi, grand-niece Cynthia Dorazi and grand-nephews. A memorial in her honor is planned at HBO in the near future.

Valerie Estess tells me they are getting closer and closer to finding a remedy for ALS.

In the summer of 2001, I was walking along Broadway on my way home. I was just about to pass Zabar's when I looked up and saw . . . my former teacher, Margie Gold. I slowed. She was walking toward her car and passed directly in front of me. I hadn't seen her in forty years or so.

"Miss Gold?" I said.

She stopped, turned toward me, a blank look on her face.

"Yes . . ." she said, obviously bewildered.

"I'm Philip Carlo," I said.

A blank stare.

"You were my teacher—do you remember?"

"No, I don't."

Before I knew it, this slipped out of my mouth: "You remember me. We fucked!"

"Oh," she said. "I was very wild back then. Now I'm a born-again Christian." She walked away dismissively. I didn't know how to react.

I didn't know if I should be insulted, pleased, what. I walked on, laughing to myself as I went.

In December 2009, Joe Pesci contacted me, wanting to know what, if anything, was happening with *Stolen Flower*. I told him nothing, that the film rights were available. He asked me to write a script based on the book for him. I finished the script in March 2010 and *Stolen Flower* is slated to be made into a feature starring Joe Pesci as Frank DeNardo. I'm pleased.

In June of 2010 Kelsey and I parted ways. She wanted to go live in Paris and write. "I want to write my *Stolen Flower*," she said. We miss her and wish her the best of luck.

You can learn more about the author at www.philipcarlo.com.

Acknowledgments

There are so many people I want to thank this might, if I am not careful, become a book unto itself. As always, my heartfelt gratitude goes out to my dear friend, confidante and agent, Matt Bialer. My family, Dante and Nina Carlo, my sister, Doreen and my brother-in-law, Joe, for their love and support during this difficult time. Thanks also to James Sliman for his help in getting the word out. I wish to give my heartfelt thanks to my health professionals—my lifelong friend Dr. Richard Ash, Dr. Ray Onders out of Ohio, Dr. Mark Sivak at Mount Sinai Hospital in New York, Drs. Hiroshi Mitsumoto at New York's Columbia University and Dr. Jeffrey Rothstein out of Johns Hopkins University, all of whom have been thoughtful and helpful, gone above and beyond the call of duty. It was Dr. Ash who first gave me the key to dealing with a fatal illness—ignore it, go on with your life. I would be remiss if I didn't mention Dr. John Bach, Dr. Alfred Hartman, my caring nurse, Paul Schneider, August Smith, and Lou Saporito at Millennium. I'm still waiting for Lou's mother's chicken Milanese. Many thanks also to Sharon Wiegers, my smiling therapist; Evelyn Gomez for her loving ways; and I am indebted to Dr. Todd Narson for his very able skeletal manipulations. My friend Mike Kostrewa has been an invaluable assistant during these dire days. Thank you, Mike. Many thanks to Jonathan Meyers for always being there. Also, many thanks to Gaby Monet at HBO for her unwavering, long-term friendship. Many thanks to Valerie Estess at Project ALS for her good cheer, friendship, and her excellent work in trying to slay the fire-breathing dragon that is ALS. My gratitude goes to my gracious friends at the Savoy Hotel in South Beach—Carlos Mendes,

Fernao Carvalho, and Vicki Bailey. Many thanks to our friends the Boucher brothers, Perry and Michael, Steven and James, for their warm hospitality. Without Wilson and Byron, I could not have made it to "the office."

Moreover, I wish to give thanks to the people at The Overlook Press, Peter Mayer and my editor, Aaron Schlechter, as well as Stephanie Gorton. I want to also say thank you to my new assistant, the very foxy Nicole Zelyez.

A great many thanks to my favorite Italian restaurant in South Beach—Sardinia owned by Pietro Verdau and Francesco Cavalletti of La Locanda. My appreciation to Daniel Delcastillo and Dr. Walter Bradley out of Miami Beach. Also my sincere gratitude to Dr. Johnny Kao of Mt. Sinai. I owe much appreciation to Dr. Russ Jaffe of VA for his excellent advice and brilliant mind. Thank you to my guardian angel, Dr. Laurie Edelman, who has been an invaluable friend and always there when we needed her. Many thanks to Dr. Jorge Mallea, Dr. Stuart Packer, Dr. Bill Lawson, who discovered the killer, and all of Mt. Sinai.